THE AMERICAN PRESIDENTS
without the boring bits

Andy Jones was born in Great Britain and is an award-winning filmmaker, broadcaster and author. He is the Managing Director of the film production company *Gold Pictures*.

www.andyjonesonline.co.uk

THE AMERICAN PRESIDENTS

without the boring bits

ANDY JONES

Published by L.P.I.

This edition published in 2010 by Lulu Press International.

ISBN: 978-1-4452-6144-7

Copyright © Andy Jones 2009

Typeset in Times New Roman/Palatino

This book is dedicated to every man and woman who will ever stand on the steps of Capitol Hill and promise to preserve, protect and defend the Constitution of the United States to the best of their ability.

Here's hoping that they understand that document, and will give it the respect that it so rightfully deserves.

-AJ

Introduction   11

1.) George Washington   17

2.) John Adams   25

3.) Thomas Jefferson   32

4.) James Madison   41

5.) James Monroe   48

6.) John Quincy Adams   56

7.) Andrew Jackson   62

8.) Martin Van Buren   73

9.) William Henry Harrison   79

10.) John Tyler   85

11.) James K. Polk   91

12.) Zachary Taylor   98

13.) Millard Fillmore   106

14.) Franklin Pierce   112

15.) James Buchanan   119

16.) Abraham Lincoln   125

17.) Andrew Johnson   135

18.) Ulysses S. Grant   143

19.) Rutherford B. Hayes   150

20.) James A. Garfield   159

21.) Chester A. Arthur   166

22.) Grover Cleveland   173

23.) Benjamin Harrison   180

24.) Grover Cleveland   187

25.) William McKinley   194

26.) Theodore Roosevelt   201

27.) William Howard Taft   211

28.) Woodrow Wilson   218

29.) Warren G. Harding   229

30.) Calvin Coolidge   237

31.) Herbert Hoover   244

32.) Franklin D. Roosevelt   251

33.) Harry S. Truman   265

34.) Dwight D. Eisenhower   275

35.) John F. Kennedy   284

36.) Lyndon B. Johnson   294

37.) Richard Nixon   303

38.) Gerald Ford   313

39.) Jimmy Carter   320

40.) Ronald Reagan   329

41.) George H. W. Bush   342

42.) Bill Clinton   350

43.) George W. Bush   359

INTRODUCTION

I'VE NEVER POSSESSED SIGNIFICANT levels of patience. It is a virtue that I have never grasped. I wish that were not the case, or I would have spent more than one lazy Sunday afternoon on one of those 'trendy' genealogy websites, learning of my own family history.

In the past, I have watched my friends with envy, as they discuss with much enthusiasm the wonderful things about their own family history; the amazing people that they're related to, like historic world leaders, fascinating celebrities and so on. The serious time and care that is required to explore the depth and breadth of your families ancestry is a rewarding activity that I hypocritically recommend, having not really done it myself.

To add yet more salt into my lazy wounds, during the brief hours

I spent entering my own details online, I actually discovered a number of interesting things about my family line. Having the 'Jones' surname makes finding out about your own family somewhat tricky, but thankfully it appeared that other members of my fairly distant family had already done a great deal of leg-work, so as I entered the brief information of my grandparents full names and dates of birth, etc. suddenly aspects of my family tree (mostly on my fathers' side) went flying up on the screen.

If I've got this right, two of my blood-line family members (who were 2nd cousins 6-times removed, if I assume I was using the genealogy website calculator correctly), were a certain Allen and Willie Jones. They were brothers from the state of North Carolina. Their father, Robin Jones, was the agent and attorney to Lord Grenville, who was one of the lord proprietors of North Carolina. Their fathers' success with Lord Grenville allowed him to afford the luxury of sending his sons to Eton College in England, with great encouragement of the 'movers and shakers' of the day. The idea being, one supposes, that the powers-that-be in the American colonies wanted to educate the next generation of Americans in the ways of aristocracy and, more importantly, in loyalty to the crown.

On the whole, that plan seemed to initially work. Willie (he insisted it was to be pronounced "Wiley", which is fair enough – isn't that how you would want your name to be pronounced if you were called Willie?), played his role as the monarch wanted. He helped put down the Regulator Rebellion of 1771, a movement dedicated to opposing increased taxation.

However, things weren't all that rosy. Allen, the elder brother by one year (born in 1739), was a member of the colonial assembly between 1773 and 1775. Allen and his brother were comfortably on a fast-ticket to the easy life as aristocratic planters. However, both, it is suggested, aided a certain chap called Thomas Jefferson in writing the Declaration of Independence. Allen served throughout the Revolutionary War, eventually rising to the rank of Brigadier General. He served in the State Senate 1777-1779, 1783, 1784 and 1787. He became a member of the Continental Congress in 1779 and 1780.

Allen was a true solider; fighting for a freedom that many believed just couldn't work. His son-in-law, Founding Father William Richardson Davie was a committed Federalist, very much against the libertarian view of the Jones brothers, but even Davie couldn't match the passion for a free democratic republic that his father-in-law possessed. When Allen died on November 10th, 1798, there was a large service at his burial ground on his plantation (Mount Gallant), near Roanoke Rapids, Northampton County. The mourners knew full well that they had lost a truly important human being in the shaping of the future of a nation that would grow to become the world's one great hope.

Willie was a member of the Provincial Congress in 1774 and 1776, President of the N.C. Committee of Safety in 1776, a leader of the State Militia and the first Governor ex-officio of North Carolina. His time spent in the Continental Congress was, arguably, amongst the most important of all the others who were there and argued their points of view. It could have been very easy for the Congress to shift to a system of greater centralized control, were it not for many of the actions and objections of the Joneses, Jefferson, Madison, and the like.

Believing that both states' rights and (especially) individual rights were the most important, and therefore should be where the majority of freedoms and control needed to be held, made Willie a fly in the authoritarian ointment of the Federalists. In the Continental Congress, Willie frequently aired his concerns that the proposed Constitution created, amongst other things, the possibilities of a standing army and a federal government that regulated (i.e. controlled) the economy to the benefit of a few commercial interests. Of the many titles Willie was given by those who knew him (and occasionally argued against him), the "Jefferson of North Carolina" was, I imagine, one of the most appropriate.

Willie's continued insistence, (along with his brother and others such as Thomas Jefferson), for an elucidation of individual rights in the Constitution contributed greatly to the eventual adoption of the Bill of Rights. Willie felt that North Carolina could only ratify the Constitution when certain individual rights were guaranteed. His fellow libertarian, Thomas Jefferson, worked out the strategy with Willie: at least 9 states should adopt the Constitution, and at least 4 should not adopt it. For the sake of freedom throughout the United States, Willie bravely undertook this responsibility for North Carolina. As Willie rather articulately put it himself; "I would rather be eighteen years out of the Union than adopt [the Constitution] in its present defective form."

Willie managed to rally his fellow delegates in North Carolina not to adopt the Constitution. His resolution not to approve the Constitution passed 184 to 84. His passion for individual freedom and the way he was able to articulate those freedoms as a rational force for good won the argument, (considered by some to be the most important argument ever won in a political debate), and that passion is the reason we have a Bill of Rights in the United States today. As his Federalist rival Archibald MacLaine put it in 1789; "We might have carried our point, but for Willie Jones".

Willie then worked tirelessly with Congress. When the Bill of Rights, which he had a not insignificant hand in authoring, was finally passed, North Carolina voted for the Constitution, with Willie's enthusiastic support, 195 to 77.

The Bill of Rights was not all it could have been. Like most planters of the day, Willie was a slaveholder, with 120 slaves in his possession. Yet Willie, like Thomas Jefferson (another slave-holder), did attempt, unsuccessfully, to abandon slavery in the Union as part of the Bill of Rights. For me, contradictions such as this make the man all the more fascinating. Willie believed that in a free market, paying for all labour would be the natural direction the market would take. The natural abandonment of slavery in Europe and the northern states in America show how right he was. It's incredible. The deep understanding that slavery could die out in this 'free and moral' way came from these slave-holders. It still remains for many a testament that the free market works as a force for good moral change. The evidence of that was still not apparent however, when Willie Jones died in his summer home in Raleigh (a North Carolina city he helped to found) on June 18th, 1801. He lived just long enough to see Thomas Jefferson take Presidential office, a few months earlier.

The story of the Jones Brothers from North Carolina would make a great movie. Fighting for freedom, standing up for what you believe is right, and taking on the responsibility of office and making changes for the better, even in the face of fierce and even deadly opposition are not character traits that we all possess.

But one group of people have needed to possess those traits more than most in history. I am talking of course, of the Presidents of the United States.

As we know, many have not been quite so libertarian. What kind of person would even want to shoulder the burden of the position of head of the executive branch in the first place? My cousins had quite a significant part to play in making sure that the power of the Commander-in-chief was quite limited. In fact, it is sometimes said that of the three branches of government, the executive branch has much less power than either the legislative or judicial branches.

The purpose of this book is to scrape away all the boring clichéd (and often inaccurate) bits of American Presidential history and show you a truth that rarely gets an airing. I made an important discovery in the writing of this book that I wish to convey to you. I hope to reveal one simple fact. The fact that those Presidents who embrace the limitations of office, who operate within the margins of their Constitutional power, rather than those who try to push the boundaries of what they can get away with, frequently end up leaving incredible legacies of greater freedom, and prosperity in the country and the wider world. But history often judges them with less respect.

The other problem with history is that it's frequently boring. And watching defective documentaries about those who have shaped so much of the world are usually rather dry affairs, as any history student – stuck in the classroom with their technology-baffled history teacher as he/she tries to operate the VCR – can attest.

But it doesn't have to like that: the histories of the American Presidents are actually quite fun. They have often lead exciting lives and achieved things that most of us can barely comprehend, let alone achieve ourselves.

So together let's try to find out who these people were, what motivated them and what they achieved. Only by looking at it in this way, can we bypass the tedium of the dry history textbook and discover more important qualities. Perhaps we can learn something about ourselves and our decisions, and maybe even what 'sort' of people we want to send into elected office in the future.

But in undertaking this little adventure, I ask only one thing: if, as we go on this journey, you ever finding yourself thinking that a President can fix social and economic problems better than freedom can, try to remember Allen and Willie Jones.

ONE
GEORGE WASHINGTON

Took Office: April 30th 1789
Left Office: March 4th 1797
Party: None/Federalist
Terms: 1 & 2

THE BARE MINIMUM REQUIREMENTS on the résumé of anyone who wants to be the President of the United States of America, should, most would agree, include fairly significant levels of intelligence and political savvy. General Washington had little of these traits.

He was not the smartest, and not the most politically aware. However, he is the only President to be unanimously elected, and he did it twice. As we shall see, it would appear that other qualities are arguably more important after all.

George Washington was born on February 22nd 1732 on his family's Pope Creek Estate near present-day Colonial Beach in Westmoreland County, Virginia. And parents who are making choices today about which school will be appropriate for their children, may be interested to note that the first President was homeschooled. His mother Mary Ball and father Augustine, thought that young George would go through life as a surveyor and planter in Virginia. A simple, yet well-paid life.

There is little about Washington's early life that indicates he was destined for greatness. But in the theatre of war, his natural leadership qualities shone through, and it became clear where his talents would lie. But even then, Washington would be unaware of the curveball that fate was to throw in his direction.

When the revolution was in its early stages and the fighting had already broken out, Washington appeared at the Second Continental Congress in full military uniform, signalling he was ready for war. It was just the rallying gesture that the likes of Ben Franklin and Thomas Jefferson had hoped for. Their hopes paid off. On June 14th, 1775, on the nomination of John Adams, Congress appointed George Washington to the rank of Major General and Commander-in-Chief.

The year after his appointment, General Washington forced the British out of Boston. He lost New York City, but crossed the Delaware River into New Jersey and defeated the surprised British army units later that year. Washington, like many who made up the Continental Army and state militias, was out-gunned and out-manned. Yet they fought for their freedom and frequently beat the odds.

On paper, there was no way that the Continental forces should have secured victory and independence, and many don't realise that they did actually lose more battles that they won. But they won the *right* battles, which is all that counts. There are endless books on Valley Forge and other crucial turning points of the revolution that detail the nature of the American victory. A victory far too complex to describe here. But put it this way, if the British put up 2,000 soldiers against 200 American minutemen, and by the end of the battle all but 20 of the minutemen are dead, and all but 200 of the British army are dead, is that *really* a victory for the British? The desire for freedom means that even when the odds are stacked against you, the odds simply don't apply.

THE FIRST PRESIDENT

George Washington took office in New York City, on April 30th, 1789. He was the first President of a broken down, third-world nation, that had barely survived the onslaught of a war of independence. And all because of a relatively untested notion of liberty. There were many, including King George III, who simply felt that the United States of America would crawl back to its master in time.

So it's no big surprise (and indeed, it's something of a relief) that Washington was tentative and almost apprehensive in becoming the first head of the executive branch of government: "My movements to the chair of government will be accompanied with feelings not unlike those of a culprit who was going to the place of his execution," he confessed. "I greatly fear that my countrymen will expect too much from me."

John Adams, a Federalist, wanted the President to be called "His Mightiness, His Excellency, His High Mightiness, The President of the United States and Defender of Our Liberties." That'd be quite a mouthful to say in casual conversation. But one supposes that Adams felt that no one should ever engage in casual conversation with the President, just as they wouldn't do with a king. But Washington just wanted to be called 'Mr. President', like how the Chairman of a board of directors in a business would be Mr. Chairman. It was a title that properly respected the office, without the fraudulent grandeur of a monarch. It is in those attitudes that Washington's greatest traits can be understood.

However, just one tiny microorganism could have destroyed any chance of mankind's greatest hope for freedom. Only weeks after taking office, Washington came down with a rare bacterial infection, which could have ended his presidency all too quickly. Some believe it was anthrax, picked up on a farm. Thankfully he recovered, and the Republic as we know it survived.

Washington had flaws, of course, and these were mostly centred on some of his instinctive reflexes for military-style management. But there were other, well, 'quirks' as well. For example; he refused to shake hands, as he thought it was "beneath the Presidency". Maybe that's why future Presidents like Barack Obama prefer to bump-fists instead. Though I doubt that's what Washington would have done. Be honest though – don't you kind of hope that he did?

Quirks aside, he was the 'action man' of the Founders. An icon that the others needed to rally the people. Jefferson said Washington was the best horseback rider of the period. There have been many portraits of Washington, atop or standing by his white horse, Nelson. Nelson was used by Washington as a PR stunt: Washington could ride into town during the elections looking very manly, to impress the constituents. Yep, spin and PR were alive and well even then.

BUT NOT JUST "THE FIRST PRESIDENT"
His military achievements were one of the main and most impressive things that brought him to high office, and many were reminded of this as he went around the country (and he DID travel extensively during his time as President). He made sure he visited every state in the new union, as he felt it his duty, rather than just make arbitrary decisions in an isolated bubble. It was during this time he became the first American patron of the arts, collecting lots of American land-scape paintings along the way.

In fact, he was first at everything. When it came to those turning points of the American revolution, he was the first at wading into battle. But then using all the diplomacy skills at his command, he was always the first to broker peace as soon as possible.

Washington was also first to take to the dance floor (he was the John Travolta in *Saturday Night Fever* of his day, only with a 'slightly' less embarrassing wardrobe). He was the first major interior decorator. He'd have a makeover reality TV show if he were around today. He was a real DIY guy, always fixing up Mount Vernon, even during the revolutionary war. Also, rather oddly, George Washington, the 'first in war' was also the 'first in fashion': Some historians say he was the Calvin Klein of his day, because he designed many of the military uniforms that the US soldiers wore. However, unlike Calvin Klein, he never went into the 'fragrances' business. Kind of a shame though; I bet everyone would have bought *"GW-One: the new fragrance for the minuteman in your life"* for their partners at Christmas. It would appear that Washington failed to cash in.

But, he 'cashed in' in other ways: Washington was also first to the gambling table, and was always wagering a bet on something or other. ("Hey Hamilton, I bet you five bucks I can chop that cherry tree down with one axe-swing!")

VITAL TALENT

His abilities to bring people together and develop an accommodating consensus were extraordinary. He probably didn't know exactly what his job entitled, (having had no previous people to serve as a guide), but he was a man accustomed to commanding, and he drew respect to himself like a magnet. As a General, he would have frequent councils of war and debate what was to be done in a rather democratic fashion, so he could get his hands on all the available evidence and opinions before making informed judgements. We must be thankful that he decided to run his administration the same way. Fact and reason became the main principles that counted under President Washington.

He possessed a keen sense of character and talent. By getting the right people to do the right things, he would make himself look good. We should be thankful that his first executive cabinet happened to be (arguably) the best in US history. Jefferson as Secretary of State, and Henry Knox as Secretary of War. The list goes on. And as the wheels of history turn, it is harder to find people to live up to the brilliance of these original cabinet occupants.

Many say Hamilton 'set the economy off' in many ways. He built the Federal Bank under Washington's guidance. This appointment by Washington has been recorded as sensible, but I'm not so sure.

Accumulating the individual states' war debt helped some of the states in the short-term, but hindered, as Jefferson pointed out, a possible freer and wealthier future. Free-market economists still argue this valid point today. Virginia had been productive and laboured under the free market and had pretty much paid off its war debt by the time this Federal Bank was put in place. Understandably Virginians like Jefferson and James Madison were not happy. There are those (including me), that believe that if individual states had been allowed to pay off their own war debts and keep financial independence based on liquid assets (which would pretty much mean the 'gold standard'), then some of the future recessions the and economic turbulence that was occasionally experienced for many years afterwards would possibly not have occurred.

A compromise was reached. In order to keep Virginia happy, the new nation's capital would be built on land in the state of Virginia, but it would be an independent district; the District of Columbia. The swamp-land that Washington picked for the capital was called 'Foggy Bottom', and wouldn't it have been great if it had stayed that way. Alas it didn't: the designated capital was increasingly being referred to as "the city of Washington", and the name stuck.

Washington micro-managed virtually everything that needed to be done in the new capital. He helped lay out the roads, civil infra-structure and the like, and put the finishing touches to the blueprints of the Presidents Mansion, though he was the only President never to stay in it. In fact, Washington is the only President never to run executive office from Washington D.C. at all.

OVERCOMING PROBLEMS

There were many times when Washington had to handle difficult moments. They helped both shape his presidency, him as a man, and set a precedent for future heads of the executive branch. One such crisis was in 1793, when war broke out between England and France. The US was asked to choose sides. Washington chose neutrality. While there are many good reasons for this, it did lead to trouble for future Presidents.

Then there was the whiskey rebellion in his second term. In 1794, Pennsylvania farmers were angry at a Federal taxation on liquor. The old familiar rebellious cry of "no taxation without representation" could be heard throughout the state. If the rock band *The Who* were around back then I suppose they'd sing (perhaps unfairly) "Meet the new boss, same as the old boss."

Of course, Washington understood that this was not an 'unrepresented' tax – the original taxation without representation came from Westminster in England. There was no representation for the American colonies in that institution. But here, the taxation was raised by the Pennsylvania government who directly represented the people of the state. He was having none of it. He mustered 12,000 Federal soldiers to Pennsylvania. This was all that was needed to put down the rebellion.

HOW THE FIRST COMMANDER-IN-CHIEF SHOULD BE JUDGED

Washington was all too keenly aware that the choices he made would set precedents for future heads of the executive branch. He also knew the eyes of the world were watching him. Two main questions were asked: Would he become a new monarch? Would he gain increasing authoritarian control?

The answer to the first question is definitely no. The second is a slightly weaker 'no, not on the whole'. He started the first two years of his Presidency as an independent, with a libertarian bent. During the last two years of his first term, and the first two years of his second, he was very much on the path of the more centralised and authoritarian Federalists. Then, in his last two years, moved much more to the Jeffersonian-style libertarians.

And as a libertarian, the most important thing that George Washington did during his presidency was to leave. He made the decision to step down in his second term, though he could have stayed and kept getting elected for the rest of his life. However, he understood that he was getting older, and freedom couldn't reign with one man in power for life. Also by his mid-sixties, enough was enough.

To his eternal credit, we have to acknowledge this increasingly 'Jeffersonian spirit' about President Washington as he got older. He wanted to teach the world and the next political generation in America that the power to represent the people is an honour and should – no, *must* – be relinquished after relatively short periods of time. What if John Adams was the first President and not the second? What if Hamilton had taken office? Would these men have felt the same way about the power that they could have held on to indefinitely?

Stepping down, and therefore demonstrating what the limited power of the executive office should be, was the greatest thing that George Washington achieved. And America is all the more greater today because of it.

TWO

JOHN ADAMS

Took Office: March 4th 1797
Left Office: March 4th 1801
Party: Federalist
Term: 3

IF THE WEATHER REVEALED any real symbolic significance for the Presidency of the second ever Commander-in-Chief, John Adams was destined to have a tough time in office from the beginning.

The weather in Philadelphia on his inauguration day was frankly dire. So, I'm afraid, was the majority of John Adams' time spent in office. But what went wrong? Were there no achievements at all? And how was he different from those who came and went before and after him?

First of all, there was always going to be what can only be described as the "George Washington issue". Everyone was very moved that Washington had actually left office and not stayed on indefinitely. Throughout the rest of the world, leaders came to power and stayed there for the rest of their lives, if not longer, as they would leave their 'kingdoms' to their sons and other family members after they had kicked the bucket. But Washington, by stepping down after two terms, had set the precedent that showed America was radically different. It was symbolic of the American lack of authoritarianism and how it was a better place because of it.

However, to John Adams, Washington stepping down was nothing short of, well, odd. It is in this attitude, and many others, that Adams found himself out of step with the general consensus of America. While they were celebrating Washington's commitment to democracy by stepping down, little John Adams was sitting in the corner, scratching his head in bemusement, wondering why Washington did not cling onto power.

But of course, the big question that was going to be tough for any successor was simply 'how do you follow George Washington'? I mean, just think about it. John Adams must have felt pretty gutted. It would be very hard for anybody to live up to the legacy left by Washington, and Adams knew it. I guess my point is this: many of the early Presidents would have stepped up the challenge, but in so many ways, Adams just kind of, well, sulked.

And I suppose that his character informed his politics. John Adams was a man of many contradictions. He was Harvard educated, but highly insecure. While he wielded authoritarian convictions, to understand that he did so from a position of such insecurity makes his convictions all the more curious.

He spoke with a lisp and had very poor people skills. This short fat little man was always going to have it tough in comparison to his predecessor and the better men around him. His humble nature may have earned him more respect in certain circles, (usually those circles contained people who agreed with his brand of politics), but others found him rather abrasive, uncompromising and even oafish.

His demand for more authority in the Presidency was frequently, (and poorly), delivered in the biting, almost vicious ambitiousness, that ran through his veins. Herein lay the problem. John Adams represented the old way of doing things infinitely more than the new way. He wanted America to be more like the European nations with aristocracy and not with an unconditional level of social mobility. He never seemed to understand that the US was a country with the courage to say goodbye to all that and embrace freedom instead.

Both Adams' lack of understanding about what the classical republican nation was all about, coupled with so many people not being able to understand what Adams wanted America to be, manifested itself in the form of mood swings. With regard to his temper, Adams was very up and down. He craved fame and power but always pulled himself down in some odd puritanical desire for self pity and sacrifice. I'm no psychologist, but I'm sure you'll get my drift if I call it 'oh woe is me syndrome'. Some days he acted like he was on cloud nine, others he felt like the biggest loser in history.

TICKING THE BOXES

The funny thing is, Adams had everything on paper required to be President at the time. He had (just about) the right level of support, as so many Federalists felt he was the only one of them who could have beaten Jefferson, a dangerous man (or so they thought), with too many 'radical' libertarian ideas. It turned out, of course, that those libertarian ideals were much more popular amongst the people than the more authoritarian ideals that the Federalists promoted.

But Adams had more going for him that that. He was a signer of the Declaration of Independence, as well as a member of the Continental Congress. He understood enough of the rest of the world, and this was evidenced during this time as a minister to both France and England. During this time in England, the very vicious King George, deeply unhappy with the separation of America from England, told Adams that he hoped the "American people would not suffer too much without a monarch." It could be speculated that Adams had frequently pondered the very same question.

Of course, in terms of qualification to office, it's worth remembering that John Adams was the first Vice President, serving under George Washington. This was an important box to tick, in terms of Adams' practical eligibility for Presidential office.

The ability to micro-manage things was quite an asset to John Adams. He had a real talent for some of the levels of administration that political office requires in order to get things done. Adams understood that in order for America to be safe, it would need its own Navy. John Paul Jones is (rightly) known as the first Head of the US Navy, but the actual political process of creating such an entity was all down to John Adams.

But, as we've said, he didn't have the personality and the social awareness needed to be the inspirational executive that Americans craved. He was prone to fits of anger that he unleashed on subordinates.

His social and management skills were very lacking. He seemed incapable to bringing others into his 'big tent'. He was highly opinionated, thought he knew best, and very rarely sought council from his executive cabinet or anyone else for that matter. Members of the Democratic-Republican Party were especially excluded from the John Adams White House.

The hardest aspect of his attitude to grasp, might be described as almost monarchist. He felt that the President should be more like an aristocratic leader, with unconditional support. This attitude, as we shall see, was used to very dangerous ends. He believed that while there was room for some social mobility, that there was always going to be (and also must be) a hierarchy and order. This ran in the face of the majority of American opinion. Most citizens in the new republic simply saw the US as a place of freedom where every individual could be the architect of their own destiny. It's not often said in the history books, but Adams didn't seem to share that 'libertarian' view quite as enthusiastically as many of the Founding Fathers did.

POLICY PAINS

Two big issues plagued Adams' time in office. These were the so-called XYZ Affair, and the Alien and Sedition Acts. We'll get to the second one in a minute.

As it always does, war was escalating between England and France. In fairness to Adams, Washington had left the US position on this rather too open, by remaining neutral on the matter. By the time Adams came into office, the French were being rather obnoxious towards the American attitude to war. I guess that some things never change!

It wasn't long before reports got back to Adams that the French had started seizing US ships. The reason was simple. The French didn't want America trading with their enemy.

Adams sent a diplomatic envoy out to France to negotiate a settlement. The French agreed to cease and desist, but only in return for a bribe. Again, nothing changes! When the news of this bribe-request came back to the US government, instead of referring to the Frenchmen who wanted this bribe by their real names, they used the letters X, Y & Z. hence the XYZ Affair.

The powers-that-be in Congress were very unhappy by the way that the French were treating America. Adams was never a big fan of the French anyway, and his plan for solving this was simply to send another delegation to Paris. Some of the US war-mongers, (most of them were from Adams' own more authoritarian party, the Federalists), were very unhappy with Adams for not simply declaring war on France and finally wading in on this conflict. Finally though, to Adams' credit, it paid off and in 1800 America and France signed a peace treaty. However, by then, Adams had already screwed up, big-time.

DEALING WITH DISSENT

Ridiculing, patronising, and condemning government figures. It's totally commonplace now, so much so that we don't even notice it, but back in the late 1790s, it was a fairly new phenomenon in a republic where free speech was a fundamental right.

Many Americans in the new print media and so on, were already voicing their lack of respect for Adams' Presidency. This level of dissent and questioning of authority was a perfect example of the principles and freedoms that America was founded upon. But grumpy Adams was very unhappy about it.

Adams, growing ever more authoritarian, felt that the political attacks on him were seditious, and therefore, dangerous to national security. And no, I'm not making this up. So in 1798, he signed the Alien and Sedition Acts into power. It was now a crime to 'falsely' speak/write against certain holders of federal offices (including, of course, the President). This was a clear violation of the Constitution's 1st amendment, and one of the worst public policies in the history of America. It only heightened the view of Adams as the aristocratic dictatorial figure.

COMPLEX REIGN

On the one hand, had Adams not negotiated a peace with France and signed that treaty in 1800, America would have been a much weaker nation, scarred and possibly ruined in a war between two European imperialist powers. On the other hand, his authoritarian nature flew in the face of what this idea of an American republic was so desperately about. In a democracy, inventing rules to undermine your rival party and any other voices of dissent deserves, and even to an extent guarantees, that your time in office will be reduced. And, though he was rather bitter about serving only one term, that's what happened to John Adams. And I bet he never really took the time to understand why everyone had had enough of him.

You know what? If he had kept getting the Electoral College votes, I bet that Adams would have remained President for life, refusing to leave office. But America was built for bigger hearts than that of the second President, and on March 4th, 1801, without Adams even being gracious enough to be present, Thomas Jefferson took the oath of office, and became the third President of the United States.

THREE
THOMAS JEFFERSON

Took Office: March 4th 1801
Left Office: March 4th 1809
Party: Democratic-Republican
Terms: 4 & 5

IN THE INTERESTS OF honesty, I am required to issue a disclaimer at the start of this chapter: Thomas Jefferson is not only my favourite President of the United States, but also he's definitely, (my own family lineage accounted for, of course) my favourite Founding Father. I hope over the course of this chapter, to help you understand why.

It is often understandably said, that George Washington was the 'father' of America. But a cursory glance at the influence of the third President, not just during his two-term Presidency, but way before he became the Commander-in-Chief, (just think; this is the author of the Declaration of Independence, the major fighter for the Bill of Rights, etc), shows that Jefferson is arguably the real father of this great experiment in liberty known as the United States of America.

Most of the acts of his Presidency continue to affirm this perspective.

Constantly ranked by scholars and boffins as one of the greatest American Presidents and political leaders of all time, (see, it's not just me – people who know what they're talking about say it too), Jefferson deserves every bit of the respect he is given. He was a polymath whose genius was quite magnificent. When President John F. Kennedy once welcomed forty-nine Nobel Prize-winners to the White House in 1962, he said "I think this is the most extraordinary collection of talent and of human knowledge that has ever gathered together at the White House – with the possible exception of when Thomas Jefferson dined alone."

His views are still controversial, but in keeping with the libertarian attitude of reason. Like many Founding Fathers, he was a deist who once suggested that eventually the human race would shrug off their backwards religious beliefs, (or "monkish attitudes" as he delightfully called it), and then be truly free. Time may still show that he was right about that as well.

Any description of an America that was democratic, free, with equality of opportunity, is still described as Jeffersonian. Still today, the limited government pro-freedom politicians in America are often known as Jeffersonian. It's a badge of honour, that is sometimes (in the case of several politicians we could name) unfairly handed out.

TRANSITION OF POWER

The ill feeling that his predecessor had for him cannot be emphasised enough. Though they grew to be good friends in old age, it must be said that it was a bitter defeat for John Adams. In fact Adams left Washington D.C. in the middle of the night. This undignified exit sealed the end of the Federalists major influence over the executive branch of government, as well as the beginning of the end of their influence in shaping America more generally.

You can just imagine the aristocratic contempt for Thomas Jefferson's overwhelming election victory can't you: "Damn it men, that infernal 'freedom man' is in office." And you can bet that they were not going to like it.

It's also worth noting that the election of 1800 was the first where the printed media played a big role. The honest exposure of Adams' less freedom-friendly way of doing things took a real bashing in the press. And Jefferson's ideals of liberty seemed to resonate more with the Electoral College, and indeed, with the people themselves. People were debating the issues in the streets of Washington and across the United States. It's something that we take for granted today, but was quite revolutionary in its day. What exactly the early Americans would make of the daily commentaries on the blogosphere is quite another issue.

Also, very importantly, for the first time in this new republic, power was shifted (peacefully mind) from one party to another. Observers were all saying the same thing about Thomas Jefferson. There was a feeling that this 58 year-old Founder from Virginia would finally set the standards of freedom that all other Presidents would have to follow. And in so many ways, he did not disappoint.

Jefferson was the first to be inaugurated in D.C. The imagery that this conjures up still causes the hairs on the back of my neck to rise. On the day of his inauguration, Jefferson walked to the (unfinished) Capitol Building, and, as we have seen so many do since, and gave his inaugural address. In one of the most important statements ever made by any Commander-in-Chief in the history of America, he boldly told those assembled there, that "We are all Federalists. We are all Republicans."

It was an honest recognition that America's strength is its diversity. Everyone is different and those differences are to be celebrated, not because of tokenism or political correctness, but because it's the only way for America to finally be free. It was a call for unity, while respecting and tolerating for everyone's differences. It was an acceptance that in a free society, you do not have the right to live in a bubble, where you cannot be offended by other people's opinions. It was an eloquent nod in the direction of Voltaire's declaration that "I disagree with what you say, but I'll fight to the death to defend your right to say it." Finally, it was a call for America to become what it was always destined to be and now finally could be.

THE SECOND REVOLUTION

Jefferson believed, as did many Americans at the time, that his election was the second revolution that America needed to be truly free and to have the prosperity and liberty it deserved. It really was the concluding piece of the puzzle.

There was a sense that things could continue under Jefferson to get better and better. That was sort of the point. Jefferson set out an example of freedom, that every other President and person in public office would have to follow if America could make significant progress. The more 'Jeffersonian' a leader would be, the more successful their time in office. The more 'authoritarian' they acted, the less triumphant they would be.

America needed saving, Jefferson thought. And the best way to do that was simply by taking the power away from the Federal government and giving it back to the people, as he originally envisaged. As he said himself; "Government is best that governs least." It should be noted, though, that some of his decisions in office appear to contradict that view. By the end of this little intellectual exercise, I hope to show a slightly different outlook to some of Jefferson's bigger decisions.

Jefferson's attitude to freedom and how that should be presented was pretty consistent. In the White House, he often greeted guests informally in his pyjamas and slippers. It was often said that if you had to visit the White House for whatever reason, or even if you were a regular civilian and wished to pop in unannounced, quite often it would be Jefferson himself who would open the door and welcome you in – can you imagine that today?! What a shame that this one tradition can no longer be practically applied. Also, I've heard that the current incumbent at the White House wears P.J.'s with little bunnies on them; that's probably not a sight you'd want to see.

The third President also put an end to the formal White House dinners that Washington and Adams insisted upon. Instead he hosted informal supper parties, where guests could sit anywhere they pleased. Poor Thomas Jefferson, that he did not live in the age of the microwave and Chinese takeout, otherwise international diplomacy meetings would have been conducted with chicken chow mien and egg-fried rice.

He felt the pomp of a monarch-like Commander was not what the President should be. The whole point was that the President was not some great person, chosen by god, but a man of the people, chosen from the people. His wealth set him apart from most Americans, that is true, but his character and lightness made him very identifiable as a man of the people. A trait many seeking political office have tried (and failed) to emulate ever since.

While being this informal, Jefferson was also busy being very effective as the head of the executive branch. He was quiet but productive, and enjoyed 'getting things done' by working hard in his office instead of loudly doing nothing in the public eye, like so many of today's politicians. With his soft voice and slight lisp, he wasn't the best public speaker in the world, (he would send his addresses to Congress in letter form than turn up and give a speech), but actions spoke louder than words.

Unlike John Adams and his constant fight with the press (and his undermining of their freedoms), Jefferson did things very differently. He was very good at handling the press. He knew that in order for America to be free, he couldn't dismiss them, he had to work with them as best as he could. They loved him, (mostly because of the freedom they enjoyed under his Presidency, a stark contrast to his predecessor), but that didn't give him a free pass, and, I'm sure Jefferson would say, nor should it.

One of the biggest scandals that came up, was his alleged affair with one of his slaves, Sally Hemmings. Freud would have been able to write a book putting this information together: Sally Hemmings was the half-sister of Martha Wayles Skelton, Jefferson's late wife. How did Jefferson handle this accusation with Sally Hemmings? Nothing. He felt that because it didn't concern his duties of office, it wasn't anyone's business, rather like a person's religious beliefs, for example. So he did nothing and it died down. Simple but brilliant. Again, I wonder what scandals would have turned to nothing if the politicians involved just ignored them and continued to govern as best as they can?

DOUBLING THE SIZE OF AMERICA

Now, onto the controversies: One of the biggest things Jefferson did that seem to contradict his libertarian, limited-government view, was the Louisiana Purchase. For the paltry sum of $15 million, Thomas Jefferson bought the French territories in America (and the French barely even knew what they were selling – it was the bargain of the century, and January sales hadn't even been invented then).

This massive expansion came about, some could argue, *because* of Jefferson's ideals for the expansion of Freedom. I know that's not what you normally hear, but indulge me on this. Jefferson felt America could be safer, and freedom could be granted to more people, if America's border ranged from sea to shining sea.

He was worried that it might be unconstitutional. In fact, he came to the conclusion that it's not. The Federalists attacked him for it, because Jefferson was proposing to rule the new territories, (though some argue temporarily until things can settle down), under the leadership of military governors. It is my opinion that Jefferson simply wanted more of the continent to live in freedom and the only thing that might stop this libertarian nation from being destroyed by jealous people of other nations, was to expand it until the border was large enough, and the population big enough, to prevent any such attack. We will never know if he was right or wrong, as America got too big and too prosperous to ever be under any real threat. Maybe that means he was right.

I honestly think that had Jefferson not expanded the size of America with the Louisiana Purchase, then by the time the next war with Britain rained down on the US, America would have been swallowed up and the experiment in freedom would have been consigned to the ash-heap of history.

He didn't stop at the Louisiana Purchase though: he allowed a secret expedition, the Lewis and Clark Expedition, to explore the continent further. His critics were unhappy about this as well. They declared it an unconstitutional military expansion, but I think that history judges the Lewis and Clark expedition as 'great American adventure', in which peace and exploration seemed to be the order of the day.

So the real question is, did Thomas Jefferson, the man who claimed to love small government, massively expand the size of government? I believe that in many ways, he didn't. He simply expanded the size of the United States of America, which is a different thing. He didn't make the executive any more authoritarian, which *would* be an expansion of government. But heck, I appreciate that that's a debate for the ages.

THE SECOND (AND FINAL) TERM

The people overwhelmingly re-elected Thomas Jefferson in 1804.

Things appeared to be going well. The promise of a Jeffersonian America was granted. However, he had a hard time dealing with the rising international crisis. Yep, it's England and France at war again, (do they ever learn?), and America looked like it was going to be sucked in. Jefferson believed in non-interventionism in this instance. America need not be sucked into all the petty grievances of Europe.

But of course, how could the United States not be affected? American merchants traded with both England and France, which enraged both countries. The French were angry that America traded with England, and England likewise with France. War with one of these countries was inevitable.

Jefferson tried to ease things, mostly in vein. Eventually he created a temporary measure in the form of the Embargo Act of 1807, which ceased trade with all foreign nations. It was his worst decision, but he felt helpless to do anything else. And what else could he have done? The diplomacy wasn't working, and war appeared to be the only other choice, a war that could have destroyed the United States. The blossoming of liberty in America was such a success, but the old countries were dragging things down. He must have felt like Al Pacino in *The Godfather Part 3*: "Just when I thought I was out, they pull me back in!"

Mostly due to this, despite his huge popularity, it is the understatement of the century to say that he didn't enjoy the second term as much. The criticism of his diffusion of war got him down, but the lack of being able to solve it got him down more. This wasn't something America could fix and have sorted overnight, regardless of who was in power.

However, let's remember that the kind of free-market democracy that Jefferson was at the heart of putting in place was a beacon of light to the rest of the world, and this eventually extended to England and France to. So how did these two European neighbours finally settle their differences? The American way – trade.

Jefferson had done most of the positive things he needed to do, and therefore set the groundwork for a President that was not a dictator, that was wholly accountable to the people, and that while some Presidents would be more authoritative, others would be less so, and the hope was that there would never be any extremes of oppression ever more in America. That single reason, is why Jefferson was such an important President. It was the standards he set.

And while Thomas Jefferson was in government, it must be noted that the standard of living for the citizens and residents of the United States overall rose to incredible levels. Despite the difficult but, for the time, necessary governing decisions that Jefferson undertook, we have to recall all of this in one context: at the time, with Jefferson as President, the American people's prosperity, opportunities and potential was raised at a pace that no society on earth had ever known.

As a Founding Father, Jefferson was the chief architect in setting the groundwork for freedom and success. As President, he made sure that no matter how authoritarian or libertarian future Commanders-in-Chief would be, (within reason), the American people could still pursue happiness and enjoy the blessings that being the architects of their own destiny would provide. Jefferson wasn't just an enthusiastic supporter of this idea that they called America. Thomas Jefferson *was* America.

And Jefferson was such an influence and inspiration to America and to what the country could achieve, that it came as no surprise that Jefferson's number two, the guy who was his right hand man for over twenty years, was overwhelmingly elected as the fourth President: committed Jeffersonian Democratic-Republican, James Madison.

FOUR
JAMES MADISON

Took Office: March 4th 1809
Left Office: March 4th 1817
Party: Democratic-Republican
Terms: 6 & 7

As SECRETARY OF STATE, the Virginian James Madison was very successful. The American people still had a lot of love for Thomas Jefferson, and it was somewhat obvious that his successor would have to be someone who shared a great deal of his values. That is precisely what they got.

A cursory glance at his personality résumé, (if there were such a thing), showed that he ticked all the boxes for office: James Madison was an honourable veteran of the revolution, as well as a significant author of the Constitution. In fact, today he is still known as the 'father of the Constitution' by most. Of course, as should be clear by now, he was very much a Jeffersonian democrat.

Let's be honest. Maybe didn't have the huge intellect and the same 'beautiful mind' that Jefferson possessed, but he was very intelligent and his mind was certainly more disciplined. Though he had a coarse sense of humour, this was offset by a calm demeanour. Very rarely did rage overtake him. Actually, I have to be honest, I couldn't find a single major account by the political commentators of the time, of him getting irrationally angry over anything. Philosophically I suppose you could argue that he was almost an 'objectivist' in his attitudes – most of the time, he would measure his decisions based on the facts and reason.

A look into the clothing of all the Presidents shows how fashions can change over time. But I think it's fair to say that fashion-wise, Madison was the first 'goth' President. Think about it: have you ever seen a picture of this guy where he's _not_ dressed in all-black?

While it's true that he was very funny socially, the paradox lies in the fact that he was not really all that into small-talk. He could be rather bluntly spoken when he wanted to be, but was never rude and always personable.

Jefferson lost his wife at quite a young age. Madison however, was still happily married at the time of entering office, so the White House was home to a first lady again. Dolly Madison was young, vivacious and very colourful character. You know those sort of people who just light up any room they are in? Yep, that's what Dolly was like.

She was into lavish parties (involving lots of ice cream, a delicacy of the era). Her favourite flavour wasn't chocolate, strawberry or vanilla. It was 'oyster flavour' of course! I think I'd have to pass on that. In many ways, she added the much-needed sparkle to James Madison's rather calm demeanour.

Madison was always well prepared. This only added to his calm demeanour and rational thinking. He was as committed to the principles of liberty as Jefferson was, and interestingly, his passion for freedom only increased his sense of rationality and fairness. It wasn't just that he was incredibly smart; he was also incredibly studious. Frequently was Madison to be seen pacing all over the White House, thinking about the deeper issues. He 'got' America, in the same way Jefferson did, and perhaps in the way someone like John Adams did not (sorry about having a dig at poor John Adams again!).

We can conclude therefore that President James Madison was always prepared for any eventuality. Anything except that is, for war, which rather blindsided him.

THE WAR OF 1812

It must really suck to be a President who has to see a war defining their time in office. Especially if you're not exactly looking for a fight to begin with. But unfortunately for James Madison, the War of 1812 was what shaped his Presidency.

And it was a real topsy-tury affair as well. Half of America was pushing to go to war with England, half with France. He was in quite a predicament. Poor James Madison would've rather not gone to war with either, but it became increasingly clear that there was something of an inevitability about America's involvement in the English/French cat-fight. What is it with Britain and America – couldn't these two countries just get along?!

Eventually it became clear to Madison (and everyone else) that England was the main country that seemed to be at the root of this dispute. It was the old empire flexing its muscles again, and boy, what muscles. Some historians feel Madison also possibly feared that if America were to join alongside England against France, then the new republic could sleepwalk its way back into the oppressive empire. The problem was, if America fought against England, then the same could happen because the mighty British army could crush America with a series of swift blows. Luckily that danger was less likely. Jefferson's Louisiana Purchase had increased the size of the republic as well as the number of people willing to fight for it.

With options quickly running out, it turned out that Madison wouldn't really have to make a decision. The British would make it for him.

The war itself was sparked on the high seas. Not long into Madison's first term in office, British vessels started seizing American ships. It was clear that England was determined to drag America into this war, whether she wanted to be involved or not. Madison's diplomatic efforts to solve the crisis came up empty. Finally on June 18th, 1812, Madison became the first President in the history of the United States to exercise the Constitutional requirement to go to Congress and ask for a declaration of war. Though the circumstances were quite terrible, the one positive note to take from this is rooted in the American form of limited government: the head of the federal executive branch had to ask the elected members of Congress before initiating a war. Had that ever properly happened anywhere else before?

There was much debate in Congress, but eventually the votes were in, and it was clear: Congress accepted Madison's request, and America officially declared war on England.

Let's time out for one second to ask a very serious question: How could America have possibly won this war? England was fighting (and in many respects, soundly beating) Napoleon's army and the United States could barely string together a militia to fight. The neutral at the time would have to admit that America wasn't going to stand a chance.

To say that things didn't go well, is rather an understatement I'm afraid. America suffered from humiliating defeats all over the place. Detroit, upstate New York, all fell to the British prowess. Some may have said 'if only General Washington was still around to save the day', but even Washington couldn't have done much about these total defeats.

Things got so bad, that there was almost a civil war in New England in 1814. The state of New England massively depended on shipping and trade to survive, and this war was crushing their commerce. Many influential politicians in the state threaten to secede from the Union. Great, that was just what Madison wanted. Thankfully, lots of diplomatic talks eventually calmed the fires of anger in New England.

The ultimate low-point for America came in 1814. It was somewhat inevitable, but the British finally invaded Washington DC. They ransacked the place. And worst of all, they burned down the White House. Madison was driven from his home and was the first (and only, to date) sitting President to directly face the onslaught of enemy fire. His wife Dolly, to her credit, was able to save the famous portrait of George Washington that hung in the White House. But that was pretty much all that was salvaged.

James Madison took command of a militia that was posted just outside of the capitol. However, as with so many of these battles, even Madison's army was forced to retreat. There was no doubt, this war was well and truly lost. We have to look at the context: America was still really a third-world nation in terms of its wealth and influence and was just not strong enough to fight off what was at the time, the greatest army in the world. England defeated America on land and sea, it was a total thrashing. This thrashing burdened Madison and the entirety of his Presidency.

But, it was under his second term that finally Madison ended this war. He sent James Monroe to seek any and all diplomatic routes to end the destructive conflict. Monroe, like Madison, was a man of great intelligence and, to the surprise of many, succeeded with the December 1814 Treaty of Gent. Finally, the war was officially over. There were those in England who did not favour this treaty and felt that America could be retaken again with just one more victory on American soil. However, thankfully they did not get their way...

HANDS OFF NEW ORLEANS

Before the age of the internet and high-speed communication, news travelled slowly. This peace agreement was no exception. It took some time before the news of the treaty came to America. As such, there was still some fighting going on after the treaty was signed. Many of the English hoped that a key victory in New Orleans could finally end the solidarity of the entire American republic and America would be British once more. New Orleans was part of the Louisiana Purchase. If America could defend their new soil there, then maybe Jefferson's purchase would prove to be the right choice to make.

So the British Army was desperate in its attempts to take over the city and possibly retake the entire republic with it. But the Americans fighting to defend New Orleans had other plans. They beat the British army with a stunning victory. However, as was the case so many times before during the Revolutionary War, the odds were definitely not stacked in America's favour. Again, the American spirit prevailed and at the crucial time, the United States stood firm.

A man of note in the victory was a General by the name of Andrew Jackson. Jackson received a 'George Washington-esque' reverence from those who fought with him. This would serve him well in the future.

The victory however, did little for James Madison.

EVENTS SHAPING THE PRESIDENCY

Let us be totally clear: James Madison was a great man, and should have been an amazing President. However, the War of 1812 stifled most of what he wanted to do and also signalled the end of his

Presidency.

However, Madison's time in office did gesture a change in America. It was no longer an isolated country, that could escape the rest of the world. America was now a nation at the centre of world events. It was America's first venture into the politics of international diplomacy. No longer could the outside world beyond America's borders be ignored. It was a vital exercise for the new republic in growing up and reaching a maturity. America now had a better idea of how to deal with the rest of world events.

Under President Madison, American prosperity and social mobility continued to skyrocket. But despite this, and despite his character in the face of adversity, and despite his enormous potential and incredible ability, history remembers Madison simply as the reluctant wartime President.

FIVE
JAMES MONROE

Took Office: March 4th 1817
Left Office: March 4th 1825
Party: Democratic-Republican
Terms: 8 & 9

AS WITH PREVIOUS ELECTIONS of the time, the Presidential election of 1816 occurred peacefully, democratically and without drama. Hey, America was getting good at this! The Federalists were all but finished, and it seemed that the winners would again be some variant of the Jeffersonian wing of the Democratic-Republican Party. In the selection of the fifth head of the executive branch of federal government, America yet again turned to a Virginian founding father, James Monroe.

As George Washington was a President of firsts, President Monroe was a President of lasts. He was the last of the Virginian/revolutionary dynasty to be the President.

However, the reverence reserved for the previous 'revolutionary'

Presidents seemed to be absent when it came to President Monroe. Going over the writings and commentary of the day, no one seemed to hold him in that high regard. However, as another war hero, there is a certain level of respect, and there have been numerous writings about his virtues as a patient and honest man.

But the passionate feeling that was written about Washington, Jefferson and Madison is somewhat absent when it comes to the fifth Commander-in-Chief. Some say he wasn't the smartest man in the world, yet he won two elections to the Presidency and won them with very significant margins (though in fairness, he ran unopposed in his second term, possibly because of his amicable nature and the fact that he was widely tolerated by many Americans). He was a brilliant man though. It's unfair how history records things sometimes, isn't it?

PEACE MAN, PEACE

In many ways, quite a bit of the hard work was done. Expanding the United States' borders to ensure, amongst other things, the security of the nation was a necessary action already achieved by Jefferson, as was the general principle and application of free trade and the mantra of 'life, liberty and the pursuit of happiness'. Dealing with the immediate difficulties of a new fragile republic was already handled by Washington. The war against Britain was dealt with thanks to the diplomatic talents of Madison and his staff. Though Monroe was probably the most significant player in that diplomacy.

So the new President entered office with the peace and prosperity the other Presidents had worked so hard to achieve. He wasn't so foolish as to take credit for it all, but we have to credit him with the fact that he could have greatly interfered with the freedoms that finally were beginning to show fruit in America, but chose not to.

Monroe wasn't a very controlling President at all. He would delegate work to his cabinet, in the way that the Founding Fathers assumed the President would. This attitude, very much in keeping with Monroe's hands-off management style, came in very handy. He hired the best people and entrusted them with doing the right thing.

The President was never supposed to be a great authoritarian leader, the general idea was that they were supposed to have great minds advising and implementing executive orders, and the President was supposed to serve the will of Congress. The Founding Fathers ideas were being very well implemented by Monroe, and they grew to serve him well for the moments that defined his Presidency.

MISSOURI RISING

Right at the start of Monroe's first term, the territory of Missouri petitioned for statehood. America's insistence on the right to life, liberty and the pursuit of happiness was becoming a catchy idea, with more and more evidence of prosperity behind it, and many in the outer territories understandably wanted in.

In isolation, simply welcoming more people into the fold of this great new republic should have been a cause for celebration. We add a new star to the flag, and then go eat cake. But the cake was on hold this time. Which was a shame, because I love cake. Missouri's petition for statehood ignited the first big political hot potato for Monroe, a hot potato that stained American politics for generations, and still, (in other forms), lingers in some corners of the political spectrum. The issue was slavery.

The question that needed answering, was 'will Missouri be a free state, or a slave state'? Congress took this question and debated it over and over. It seems so abstract to our values now. How could anyone even contemplate the notion of a slave state today? But it was a 19th Century question that's very hard to see with 21st Century eyes. Monroe, (a slave-holder himself), made it clear that any state that would be excepted into the Union would be allowed 'self determination', or to put it another way, the issue of slavery was an issue for each individual state to make its mind up. If Congress pushed a law forward one way or another for Missouri, he would veto it.

Eventually, Congress passed the politically awkward and uncomfortable-sounding Missouri Compromise of 1820. So Missouri entered the Union as a slave state. At about the same time, Maine entered the Union as a free state.

It might sound like an uncomfortable situation, and in many respects it was, But the Missouri Compromise of 1820 does put a bit of common sense into the mix. Upon welcoming Missouri into the Union, restrictions were put on the expansion of slavery. As solutions go, it's like putting a band-aid on a gaping wound. But it was only ever meant as a temporary solution to what was at the time, a very fiery and divisive issue. However, as we shall see in Presidencies to come, the growth of government interference on the issue of slavery, and regulation both for and against it, (instead of the free-market collapse of slavery that the likes of Jefferson rightly envisaged happening – that's what was happening across the rest of the world), led to very ugly and violent times across American history.

Monroe had his own plan to solve the 'slave problem'. He had the idea of returning slaves back to Africa. This idea led to the formation of the American Colonisation Society. It had quite a bit of support in certain circles. Those former slaves who wanted to go back home, would be free to do so. Slavery was seen by many of the Americans as an ugly virus of the old British monarchist, hierarchy-obsessed, authoritarian way of doing things.

Monroe's plan led to the founding of Monrovia in Liberia. Yep, it was named after President Monroe. It was the only foreign capital to be named after an American President. It's a shame in a way, because I reckon that 'Jeffersonia' sounds like a cool place to live.

However, the American Colonisation Society did little to settle, or minimise the domestic slavery in the United States. Governmental interference of any kind on either side of the debate just seemed incapable of making any significant changes for the better. I could copy and paste that sentence over and over throughout this book, or indeed any book on political history. It would almost always be true.

HEY – STICK TO YOUR OWN BORDERS

As the issue of slavery continued to be a source of great difficulty for politicians and the American people at large, the President suddenly found he faced another issue that required urgent attention: Florida. It was one of the first significant problems involving American borders for a President to deal with. The Floridian territory was still under the rule and ownership of the Spanish empire. An empire not too happy with this new free American republic (a jealousy that other nations have for the USA that continues to this day).

However, Florida was only technically under Spanish control. In actual fact, the Spanish authorities only marginally controlled what went on in the territory. As a result, it became a haven for criminal activity. If you go to Disney World in Orlando, Florida today, the Pirates of the Caribbean ride was a pretty good representation of Florida activity back in the early 1800s. Well, you know, sort of. It was probably a little less animatronic back then. The whole state was rife with pirates, crooks and villains. And just to make it even more exciting, the state was populated by dozens of Native American tribes. Those guys certainly weren't governed by the Spanish!

By 1818, illegal (and violent) border incursions into the United States were all-too frequent. While occasionally the incursions were committed by pirates and the like, the Native Americans were particularly to blame.

Poor Georgia – that state was the biggest victim of these incursions. The Native Americans would frequently raid and loot the white settlements, and they would usually do so with the encouragement of British privateers, whose boats and trading activities were usually done just off the Florida coast. (Boo! It's always those nasty Brits in some form or another isn't it?!)

President Monroe was having none of it. He ordered troops to the area to tighten up security. American border-patrol to the south was finally born. And this was probably the only time that it had any significant effect of dealing with the problem at hand. Also, worthy of note (we've mentioned him already in this book, and we've not even gotten to his chapter yet), is the fact that the army was led by a certain war hero by the name of Andrew Jackson.

Jackson had orders from President Monroe to prevent the Native Americans from invading the settlements. It didn't take him long to realise that the British privateers were behind it all, (think James Bond villains, stroking white cats in the background and you get the idea), and if he didn't do something about them, the Native Americans would just keep coming back and back. So he decided to invade Florida. Though not in the way that millions of tourists do every year these days. The Native Americans wore a lot less Mickey Mouse hats.

Andrew Jackson found the British men responsible and had them hanged. Job done, except for the little matter that he basically has caused a massive international incident involving America, Spain and Great Britain. Oops.

Some in President Monroe's cabinet were furious. Monroe's Secretary of War, John C. Calhoun, (the angriest looking man in the history of American politics – even more so than the great Warren G. Harding), insisted on General Jackson being reprimanded for his actions. However, John Quincy Adams, (remember that name too), Monroe's Secretary of State, stuck up for Andrew Jackson. Adams was the son of the second President, the authoritarian John Adams.

John Quincy pointed out that the actions of the British privateers was utterly reprehensible. The Spaniards ought to have stopped them and so failed in their duties. He also pointed out that Congress had ordered the President to stop this activity by any means, and the head of the executive branch had rightly given that order to his General. So no real rules were broken.

Monroe was convinced by John Quincy Adams' argument. In fact, rather than reprimand Andrew Jackson, he instead spoke to the Spanish and tried to cut a deal in purchasing Florida from them. Heck, why not – it'd stop America from being constantly invaded and the Spanish weren't really using it anyway, right? In 1819, the Spanish, though they weren't the biggest fans of America, really couldn't be bothered with either the Florida territory or having a fight over it, so, with the native population kicking up very little stink, the Spanish peacefully allowed Florida to join the American Union.

DEFINING THE MONROE PRESIDENCY

Despite yet more rising standards during his time in office, border issues were rife under Monroe's Presidency. Poor guy, what did he ever do to deserve that? Though he didn't want it to be the case, as is often the way with these things, it was disputes over borders that defined his legacy. As well as having trouble down in the Deep South with Florida, America was having a dispute right up north with the Russians over Alaska.

In his December 1823 address to Congress over the issue, he made his most important speech. The speech was not just for Congress' ears. It was a speech that was also addressed to the rest of the world. A line of that speech became the most significant line he would ever speak during in his time in office. The line he is remembered for: "The American continents are henceforth not to be considered as subjects for future colonisation by any European powers." The now infamous 'Monroe Doctrine' was born. But in a grand way, it was the Americans telling Europe that they could no longer come in and take new territories from the American continent. In more simple terms, Monroe was saying to Europe "this be our hood now, so back off, y'all".

Of course, it wasn't until 1852 that people started calling this concept 'The Monroe Doctrine'. President Monroe had long since left office. Even today, it is widely considered the greatest achievement of this pretty decent American President. However, it's worth noting, that even though the defining line in that speech he made in 1823 perfectly summed up Monroe's beliefs in the matter at hand, he wasn't actually the author of the speech. That credit goes to the gentleman I mentioned earlier. John Quincy Adams.

SIX
JOHN QUINCY ADAMS

Took Office: March 4th 1825
Left Office: March 4th 1829
Party: Democratic-Republican
Term: 10

HAVING ALREADY MADE HIS mark as Secretary of State, John Quincy Adams was considered an ideal candidate for President. It appeared that the Secretary of State cabinet position was becoming the big shoe-in role for the top job. Before John Quincy Adams, Thomas Jefferson, James Madison and James Monroe all had undertaken the Secretary of State role before becoming President. While almost all aspiration-filled politicians wanted to be the Commander-in-Chief, it's not surprising that many wanted the Secretary of State job too.

However, it wasn't going to be a shoe-in this time. The election year of 1824 was quite different. And by 'different', I mean completely barmy. Looking back, today the whole story would be considered even too over the top for a dire soap opera.

John Quincy Adams faced pretty stiff competition. Amongst those putting themselves forward for the top job, was John C. Calhoun (the Secretary of War in Monroe's cabinet), as well as Treasury Secretary William Crawford. But the Monroe cabinet was not the only place that John Quincy Adams had competition. In Congress, finally more vocal men of stature were being hotly tipped, including Henry Clay, the Speaker of the House. Along with state governors, one of the most frequent positions people would make a bid for President from would grow to become Congress.

And of course, we still can't forget one chap who keeps turning up in everyone else's chapters: Andrew Jackson. We'll get to his main story soon I promise, but he plays a big part in this one too. The General was gaining huge public support, and many felt that he could become the sixth President of the United States. They were almost right. And they should have been right.

The fact that the 1824 election for President was going to be the first election where states were counting the popular vote, should have been a cause for great celebration and the advancement of democracy in the United States. Finally a candidate could measure their popularity amongst the people they were vying to represent.

When the votes were counted and tallied up, it must be stated that with 151,271 votes, Jackson was way ahead of John Quincy Adams' distant second place score of 113,112. Game over, right? Well, no, not really. Under the constitution, the Electoral College system was still where the decision was made. And despite Andrew Jackson's significant victory in the popular vote, the Electoral College system said it was too close to call.

Electoral College votes put Andrew Jackson on 99 votes, John Quincy Adams on 84, William Crawford on 41, and Henry Clay in fourth place on 37. Again, this should be straightforward. Jackson won it, right? Nope. Under the rules, he needed an overall majority of votes, which he clearly did not get.

So how did they resolve this? The constitution was pretty clear. The top three had to go to the House of Representatives and it was the House that got to decide. Now things got interesting. Because the top three went through to the next round, (it's like a quiz show!), the fourth-placed Henry Clay was dropped. But here's the odd twist: remember, Henry Clay was the Speaker of the House of Representatives. So Clay would be the king-maker, and not the king.

But we're not done with this saga yet. Out of nowhere, William Crawford goes and has a stroke. So then it became a two-man deal. The contest was between the very popular Andrew Jackson, and the not as popular John Quincy Adams. With the whole contest going on under the nose of Henry Clay, presiding over the madness from his pulpit. You couldn't make it up.

We'll never quite know if a deal was made between Henry Clay and John Quincy Adams. But let's put it this way; despite his lower popularity and the fact he got less Electoral College votes than Andrew Jackson, John Quincy Adams somehow won the House of Representatives ballot in the first round, and appointed Henry Clay to the cushy (President-making) role of Secretary of State. If you don't think a dodgy deal was made between these two, then you're a lot more trusting that I am...

Rather unsurprisingly, Andrew Jackson, as anyone in his position would, screamed 'scandal' from the top of his lungs. His supporters were outraged. On the whole, the American people were frankly disgusted. Many feel this 'corrupt deal' was a cynical bid for power on the part of John Quincy Adams, a man who was of course, son to the second American President, a man who also had a little too much thirst for authority and power. John Quincy wanted to take office and prove that his father was right in the way he wanted to run things all along. Well, he was certainly doing things his fathers' way, but it definitely wasn't proving his father 'right' in any way. Even before he took the Presidential oath, it wasn't going well for John Quincy Adams. And let us be clear; it was his own fault.

AMBITIONS FOR THE REPUBLIC

John Quincy Adams had a number of ambitions for his time in office. He wanted to fund public education. He wanted more progress in the field of scientific advancement. He wanted Americans to venture even further than they had before and discover more of the Western territories. And in the areas of the continent that were already part of the United States, he wanted better civil infrastructure, such as roads and bridges. Or to put it in a more clear way, he wanted a bigger Federal government.

A quick side-note to these plans: Many believed, and many still do, that there was a significant problem with these ideas. For example: improving civil infrastructure is a great idea, sure. But why not allow the individual states to do that? Eventually the Federal government did take control of many of these things. However, anyone who's driven down a pothole infested road in Middle-America today knows that the Federal mandates to improve roads and so on, are so bogged down in waste and red tape, that many never get fixed.

If each state had the obligation, then the competition between them to have the best infrastructures, etc. would have probably led to a much more efficient and competent series of road-management schemes, with each state learning from the others' successes and failures. And because the regulations to manage the roads would be decentralised to the states, then there would (hopefully in most cases) be a lot less bureaucratic waste.

However, a great deal of the things John Quincy Adams wanted to implement, almost all of them in fact, were pretty much scrapped from the get go. The nature of the politics in Washington DC prevented the new President Adams from achieving much of anything. The growing supporters of Andrew Jackson were still very sore at the awfully anti-democratic way that John Quincy Adams grabbed at office. They were very upset at the 'cronyism' that Adams had utilised in order to gain power.

But power for the President was limited by the rules of office. Congress had the real power to make and vote on the laws, and with John Quincy Adams as the head of the executive branch of government, boy did they use it. They knocked down virtually every proposal and policy that he wanted to implement. Many of them were proud of the free democratic values that the likes of Jefferson and Madison had instilled in the country, and were still disgusted at the nasty back-door way John Quincy Adams managed to sneak into the White House.

And to top it all off, Congress knew that John Quincy Adams was a 'big state' guy like his father. He wanted massive increases in government spending and he wanted considerably more power to achieve it. Thankfully for the people, in virtually every occasion that he wanted yet more power or control, the defiant Congress, acting as the Founding Fathers would have almost certainly wanted it to, denied his requests.

Of course, a great President needs to be endearing and inspirational. As a character, John Quincy Adams held none of these traits. Though he was of great intelligence, he had the humour of a dead fish and a point-blank refusal to accommodate others. It was frequently said by both those in Congress and (after the fact) those in his cabinet, that John Quincy Adams simply wouldn't 'meet you in the middle' on anything. But if he wasn't going to play the democratic game, then no one else would play with him.

John Quincy Adams, true to his father's form, wanted the office of President to be a more 'monarchist' device that would be of such authoritarian power that Congress would be forced to carry out every single whim. Unfortunately for both of the Adams men, (though fortunately, I dare suggest, for the rest of us), freedom doesn't really work like that. And as such, it is often said that John Quincy Adams suffered from the most miserable and snivelling Presidency in history. And I'm sorry to say it, but he kind of deserved it.

There was a general sigh of relief in Washington and around the United States, when, despite John Quincy Adams trying for a second term, (why on earth did he bother?), finally the man who the people wanted to be the sixth President became the seventh instead. It was a bitter election, but Andrew Jackson finally stepped up, and John Quincy Adams shuffled off into the dark corners of history. Only for a while though. His time in Congress (where he returned after a bit of a sulk) saw him achieving quite a bit in the areas of civil liberty and the increase in abolitionist policies.

SEVEN
ANDREW JACKSON

Took Office: March 4th 1829
Left Office: March 4th 1837
Party: Democratic
Terms: 11 & 12

THE BATTLE FOR OFFICE between Andrew Jackson and John Quincy Adams was a very bitter one. There's no point in denying it. These guys would never be friends. And, in the beginning anyway, you can't really point the figure at Jackson. He should have been the sixth President and it was taken from him in a very cynical and rather suspect deal. When Jackson stood again, it was on the ticket of a new party. It was basically a modification of the Democratic-Republicans, known simply as the Democratic Party. His political opponents at the time called him a 'Jackass'. Jackson liked the name so much, he made it the emblem of his new party. That's why the Democrats today still use that donkey motif.

The dirty campaign tactics in the second Jackson/Adams election were the most brutal in American history at the time. Andrew Jackson's plan for the 1828 election campaign was pretty simple. He was a very successful General in the US Armed forces. He embodied the struggle that underpinned the American Revolution. And most of all, he was a people's favourite. However, Jackson had some skeletons in his closet, and the John Quincy Adams campaign team had no qualms about exploiting them.

Jackson liked to gamble. That was frowned upon by certain Americans and so was used by John Quincy Adams to paint a less savoury picture of his opponent. Andrew Jackson's skills as a military General were a winning plus-point for him, but John Quincy Adams tried to use the politics of fear on this issue. He wanted Americans to believe that Jackson would act like a military dictator. At one political rally, John Quincy Adams even went as far as to call Andrew Jackson nothing more than "a barbarian." Handbags at dawn.

But not only did John Quincy Adams attack Andrew Jackson in any way he could, he also overstepped the mark elsewhere. His ugly campaign also concentrated in part, on Jackson's wife, Rachel. Poor Rachel – what on earth had she done? The main argument was that many years ago she married Andrew Jackson before obtaining a legally-binding divorce from her previous husband. Now technically that was correct. There had been a mistake made in this area. But it was a mistake made toward the end of the previous century. No one in the Jackson camp could even believe it was being brought up as an issue. Finally when a Cincinnati newspaper published all the lurid details, Jackson flew into a rage. He was particularly angry at Henry Clay, who he blamed for revealing the information in the first place.

Unfortunately, the main political issues that should have been at the forefront of the debate, (such as the role of government in society, the tax rate, and so on), were cast to one side. The vicious tactics used by John Quincy Adams' team meant that this became an election based on character. In some ways, maybe that was good for both candidates. If either of them had to spend too long on the real issues, there were arguably plenty of far superior potential candidates who could have swept in from relative obscurity to win the top job. As a matter of a fact, I can't help feeling that it was a shame there was no decent alternative candidate at the time. Maybe if there was, the American people would have gotten a better deal.

John Quincy Adams may have started this particularly ugly fight, but Andrew Jackson didn't exactly shy away from it either. In his campaign literature, Jackson would imply that John Quincy Adams lived with his wife 'in sin' before they were married. Also that he purchased a pool table for 'gambling purposes' and that he had broken the Sabbath on more than one occasion. I know, I know. But these things were a big deal back then. However some of the allegations would make your toes curl even today. Check this one out: Jackson implied on more than one occasion that John Quincy Adams had somehow 'provided' a visiting Russian VIP with a young American virgin girl to do with as he pleased. Not only was this a horrific accusation, but also as far as I could research, utterly untrue.

Both men spent a great deal of time smearing the others character. For years to come, this sort of electioneering has easily become one of the main causes of apathy amongst voters.

And ultimately, none of it mattered anyway. The outcome that many had predicted before the race had even started turned out to be exactly what happened. Andrew Jackson won in a landslide. Regardless of the bitter personal accusations made by either candidate, (though it has to be noted that most of the accusations made by John Quincy Adams were true, where Jackson's were not), the people and the Electoral College still remembered the awful way Adams won the previous election. And they did not forgive him for it.

WHAT A WAY TO START

Unfortunately for Andrew Jackson, before he was even sworn into office, tragedy struck. His wife, who commendably held her head high during the whole awfulness of the campaign, died suddenly of a heart attack. Apparently she was picking out a gown to wear for the inauguration at the time.

Andrew Jackson wasn't just devastated. He was almost brought to a position of mental breakdown. It affected his entire mental state, and it did so for the entirety of his Presidency. He declared that he would unconditionally forgive all those who attacked him during the campaign, but never anyone who attacked the character of his wife. And he meant it.

And if you were thinking that John Quincy Adams couldn't be any more awful, any more like his father, think again. Like his bitter father after he lost the election to the great Thomas Jefferson, John Quincy Adams refused to attend Andrew Jackson's inauguration. If I was Andrew Jackson, (and the American people can breathe a sigh of relief that I was not), I'd be perfectly happy that John Quincy Adams wasn't there. Good riddance.

Or maybe not quite. Unlike many other Presidents, John Quincy Adams didn't just shuffle off into the pages of political history after leaving the white House. To his lasting credit, he returned to Washington DC two years later, having been elected to the House of Representatives, and spent his later years fighting the good fight against slavery. It's his saving grace. The authoritarian President, spending his twilight years fighting for liberty. Good on you, J.Q.

JACKSON'S WAY

It's interesting that Andrew Jackson called himself a 'Jeffersonian Democrat'. Interesting only in so much as the fact that Thomas Jefferson actually called Jackson a 'dangerous man'. Jefferson respected men of passion, conviction and reason. However, he felt that Jackson was a man who bordered on 'fanaticism'. Jefferson thought that Jackson had his beliefs so ideologically ingrained that no rational reason-based counterargument could sway him. This is the 'danger' that Jefferson so rightly talked about. The only question, was could Jackson step up above the character flaws within himself to be the 'Jeffersonian Democrat' that he so desperately claimed to be? The answer turned out to be simply "In most ways, not at all." It would turn out that most of the fears Jefferson had would be very valid.

Jackson was not an easy man to sum up. The basic two-dimensional character-smears of the 1828 election aside, this was a very multifaceted individual.

Unlike his Presidential predecessor, Andrew Jackson, the first President to be born in a log cabin, despised privilege. During his time as the Commander-in-Chief, he insisted that people continued to call him 'General', (in terms of affection more than title), rather than the normal "Mr. President." He was a 'bruiser', a bar-room brawler, a gambler and would smoke his tobacco pipe whenever he felt the urge. He even had two bullets lodged in his body from duels. He'd fight at the drop of a hat. As one historian put it, if Andrew Jackson were around today, a psychologist would probably deem him a troubled man and give him medication, but Jackson "would probably not take it."

He loathed the idea of monarchs and people within the American system who wanted to be like them. He was perfectly happy, (in fact he was a big supporter), of people who rose above their 'station' to make a success of themselves. But he understood the difference between 'old money' and the Jeffersonian spirit of American social mobility.

But Jackson, like Jefferson, was not the sort of President who wanted to know every ounce of feeling and opinion that the American people had and act upon it. Quite the contrary. Like his idol the third President, Jackson wanted to understand public opinion so that he could shape it. And his determination to shape public opinion was achieved by his strong will.

However, that's where the Jeffersonian democrat in him ended. Unlike the highly personable Thomas Jefferson, Jackson was a pretty intimidating guy to be around. He would boom and rage when he wanted to, and was rather a belligerent so-and-so. But he used his anger as a rather effective, if brutal, management tool. As such, those who met and worked with him never sat on the fence. They either loved him or hated him. They either found him very easy to work with, or would just walk out and quit. He was a man who neither knew or cared for the 'centre-ground', that phrase most often worshipped by politicians.

JACKSON'S CABINET FIGHTS

Ever the military man, Jackson started a war right away. The old guard at the White House were swept away immediately. He fired all of his political 'enemies', and hired all of his friends. This caused anger amid the political chattering classes in D.C.

And just one month into his Presidency, and Andrew Jackson was faced with his most challenging war yet. The War of the Petticoats. As the title suggests, this has to be the most pathetic dispute ever. It concerned the wife of John Eaton, Andrew Jackson's secretary of war. Eaton's wife, Margaret Peggy Eaton, was not exactly on good terms with the wives of the other cabinet members. The reason being, Margaret started to date John Eaton while she was still married to another man. Shock! Horror! As such, the wives of the other cabinet secretaries refused to socialise with the Eaton's. John C. Calhoun's wife was the one wife to be the most vocally opposed to Margaret.

Andrew Jackson, who had of course just lost his own wife not so long ago, was both angry and perplexed by this. But of course, Peggy Eaton was being given the same 'contempt' by the same political class that had given Jackson's wife such a hard time too, so he had a great sympathy for her. Jackson told his cabinet that their wives just *HAD* to socialise with the Eatons. However, the wives refused to do anything of the sort. This 'war' ran on for two years of Jackson's Presidency. It came to head when Jackson, utterly baffled by what to do, demanded that his cabinet officers resign. They did.

I know what you're thinking. Why is Andy Jones wasting our time over the historical nuances of such a trivial matter? Well think about it. This was a rather revealing aspect to his Presidency. He couldn't manage his cabinet at all. He ruled purely by force and co-ercion. And it just plain didn't work. As such, cabinet secretaries, the guys who are supposed to be his closest advisers, were reduced cas-ual workers. With Andrew Jackson in office, cabinet secretaries were like newspapers. There were new ones every day.

He went through five secretaries of treasury, four secretaries of state, six secretaries of…well, you get the idea. So instead of the cabi-net, Jackson was much more comfortable working with an informal group of advisers.

This loose gathering of friends quickly became known in the press at the time as "Andrew Jackson's Kitchen Cabinet." The name came from the fact that this 'unofficial' advisers would come into the White House through the back door, literally the kitchen door, in-stead of entering through the more formal entrances to the building. It's a shame that's where the name comes from really. Unfortunately, it's not because they actually had their meetings *in* the kitchen. I've got a great image in my head of them all just hanging out and gossip-ing by the breakfast bar with the Commander-in-Chief, while he fixes everyone up with a mug of hot java.

JACKSON MAKES SOME CHANGES

And he made them very fast indeed.

The first major piece of legislation that Jackson recommended and got past, was the Indian Removal Act of 1830. The legislation was as awful as it sounded. It allowed Jackson to forcibly evict every single Native American tribe east of the Mississippi River. Five 'Indian Nations' were directly affected. One of the tribes, the now famous Cherokee Tribe, chose to tackle this eviction in an all-new, very American way. War? Nope. Circling the wagons? Nope. They took their case to court. The US Supreme Court, no less.

And it worked, just like the Founding Fathers said it would. The Chief Justice ruled in favour of the Cherokee. He rightly stated that the action was unconstitutional and therefore the Cherokee did not have to move. Andrew Jackson however, wasn't going to just roll over on this.

Now, let's be clear, because there can be no doubts about this: Andrew Jackson indulged in one of the worst abuses in American Presidential history. He ignored the Supreme Courts' ruling. He had the Cherokee moved under gun point. Their property was seized, they were forced to leave and were taken far away to a new settlement sight. The awful and horrific truth is that 25% of all the Cherokee's died en-route. Unsurprising then, that this forced movement is called simply 'the trail of tears'. It remains one of the worst stains on American history.

It wasn't long after the Indian Removal Act of 1830 that Andrew Jackson faced a crisis so deep, that the Union itself could have been threatened. It was the South Carolina Nullification Crisis.

Officials in South Carolina were increasingly angry about the high Federal tariffs on imported goods. Such laws were great for the likes of the state of Maine, but the Southern plantation states felt they were getting a raw deal. As such, South Carolina declared it had a right to nullify the tax. Just like that.

The Vice President, John C. Calhoun was the man who was most responsible for being the advocate of this nullification. It is supposed that President Jackson was more than happy to negotiate the main issue (i.e. that the tax was too high and therefore should be lowered), but, and this is where it gets silly again, his dislike of his Vice President (who he considered an enemy) was so great, that he refused to negotiate. In fact, he was willing to ride into South Carolina with an army and put down anything that even remotely looked like a rebellion.

Thankfully, the democratic provisions that the Founding Fathers laid down were put to good use instead. Congress negotiated a fairer tariff, and South Carolina agreed and back down.

The biggest challenge that Andrew Jackson faced just at the end of his first term, was the 'Bank War'. What is it with Andrew Jackson and wars?! However, this one wasn't really his doing.

Henry Clay, (who, it must be noted, was running for President at the time), guided Congress to renew the Bank of the United States' charter, even though it wasn't due until 1836. But because the President of the Bank (Nicholas Biddle) was a big supporter of his, Henry Clay made sure its future was secure. He presented the new charter to President Jackson on the 4th of July. Nice timing Clay.

Now Andrew Jackson didn't seem to be that fussed about the banks new charter really. It was pretty much exactly as it would have been had it been presented to him in 1836. But because Clay had done it just before the election, Jackson came down hard against it on the grounds of (oh no, sorry, but here we go again) Clay being his 'political enemy'.

And in many ways, this time Jackson was right. Both Clay and Biddle thought that if Jackson didn't sign the bill, then Jackson would have no chance in getting re-elected for a second term. They hoped his irrationality would take him out of office. But President Jackson still had some electioneering tricks up his sleeve.

In his campaign for re-election, Jackson personified the Bank of the United States as being one man: Nicholas Biddle. And not only did Jackson set out to paint Biddle as his own personal enemy, but also as the oppressive enemy of the people of the United States. The public supported this narrative. He was the man who could smash the 'master bank'. It was a success.

Andrew Jackson vetoed the bill and returned it to Congress with a simple note: "The bill to continue the Bank of the United States was presented to me on the 4th of July. Having considered it with that solemn regard to the principles of the Constitution which the day was calculated to inspire, and come to the conclusion that it ought not to become a law, I herewith return it to the Senate, in which it originated, with my objections."

Upon his landslide second-term victory, Jackson proceeded to close down the Bank of the United States. He redirected funds, (after firing a couple of secretaries of the treasury first), from the 'monster bank' to state banks. When Congress found out what Andrew Jackson had done, they censured him for his actions. But once the Democrats took control of Congress, they had Jackson's censure officially expunged. Eventually, the Bank of the United States was finished. The American economy was all the more freer and healthier for it.

Andrew Jackson was a complex man. He had the principled belief of hating authority, but ruled with an iron and authoritarian fist. Both America as a nation, and the standards of living of the people in it, progressed greatly while he was in office. But again, this was mostly despite Jackson's Presidency rather than because of it. However, this did not stem his popularity as people identified (however incorrectly) that their prosperity came from the fact that Andrew

Jackson was in power at the time. Really, the fact that he was in power was irrelevant. Congress and the lawmakers were spending most of their time making sure the Constitutional rules of law were enforced, and they were not indulging in rules and bills of 'social engineering'. It was this more Jeffersonian fact, not any specific philosophy of Andrew Jackson, which was responsible for the great prosperous 'Era of Jackson.'

And while America was finally debt-free under his time in office, and even though he had great support of the people, America would not go on supporting such centralised power. As a result, by his own decision, Jackson's second term would be his last. It was the turn of his good friend, Martin Van Buren.

EIGHT
MARTIN VAN BUREN

Took Office: March 4th 1837
Left Office: March 4th 1841
Party: Democratic
Term: 13

OCCASIONALLY, AS WE SAW between Andrew Jackson and John Quincy Adams, elections for the role of President could be pretty vicious. However, the transition of power between Andrew Jackson and Martin Van Buren was a rather sedate affair. Sorry about that. After all the drama of what happened before, it comes of something as a disappointment, doesn't it?

And these 'easy' transitions of power weren't just disappointing because they contained no drama. There are many people (myself included) who fret over people who swan into political office without too much difficulty. Where is the merit? Where is the scrutiny in such a case? Shouldn't we be able to know everything about what sort of a person we're electing to government? Where are the tests to prove their worth? When someone 'inherits' political office, they usually shouldn't be there in the first place. And so enter Martin Van Buren, stage-left...

Van Buren was hand-picked by Jackson and that was sufficient for him to win the election. It's worth remembering again; despite some of the outrageous and often bizarre decisions made by Andrew Jackson, he was still the American people's favourite. As I mentioned in the previous chapter, the significant increase in prosperity that was engulfing America was occurring for a very simple reason: small government. Politicians in the legislative branch at local and federal level weren't dictating the road that Americans had to travel. People were free to find their own way in life. And when politicians let that happen, prosperity reigned.

However, the head of the executive branch of government was seen increasingly by Americans as the figurehead and (even if this were not the case) responsible for whatever was going on in their societies at the time. So if times are good, it's thanks to the President. If times are bad, then it's the Presidents fault. So many people were still passionate about wrongly attributing their success to the seventh resident at the White House.

As well as possessing the craziest hair of pretty much all the American Presidents past and present (check out the side-burns in particular – they're great), the other significant achievement of Van Buren's pre-Presidential life was that he was the true father of the Democratic Party. Jackson may have been the first President that ran and won under the Democratic Party ticket, but Van Buren was the architect of the new party itself. And thanks mostly to him, the Party was extremely successful.

A lot of this success was due to the fact that Van Buren was a very politically savvy character. He often used his very droll sense of humour to influence people. I'd love to know how he mastered that; my 'droll' sense of humour usually puts people off their lunch.

But all of this success revealed something of a problem. Martin Van Buren was the kind of guy who was very much at home scheming in the background, making deals and forging his new political Party. But these skills didn't really serve the role of President very well.

And his attitude towards the top-job wasn't very inspiring. Van Buren had worked incredibly hard all of his life and seemed to treat the Presidency as merely a figurehead role, and for him, a reward for all the hard work he'd done in life. He thought that, as President, he'd be allowed to kick back and enjoy dinner parties in his honour, shake hands with diplomats from around the world, and swan about the White House with a smug grin on his delightfully plump face. History did not allow this to play out.

PANIC! PANIC!

And history has a pretty cruel sense of timing. No sooner had President Van Buren taken the oath of office, when the Panic of 1837 kicked off. The mess and lack of any sort of banking infrastructure that President Andrew Jackson had left in his wake had finally come to roost. Van Buren hadn't rocked the boat at all during Andrew Jackson's Presidency, and even when Jackson was being so boneheaded about the reasons for dismantling the Bank of the United States, Van Buren kept his thoughts to himself.

However, this was one of those moments when a President had to stand up and make a difference. Even if the difference is largely symbolic, the President ought to try and capture or shape the mood of the people and impress upon Congress to solve the crisis in a reasonable and swift manner. Or something like that.

However, Van Buren was bewildered at how he was supposed to deal with this crisis. He was like a kid who'd just lost sight of their mother in a large department store. Utterly lost. He didn't really know what to do. Jackson had left him a real mess.

Unsurprisingly, just burying his head in the sand wasn't really working. The Panic of 1839 was even worse and again Van Buren didn't seem to know how to deal with it. If the free and decentralised banking structure had been restored after Jackson closed the Bank of the United States, then maybe there wouldn't have been a problem.

The economic trouble was really kicking off in one particular area. There was a huge surplus in the cotton industry, which was at the time pretty much the bedrock of the US economy. This caused the price of cotton to go down, and it took the economy kicking and screaming with it.

But surely he couldn't just go through his first term doing nothing, could he? How could he deal with this?

The trouble was, Van Buren had spent his whole political life being a two-handed politician, ("Well on one hand, but on the other…"), and he never had to make tough decisions. His inability to take America down one road or the other rendered any impression that his skills as a President were good enough, completely impotent.

And it wasn't just these economical panics. Another classic Van Buren example: the annexation of Texas. The issue surrounding this annexation was slavery. And slavery as an 'issue', (if you can forgive me for calling it something as trivial as that), had been brewing for some time, and many wanted to know what the President thought. He chose to just ignore the issue. Was he hoping that the debate over Texas was just going to go away? Your guess is as good as mine.

But don't worry; I'll put you out of your misery now. Of course he couldn't just act like this on every issue. He had to take hold of the reigns and (if only symbolically) lead a path to solving Americas economy crisis. So it's only fair that I point out that his eventual plan for the economy was to…erm, well. You know… actually what was his plan?

I'm sorry to report, that he just plain didn't have one. And he never grew a clue.

LET ME ADJUST MY WHIG

The Democratic-Republican Party had, by the time of the end of Van Buren's first term, all but vanished. Due to the characterised success of Andrew Jackson, and the increasingly bad image of John Quincy Adams' Presidency, the great party of Thomas Jefferson, Madison, Monroe, and many more, had vanished from the political mainstream. There was nothing wrong with the original principles of the Party, but so many authoritarian relics from the old 'Federalist Party way of thinking', were now too deeply associated with it. Which is ironic, to say the least. But they had corrupted most of the Democratic-Republican Party and its original values at this stage.

Many of the Federalist-style politicians had instead integrated themselves into the new Democratic Party. But also a (smaller) number of them were in a new Party too.

The new Whig Party was formed, so the Party members used to say, in the spirit of the revolutionaries who fought for the new American Republic back in the day.

Due to President Van Buren's utter lack of leadership and general 'limp' manner to the Presidency, it seemed like whichever candidate the Whig Party picked, would be a shoe-in for the next election. But curiously, no one told the Whigs that was the case. Otherwise, many of them would have nominated William Henry Clay. A number of them were big supporters of President Andrew Jackson's old enemy. And they'd like nothing more than to wipe the smirk of the faces of their Democrat adversaries in Congress. Many Whigs were very concerned about the sense of entitlement that was already emanating from the Democratic Party. They felt the Democrats thought they would be the Party in power forever. And nominating Henry Clay would put a strong end to that feeling.

But surprisingly, that's not what the Whig Party did. Instead, they nominated William Henry Harrison. Why? Image. Welcome to the new era of 'surface-politics', where the two-dimensional image of a candidate matters too.

As much as the Wigs really would have loved to have had Henry Clay run as their first proper Presidential candidate, they were savvy enough to understand the times, and what Americans were after.

The Whigs picked William Henry Harrison because they simply felt Harrison resembled Andrew Jackson the most. I kid you not. He was a soldier, who cut the same striking figure on a horse that the much-loved General Jackson did. You may think that such a basic and, dare I say it, dumb move might have been their downfall. But remember who it was they were running against: Martin 'I don't have an opinion on anything at all' Van Buren. So despite their motivations for picking a candidate, by a very respectable margin, it was the Whigs 'what won it', and for a very simple reason.

What's that old saying that would end up coming back again and again in the world of American market-politics? Oh yeah, that's right: "It's the economy, stupid."

NINE
WILLIAM HENRY HARRISON

Took Office: March 4th 1841
Left Office: April 4th 1841
Party: Whig
Term: 14

MYTHOLOGY PLAYS A SIGNIFICANT part in the all-too brief history of William Henry Harrison's Presidency. And that mythology surrounds his death. As you can see from the date of which President Harrison 'left office', this may very well turn out to be a very short chapter.

Both Van Buren and Harrison engaged in a rather messy election battle in 1840. There was no doubt from either camp that this one was going to get ugly. Some of the smears and silly commentary would be considered a tad unsophisticated in these times, (where politicians have much more erudite ways of attacking each other), but they were considered quite vicious back in the 19th Century. Let the war of words begin.

Harrison had a fairly impressive war record. He had fought as a Frontier General a number of times, and that seemed to go down well with the public at the time. As I explained in the previous chapter, Harrison had been picked by the Whig party for the way he looked – he was rather similar in both physique and history to the Democrat Andrew Jackson, who was still a people's favourite.

However, there was a fundamental difference between Harrison and Jackson that also relieved a few in Washington DC: Harrison was committed to re-charter the Bank of the United States again. The bank that Andrew Jackson so desperately shut down a number of years earlier.

LET THE CAMPAIGN BEGIN

In the Presidential election campaign of 1841, politics was finally becoming the sort of thing that we know and 'love' today. Some of it was great: there were proper public rallies for the first time. The people were able to hear and see the main candidates up close and personal. They could finally ask the tough questions and make those seeking office squirm, as I'm sure the Founding Fathers always wanted.

Of course, the other side of contemporary political campaigns was being born at the same time. There was a sense of a 'marketing machine' behind the main candidates this time around. There were songs (which were positive and negative) manufactured and sung about the candidates. There were planned slogans used at the rallies, and placards were doled out to the supporting crowds.

The public were being wined and dined – sometimes quite literally. Flyers were given out encouraging people to attend exciting public events. For example, in Madison County, one flyer promised free passage on the steamboat Flora to "all the friends of Harrison...and reform who wish to join in the celebration."

Whenever Van Buren or one of his people would speak at a campaign rally, Harrison supporters would do what they could to prevent the rally from going well. An image of a log-cabin (which was becoming symbolic of William Henry Harrison) would always be close whenever Van Buren wanted to make a point, which would effectively undermine any point he was trying to make. A way of rubbing in the 'earthliness' of Van Buren's rival I suppose. What is it with Presidential candidates and log cabins? William Henry Harrison wasn't even born in one, but that little factual matter didn't stop it becoming a very powerful symbol for his campaign.

The Harrison supporters also wanted to push their candidates 'man of the people' image as best they could. How would they do that nowadays? Probably by taking their candidate to a baseball match or something. But one of the biggest symbols used was that of a barrel of hard cider. Yep, they were trying to say "Look, Harrison's a man of the people, because he drinks working-class booze."

Supposedly it was the chants that really got up President Van Buren's nose. "Van Van, he's a washed-up man" was a popular one. And lots of Harrison's campaign material referred to the President as "Martin Van Ruin." Classy.

Let's not pretend for one moment that Martin Van Buren was going to rise above all of this slander. He was certainly not going to play the 'better than thou' card. His supporters rose quite happily to the gutter-speak challenge that Harrison's people had laid down, and were happy to use Harrison's Vice-Presidential running-mate, (John Tyler), in their attacks too.

They often used the nickname that Harrison acquired while he was fighting Native Americans as a Frontier General in Tippecanoe: "Tippecanoe and Tyler Too". Hmm. Great alliteration guys, but it didn't really attack the man that much did it? I guess they just wanted Americans to feel increasingly unsettled that the next Commander-in-Chief would be an Indian-fighting war-happy General.

And on the Whig's side of the political battle, just in case the symbolism of Harrison's log-cabin (that he wasn't born in) wasn't cutting enough mustard, they rolled out another slice of iconography: that of President Van Buren, riding on his rather plush English coach. It was a rather aristocratic image and, I dare say, one that rather suited Van Buren's personality. The Harrison supporters would often sing of their man "In English coaches he's no rider, but he can fight and drink hard cider."

A line of attack in a political campaign that's now all-too familiar, really began in the election of 1840. Martin Van Buren's people constantly attacked William Henry Harrison's age. He was quite old by early 19th Century standards. With this came the insinuation that Harrison was a 'phony' version of Andrew Jackson, and a cardboard cut-out version of a military General rather than one who'd really get stuck in to a battle. At one stage, a load of campaign material was produced by the Van Buren camp that depicted Harrison was the 'Granny General'. I'd have loved to have seen that picture.

By now you may have noticed something rather clear, and rather depressingly familiar with modern-day politics: where are the policies and key issues in this campaign? Ironically, although neither candidate spent much time picking through the issues of policy and matters that the public really cared about, it was in fact a particular tangible issue that swayed the outcome of the election.

President Van Buren's time had run out. As we saw in the previous chapter, he was incapable of making any decisions and people wanted to know there was security and stability, as that was good for the economy. The public were concerned and ultimately felt that the Harrison/Tyler ticket had the best solutions to the issues at hand. And with that fact, the election result comfortably went William Henry Harrison's way.

SHORTEST TERM, LONGEST SPEECH

I think he's fair to presume that President Harrison was upset about the attacks on his age. He was perturbed that people might think he was fragile and didn't have the stamina of a younger man. He had a rather impressive, (if not slightly unusual), way of answering his critics. And this is where the mythology about this Presidency starts.

On the steps of Capitol Hill, after his inauguration, Sixty-Eight year-old President William Henry Harrison proceeded to make the longest inaugural speech in history.

Alongside the rather unfair attacks on his age, his political opponent had made rather unfounded claims about Harrison being a bit of a country bumpkin. But as a college-graduating med student, he was nothing of the sort. Harrison understood he was possibly going to be the last President to have been born a British subject (and it turned out that he was), and knew that with this fact in mind, he was going to be the last President of an era. He was not one for pomp and ceremony, but understood that his inaugural speech would have to resonate in the hearts and minds of the people. He claimed to be very much a Jeffersonian democrat, but alas, we will never know just how much of what he preached, he actually was going to practice.

So Harrison wanted to dispel two key slanders against his good name: that he wasn't all that intelligent, and that he was old and past it. The content of the speech would hopefully put an end to the falsehood in the first misconception, and the stamina required for the length of the speech would rule out the second. That was the plan.

President Harrison's inaugural address was delivered on a bitterly cold March afternoon. At almost two hours, the speech was long and very effective. It was the longest address in history. Despite the cold, Harrison refused to cover up or wear any extra layers or even a hat to protect himself. He understood that image now mattered in American politics.

The myth suggests that he caught a cold that day, (unsurprising in itself), and that the cold turned into pneumonia. Now many suggest that the evidence for that is shaky. He had pneumonia, but he almost certainly caught that sometime after his speech. Nevertheless, the myth still stands. He was bed ridden before he could really do anything as President.

Treatment for such an illness was scarce and exactly one month into his Presidency, William Henry Harrison died. He was the first President to do so in office.

There was a period of dumfounded confusion in Washington at this point. What was supposed to happen? Most people understood that there should be a succession of power from the President to the Vice President. In that spirit, Vice President John Tyler should assume the office. After all, he was on the ticket as William Henry Harrison's running-mate. The people had, technically, voted for John Tyler just as much as they had voted for Harrison, and the Electoral College had effectively done the same.

But as John Tyler was about to find out, the first mid-term change in power would not prove to be an easy thing to administer.

TEN
JOHN TYLER

Took Office: April 4th 1841
Left Office: March 4th 1845
Party: Whig/None
Term: 14

THE CONSTITUTION IS PRETTY clear in this day and age, with regards to the succession of power. If the President pops his clogs, then the Vice President immediately takes over, either in a temporary fashion because the President happens to be incapacitated in the short-term, or on a permanent basis. But the twenty-fifth amendment wouldn't be written into law until 1967. And John Tyler couldn't wait that long.

John Tyler was a Southern planter of great wealth and significant political weight. He had served in both the House of Representatives and the Senate. I couldn't find out which he found to be the most enjoyable. He'd also been the Governor of Virginia. And finally, the Vice President of the United States. It's fair to say that he would have preferred to rise to the office of President by merit of an election, but fate, it would seem, had other plans.

He often said, in a Jeffersonian fashion, that too much power had been placed in the hands of the Federal government. However, as a significant player in the Whig party, some wondered if he was part of the group that seemed to be very happy with increased government economic protectionism. In a word, no. The type of power the Whigs craved would, they were to find out, be very different from the nature of government Tyler believed in.

And Tyler didn't waste time in getting right to it. He made his inaugural address within three days of taking the oath of office – very soon after William Henry Harrison's unfortunate and surprising death. The powers that be in the Whig party were not entirely sure that Tyler was their 'main choice' for President. And, as there was no real precedent for taking over the top job, many felt that someone else (Henry Clay perhaps?) would be a more appropriate choice. Basically, they wanted a Whig party 'yes man' in office. And Tyler, (to his credit in my opinion), didn't seem it.

However, in his inaugural address, John Tyler made it very clear that he was in charge. And the Whig Party would not hold any sway over him. His stubbornness on this was in many ways commendable, but it only seemed to anger the mainstream Whig party even more.

The more noble, more Jeffersonian side of John Tyler would separate him from the Party. In some circles, people described him as not being a Whig-President, but rather a President of no party, such as George Washington in his early (and later) Presidency. Eventually that would become not just a point of view from the gossiping hacks in Washington, but would become more widely understood, as we shall learn.

Tyler would frequently (and commendably) defer to Congress for decision-making. This was exactly as the Founding Fathers would have wished, and seems to be the way it should be in order for

America to prosper. However, his political adversaries had discovered that they could play a certain card against John Tyler because of his more 'constitutional' attitude towards law-making: they could paint him as being weak. And they didn't hold back.

HEY, YOU'RE NOT THE CHIEF!

Right from the start, President Tyler faced questions over his assumed authority. Some referred to him as 'His Accidentcy', for the way he seemed to have 'accidentally' become President and ascended to the role of Commander-in-Chief, purely because of the untimely death of his predecessor. Others in Washington called him 'His Ascendency' too, though probably behind his back.

Others were less cruel, but worried about the constitutional implications of Tyler ascending to power automatically. They felt that he was merely an 'acting President', a caretaker who was filling in until an election could be called. Many of William Henry Harrison's election rivals were eager to take another crack at the top spot very soon.

But others also weighed in with their views. Tyler's cabinet, which, let's be clear, was really Harrison's cabinet, tried to claim that they were entitled to the take over the Presidency, in a manner of speaking.

They were minutes into Tyler's first cabinet meeting, when the Secretary of State Daniel Webster told the new President that it was the cabinet that would make all the executive decisions for the duration of the term, through a democratic consensus. Tyler didn't exactly play the appeasement card. He calmly informed them that he required only one of two things: either their cooperation or their resignations.

And the Whig party weren't finding this fun either. Harrison had made it pretty clear that he was going to help them push all of their main bills through. He certainly wasn't going to be using his veto, at any rate. He was keen for the Whigs to implement and pass their bill for the re-chartering of the Bank of the United States. But in this way and a number of others, Tyler didn't really share the Whig perspective, or the supposed perspective of his predecessor.

This led to a situation that's practically unheard of in American politics, either before or since. The Whig party pushed through and passed two bills concerning the chartering of the Bank of the United States. Both bills were vetoed by President Tyler. He was allowed to do this, because each bill was slightly different from the other, so that technically he had not vetoed the same bill twice (which he wasn't really be allowed to do). He had good reason for doing this, in the sense that economic theory (and practise) suggest that a centralised national bank doesn't really do much good. Americans would grow to experience this more keenly over and over after the creation of the Federal Reserve in 1914.

Now this is where it gets fun: the Whigs were so frustrated that a supposed Whig President was vetoing their bills, especially ones on the Bank of the United States that they considered so important, that they held a meeting. And in that 'Great Whig Meeting', they basically decided to expel President John Tyler from their party. He was now officially, like George Washington, a member of no party. An independent President.

DOWN TO BRASS TACKS

Tyler wasn't too fazed at his rejection by the Whig party. He merely carried on regardless. And in doing so, it must be said, achieved a number of great things.

In the area of foreign policy, he was particularly impressive. He forged a significant Treaty between Great Britain and the United States, which finally resolved the dispute over the border between

America and Canada. This finally relieved tension between the nations, who could get on with the much more important (and enjoyable) task of doing what these two brethren-nations wanted to do most of all: be friends and trade with each other.

Tyler also took it upon himself to sign a treaty with the newly-formed Republic of Texas. This treaty however, was immediately struck down in Congress. Well, if President Tyler was going to veto all of the Whig parties' favourite bills, why can't they make life tough for him too I guess?

But Tyler wasn't done over Texas. He asked Congress for a joint-resolution over the new republic, basically his treaty again but in a different name. The slight-of-hand trick worked, and the resolution was passed. Tyler got his treaty, it was just under a different name.

EVALUATING HIS TERM

During his time in high office, President Tyler very much invoked the principles of Thomas Jefferson. He was a passionate advocate for states' rights, as well as the rights (most importantly) of the people. He very much believed in the classical-republic that America was founded on.

He fought with both the Whigs and the Democrats in Washington DC. And it wasn't just a case of fighting to be disagreeable, to enter into political tussles. He truly believed, as Franklin did, as Jefferson, Madison, Monroe and so many other Founders did, that the role of government was simply to administer the rule of law. I always think of Tyler as a man who felt in many ways that 99% of a Federal politicians job, was to make sure the laws are enforced: the courts, law enforcement and military, civil infrastructure that wasn't practically viable to be done by states or individuals. And that only 1% of a politicians' job was to make yet more laws.

He wanted government to be small and limited. And in doing so, the American people would continue to prosper in freedom.

And that's precisely what continued to happen. Throughout all of these Presidents, the role of the Federal government was expanding, and would continue to do so, but because there was still so little comparative interference, and so little government-based 'social engineering', the American people's prosperity, contentment and social mobility continued to grow to levels that other nations could barely comprehend. Many continued to be amazed: how could freedom bring about such a drop in poverty and rise in wealth, while increasing liberty and happiness?

The Founding Fathers knew the answer to that question. And, it would seem, so did John Tyler.

However, Tyler's political popularity continued to fade. It was becoming increasingly clear that if you're a politician who wasn't doing too much, the people's prosperity may increase because of it, but they may very well not credit you for it.

He had no major political allies in Washington. The Democrats basically didn't trust him at all. The Whigs were so frustrated with him that it got to a point that they wouldn't lift a finger to help him.

To President Tyler's credit, when it seemed clear that he'd only win a second term in his own right with the support of a full-blown political-party-based campaign, (because his overall popularity was indifferent to the American people), he decided to bow out gracefully and not run for a second term.

This meant that the fifteenth term was a walkover for the Democratic candidate: James K. Polk.

ELEVEN
JAMES KNOX POLK

Took Office: March 4th 1845
Left Office: March 4th 1849
Party: Democratic
Term: 15

As WE HAVE SEEN, elections can be brutal, fierce, and tremendously exciting. In 1844, this was not the case. With John Tyler bowing out gracefully, and the Whigs having no one of any real stature to put in his place, James K. Polk stepped in and comfortably became the eleventh President of the United States.

The reason for his election victory was simple. He had one overall mandate: to finish the work of Andrew Jackson. Jackson was still seen in tremendously high regards at this stage, and anyone who could symbolically cosy-up to the wild-haired old Democrat could do very well indeed. It's also worth remembering at this stage, that Andrew Jackson was the last President since the end of the 1830s to win more than one term. The American people had seen three one-term-wonders come and go, (though it may be a tad unfair to include William Henry Harrison in this trend) and there was increasing nostalgia for that elusive "era of Jackson."

Of course, the success of the era of Jackson really came about because it happened to be a period of economic freedom where the American people's prosperity was clearly increasing by significant levels. This was thanks to the Founding Fathers more than Jackson. The freedom of a limited federal government, restricted to basic infrastructure and the rule of law was still paying dividends for the American people. So sure, Andrew Jackson happened to be President when some of the prosperity was really shining through, but he couldn't take any significant credit for it.

However, that didn't stop the American people of most of the states giving him credit. And it was that unconditional goodwill that James. K. Polk was able to capitalise on. But what did Polk promise the people and did he manage to deliver on those promises? The answer to those questions, as we shall find, were 'a lot' and 'yes, very much so.'

DOING THINGS POLK-STYLE

President Polk had one main mission: to complete the Jacksonian Doctrine. He wanted to emulate his hero and finish what Jackson started.

He was a pretty devious workaholic, who micro-managed every inch of his Presidency. So in many ways, he was a more practical version of Andrew Jackson. He was convinced that Americans should have a 'level playing field' as that was the best way to maintain freedom. Getting that level playing field could be achieved by lowering certain taxes and allowing more wealth creation to go on. And that constant belief made him in many ways a better 'Jackson' than Andrew Jackson himself.

Despite his rather unpleasant personality, Polk was perhaps the most easy to meet President since Thomas Jefferson. We've mentioned before how Jefferson would often be the person who'd greet you if you came to the White House unannounced, and welcome you into the building. It wasn't quite as friendly as that under Polk's administration, but he was very accessible none the less.

The marine-corps band played on the White House lawn, every Wednesday regardless of the weather. The public were always invited. You simply had to show up. But that was a token gesture isn't it? Well, it gets better. As well as the free (and easy) viewings of the marine-corps band, President Polk allocated time twice a week for members of the public to see him and ask questions. I'm sure John Adams wouldn't have approved! All an American citizen had to do was obtain a card, hand it in to the White House steward, and wait your turn for some face-time with the Commander-in-Chief. Not quite as incredible as popping into the White House for a hot cup of coffee and a chat with Thomas Jefferson, but rather remarkable none the less.

With all that public access, you wonder how Polk got anything done at all. No time was ever wasted, so much so that he is regarded by many as the hardest-working President in American history. He had gas lamps installed in the White House offices so that he could work into the night. He understood that time in the White House was short, and he couldn't waste it just because the nights were drawing in. In this respect, he set the precedent of members of the executive branch working into the night.

Polk's micro-management style may have taken some of the White House staffers time to get used to. The new President made it clear that he wanted to cross-check everything that his staff were doing. Members of his cabinet had to run through their budget-figures with him, sometimes in extreme detail. In this respect, he was the first President to really get under the skin of the federal budget. Until this stage, the various members of the cabinet used to put together their budgets and send them straight to Congress for approval. Under President Polk, this finally changed. He became the one who'd insist on giving his approval before finally sending the budgets off to Congress so that the people's representatives could give their ultimate opinion.

And that workaholic attitude was very necessary for President Polk, because he had a tremendously ambitious series of plans to undertake during his time in office. If he was going to achieve them all, there was simply no time to waste.

Polk had grown up seeing more and more territories and people come to America because of the opportunities that were available. He understood the 'pull' of America. He believed that Americans should continue to labour in freedom and didn't really subscribe to any significant protectionist beliefs.

But in understanding what made America great, he also felt deeply, as Andrew Jackson had said during his time in office, that America had a manifest destiny. And the expansion that President Polk instigated formed most of the geography of America as we know it today.

MANIFEST DESTINY AND POLK'S TO-DO LIST

So much to do, and such little time. President Polk was determined to accomplish what was frequently being referred to as Americas 'manifest destiny'. Achieving such a lofty-sounding ambition wasn't going to be a straightforward affair. But what was manifest destiny?

It was all to do with expansionism. Polk had the same deeply-held beliefs as Jackson, that America's ideas of freedom could and should expand beyond their smaller borders and go west. Polk believed that America would only be truly free and safe if it existed as a continental nation from 'sea to shining sea'. Many people who lived in the territories across the American landscape wanted to be part of this great republic. However, many of the men and nations in charge of these territories weren't so happy about it.

Getting into the complications of such a task is worthy of a book (and there have been many) in of itself. But Polk, who boldly pronounced that he would only serve one term, laid out his four main actions that he wanted to accomplish.

Firstly, he wanted to settle the on-going dispute between Great Britain and America with regards to the Oregon territory. The ownership of this land was still a highly contentious issue between these two brethren nations, despite the fact that they were well on the way to kissing and making up in most areas. Tsk. Relatives huh?

Secondly, President Polk was determined to integrate California into the Union. There were a great deal of people both within the United States of America and within California itself, who wanted this grand addition to the States.

Thirdly, Polk wanted to establish a treasury that was completely independent. Ironically, this came out of a desire to end the credit-problems that his hero Andrew Jackson had created through his rather ludicrous spat between himself and the Bank of the United States. Though I very much doubt you'd have ever heard James Polk ever word it quite like that!

And finally, President Polk wanted to significantly lower tariffs on goods coming into the American economy. On that issue, a great deal of the Jeffersonian politicians were very pleased indeed. This was a prime example of one of the many supply-side booms of real-money-based rises in the American economy. Like so many similar economic moves by likeminded politicians throughout history, this helped continue the significant rise in the prosperity of many Americans, while reducing levels of poverty. Poverty always falls in America when the economy is strong and the availability of work is high. Polk understood this point as well as most. Shame so many politicians since haven't!

Polk's economic plans were achieved, and rather quickly, by him using all the influence and persuasion he could to Congress. He understood that such significant changes in the way America does things could not, and should not, be implemented by executive order. Again, wouldn't it be nice if more heads of executive governments thought like that too?! He succeeded admirably.

However, the first two items of President Polk's to-do list couldn't be achieved by the same means of persuasion, and certainly couldn't happen just because Congress accepted it. There were too many other parties involved. In order to achieve his expansionist goals, President Polk had to use force.

Firstly with the British. To gain the Oregon territory, he simply threatened force. The British knew too well that America was a passionate fighter in defence of her liberties, and wouldn't give up a claim on Oregon easily. America had grown much larger and stronger since they last fought. Also, the levels of trade and prosperity that came about from the restored friendship between the two nations, made Great Britain feel that it simply wasn't worth it. President Polk effectively carved a line that separated the United States and Canada, (the infamous 49th Parallel), and the territorial dispute was finally put to an end.

However, war was necessary for his other expansionist goal. In order to claim California and the Southwest territories, as well as establish the Texas border, America declared war on Mexico. This was the toughest task undertaken by President Polk's administration. The Mexican war lasted between 1846 and 1848. It was the toughest fight that Polk had, but by the end, he had won. And though it may still be controversial to say it, there's a significant part of me that feels that the Californians, Texans, and those residing within the Southwest territories won as well. For they were now part of a union built on the foundations of freedom. They had representation in political office, and achieved great levels of economic prosperity that come about from such freedom.

And it's quite incredible to think about it. In just four years, President Polk had taken the United States of America from just west of the Mississippi right over to the Pacific Ocean. President Polk's work was done. He stepped down as promised, and a new election campaign began. But whether a Democrat or Whig would be in office next, one thing was for sure.

The continental nation was born. From sea to shining sea.

TWELVE
ZACHARY TAYLOR

Took Office: March 4th 1849
Left Office: July 8th 1850
Party: Whig
Term: 16

IT WAS ALREADY BECOMING clear to a great deal of the rest of the world that the United States of America was a nation who's dedication to liberty was bringing about unimaginable levels of freedom and prosperity. And all in under 75 years. But alongside this shining light of hope, there was a darker narrative that had grown in importance since the birth of the nation. The ugly era of slavery was vanishing around the world, but the southern States in America were still entrenched in the buying, selling and forced labour of human beings.

Some still declare that slavery was merely a black stain on capitalism and the American free market. They say that it's the ultimate evidence you need to see that when market forces are allowed to run wild, the result can be something as horrible and degrading as slavery. That could not be further from the truth. Enslavement of any kind was the ultimate attack on the free market, not the inevitable conclusion of it. Think about it; nations or states that had very few laws one way or another governing the slave trade, also happened to be the nations that abolished slavery first. Why? Because capitalism has a way of punishing immoral and irrational decisions made in the free market. This needs to be explained and understood before we can properly analyse the roles of the many Presidents who had to deal with this issue, Zachary Taylor included.

Imagine a scenario, where you have a capitalist system under a classical republic, and a slave state that maximises the rules that authorities in power can bend, break or create. Under the capitalist system, it may or may not be illegal to own slaves (in a true classical 'Jeffersonian' republic, it'd ultimately have to be illegal because it in essence violates the moral code of individual freedom and rule of law that a classical republic espouses). But even if it's legal to hold slaves in such a state, does it make much economic sense?

In the slave state, let's say that things operate like they did in the deep south of America. So you are allowed to own slaves, but what you do with them is restricted by law. So you can't educate them, so that they learn more and therefore get more skills and become valuable to you, and you can't choose to free them to see if they become more productive by choosing to work instead of having work enforced upon them. In many of the southern states, you could only 'free' a slave if you took them all the way outside of the state and left them in a free state. That was a rather impractical (for the time) and bizarre government restriction that kept the levels of slavery high.

After a while, a cotton farmer in the capitalist state, (like one of the 'northern' states where slavery was illegal or there wasn't any rules one way or another), decides that instead of spending $1 a week on feeding, clothing, providing shelter and sanitation to his slaves, he instead offers them $1.20 each a week. In return, they can work for him or they can just not accept the money and leave. Either way, they are no longer slaves, they are free. If they choose to work for him, they can use that money as they see fit (i.e., they'll go out and buy goods and services that they want. They have to pay for their own food and shelter, etc).

Now, it's costing the farmer $.20 more than it was before, but he no longer has to worry about looking after everything the slaves require to survive. They are now employees. And he only pays them for as long as they choose to work for him, or he chooses to employ them.

The slaves in the slave state do the bare minimum work they can in order to stay alive and compliant. At the end of the week, the slave-owning farmer has a bag of cotton; let's call it the 'slave cotton', which he can sell for $10. The free market farmer's employees think differently. By working hard, they can stay in business, and even earn more money. If the farmer gets wealthier, then their prosperity can improve too. If the farmer decides not to reward them with increased pay, etc. then they are free to pursue better conditions with a better farmer who's probably more willing to reward them for their efforts. So it's well in the interests of the farmer to keep them happy.

So at the end of the week, that farmer (from the northern states), produces a bag of 'capitalist cotton', for $11. It's a little bit more expensive, but because the employees (as they now are) were happier and more productive, economies of scale brought the prices down (as more was produced) that offsets part of the extra expense. And of course, the capitalist cotton is ten times the quality of the slave cotton.

So even though some just pursue the cheaper cotton, regardless of quality, more people purchase the slightly more expensive capitalist cotton because it's far, far superior. And all of these new individual workers end up taking their earnings into the marketplace themselves and spread yet more wealth around, rather than single farmers making purchasing decisions which lowers choice, competition, quality and overall prosperity.

After a while, the capitalist cotton benefits from so much economy of scale, that it only costs $10. And the slave cotton gets an 'inverted economy of scale' because so few people want to buy it, that the slave farmer has no choice but to up his prices to $11. Now the choice is between cheaper and better quality capitalist cotton at $10, or more expensive lower quality slave cotton at $11. That, of course, is no choice at all.

And the real tragedy is that instead of getting politicians in the south to get rid of all the authoritative laws restricting famers' ability to free slaves, the citizens instead got angry and bitter towards the northern states and continued to lobby for more authoritarian politicians (mostly in the Democratic Party) who'd introduce yet more rules maintaining slavery. Special interest groups would form, who'd get politicians to restrict the freedom over slavery even more, so that their rivals in the same states they lived in couldn't free their slaves too. In return for the votes, the politicians would do what they were told.

Though it's rarely taught in such honest and blunt ways, this is essentially how slavery clung on in the southern states of America. And it's clear to see a pattern emerging throughout the western nations. Countries with a totally unregulated 'free market' approach to slavery always seemed to abolish the practice, (because it was effectively redundant, you didn't get good products and services that way), much quicker that those nations who had large special interest groups making sure politicians made lots of laws keeping slavery as a cornerstone of their market operations.

So that was how America was divided: the northern states, with unprecedented levels of prosperity and freedom (and no or very little slavery) on one hand, and the southern states, with dwindling economic prosperity and still significant amounts of slavery and resentment. One half of America sticking to the free principles of the Founding Fathers, and the other half straying away from the path.

UNITE US, PLEASE

This north/south divide was getting increasingly more pronounced. But while the north had all the freedom and wealth, the south had all the political muscle. America needed a President to save the union.

The twelfth President would not be it.

Zachary Taylor was another politician turned celebrity. He had fought in the Mexican war admirably, and people admired his competence on the battlefield. And hey, if you had helped gain over half a million square miles of new land for America, you'd be a celebrity back then too! Note to any would-be Presidential hopefuls reading: this strategy no longer works, don't campaign on the fact that you're going to invade Mexico, no one will thank you for it…

Many called George Washington the reluctant candidate. However, his reluctance doesn't come any way near that of Zachary Taylor. Taylor didn't even seek nomination. Both the Democratic and Whig Parties asked him to be their candidate. Utterly bizarre.

As a war hero, the north respected him. As a land-holder and slave-owner in Louisiana, the south embraced him as well. So maybe, just maybe, Zachary Taylor would be the compromise candidate who could keep America united. That was the theory, anyway.

Taylor appeared to have no real political agenda, which maybe would have been a good thing. After all, history has already show that when a President sticks to their limited constitutional obligations, the nation usually ends up much better off.

However, this slave-owning war hero who had never registered to vote, (and didn't even do so in his own election), had a few tricks up his sleeve.

ROUGH, READY, AND IN OFFICE

Taylor's nickname, Old Rough 'n' Ready, was due to his rather significant skills on the battlefield. But it could have been just as much due to his dishevelled appearance as well. We've mentioned crazy Presidential hair before, but Taylor may well have had the most untidy hairstyle in Presidential history, which wins him a bonus point for me, but most slick professional politicians today would probably disagree.

However, Taylor wasn't some sort of Washington outsider. The great James Madison was his second cousin, and had arranged Taylor's army position for him, after being very impressed with his skills. Jefferson Davis had been his son-in-law, and Taylor seemed to be on first-name terms with many of the movers and shakers in Foggy Bottom.

One massive credit you have to lay down at Taylor's door, was that he stated that he'd never use his Presidential veto power, and would always defer to others in such matters. He rightly saw the office of President as a branch of government and a position that should never be too powerful.

And here's where it got fun: He felt that the issue of slavery could be something that a President could wave a magic wand and fix. Taylor declared that the slavery issue was purely a national matter of Congress and not the states. Whatever the federal legislative branch would officially propose, he'd accept.

Time was of the essence. The Missouri Compromise, established some thirty years earlier to keep the north and south at peace, was beginning to crumble under the weight of new resentments.

On the southern side, certain extremists were threatening to take their states out of the union. In the northern states, the abolitionists could see what damage slavery had done to the south. They also held a very noble strong moral outrage for slavery anyway, and their vocal opposition was getting much louder.

Senator Henry Clay was still in the mix. He proposed a new set of compromises, allowing California into the Union as a free state, but giving the slave states in the south some concessions. However, this compromise did not please Zachary Taylor. He felt that California should be a free state and admitted into the Union as such. End of debate. Suddenly going back on his promise, Taylor threatened to veto the compromise.

But how did Taylor propose to appeal to those threatening to leave the Union? Well, he didn't exactly wine and dine them. He basically said that he'd hang anyone who threatened to get their state to leave the Union. And he was so adamant that he even made it clear that would include Jefferson Davis, his son-in-law. Many, including Taylors Vice-President Millard Fillmore, must have found this a risky strategy. There was a chance of solving this peacefully and even in the long-run having slavery abolished, and many felt that Taylor was putting that to risk.

AND THERE HE WAS... GONE

President Zachary Taylor, just over a year into his first term, was now turning into a formidable, (if not very effective) Unionist.

He had the honour of being the President who would declare the Washington Monument open. It was a hot 4th of July afternoon in 1850, and there was laughter and celebration in the air. It had been a great day. Suffering a tad from sunburn, Taylor decided to recuperate with some cherries and milk. Within a few hours, he complained of severe pains in his stomach. Some conspiracy theorists thought that he was poisoned with arsenic.

What was clear though, was that Taylor was ill. He died four days later. The official cause of death was gastroenteritis, but it didn't stop the feeling of foul play from lingering. It would take one hundred years before the truth was discovered. In 1991, an historian convinced Taylors descendents to allow him to exhume the body so that they could know the truth. Forensic analysis revealed no signs of foul play. The conspiracy was effectively over. There was no way Taylor was poisoned.

Meanwhile back in 1850, a new President was required. Zachary Taylor's Vice-President Millard Fillmore not only stepped into the role, but attempted to take the nation into a totally different direction than his Unionist counterpart.

THIRTEEN
MILLARD FILLMORE

Took Office: July 8th 1850
Left Office: March 4th 1853
Party: Whig
Term: 16

FOR THE SECOND TIME in the history of the United States, a Vice President had to take over the Commander-in-Chief role, after the President the Electoral College had voted for died.

The general convention, one supposes in a democracy, is that the Vice President shouldn't take over and lead the country in a new direction. When he or she has to step up and take over the role of President, they should continue down the path that they were voted in on, in the first place. Or to put it another way, they should try and continue to run the administration in the same way and with the same goals that their predecessor did. Or at least, that seems to be how the Founding Fathers would have preferred it. Millard Fillmore however, had a slightly different point of view. And the slightly more authoritarian stance his predecessor took on certain issues would not be repeated this time around.

Fillmore ascended to the top job with his wife, Abigail and two children. He was a modest chap, who apparently was very easy to get along with. He never had many airs or pretences about him, and refreshingly, unlike so many politicians, had no real sense of god-given authority.

He was a very well read man, who was in many ways infinitely more at home with a good book than playing host to lobbyists and other special interest groups that so many politicians think they have to pander in the general direction of.

And when it came to decision making and centralisation of power, Millard Fillmore was a man quite at ease with delegating authority. Every last detail didn't have to be run by his office, and the cabinet were allowed to make more of their own decisions over the direction of their respective departments. Sadly, as we will discover, this very positive trait is somewhat lampooned.

ACCIDENTAL FILLMORE

Poor old President Fillmore was a fairly clumsy chap. It seems that he may have set a trend in the executive branch of office. President Gerald Ford in the mid-late 1970s was always falling over or hurting himself in some clumsy fashion. You may well have seen the footage of President Ford falling down the steps of Air Force One. Poor guy. Though you can't help watch it over and over!

President Fillmore, many years earlier, seemed cursed with the same misfortune. At least he didn't have the steps of Air Force One to contend with. The superstitious amongst you would no doubt find this affliction for accidents pretty fitting for the thirteenth President. Due both to his accident-prone nature, and the nature of how he assumed office, it's of very little wonder why they called him the 'Accidental President'.

But as well as being clumsy, President Fillmore stands out above his fellow Presidents in other ways. But not in ways that make him look at all good. In actual fact, President Fillmore compared to the other heads of the executive branch, is rather like a beacon of mediocrity in a sea of talent. I think that's safe to say he doesn't stand out in a way that he'd like. Which is a shame, because I think the Founding Fathers really wanted the executive branch to have fairly limited powers. But what happens when a President comes to office and only uses his powers sparingly? That's right, everyone in the political scene has a go at him.

In fact, word has is that there is still a society that get together at Millard Fillmore's gravesite once a year purely to lampoon his rather insignificant Presidency. They sound like a lovely bunch of people.

Though they were running on the same ticket, incredibly Millard Fillmore never actually got to meet Zachary Taylor until after the pair were elected into office. How well they would have gotten on if that were not the case remains a mystery. Just like how Republicans and Democrats do today, the Taylor/Fillmore ticket was an evenly balanced affair. Millard Fillmore was placed on the ticket to balance out many of the views of Taylor.

Fillmore was born and raised in the northern states. And he played the stereotype perfectly. He had impeccable tastes, and was always immaculately dressed. Unlike the more radical posturing of his running mate, Fillmore was more inclined to please and serve. He always tried to strike a middle ground with his political opponents. He felt that by keeping as many of the people happy about as many things as possible, then the world would continue turning and everything would be okay. By appeasing both sides of the American politician spectrum, President Fillmore figured that the government would be physically doing less, therefore interfering less with people's daily lives, which would bring about a great deal more prosperity. For what it's worth, he was spot on.

The sad fact is, even though we're always criticising the political parties in our governments to get along with each other and leave the Punch and Judy show aside, as soon as we get a politician in power who does just that, we ridicule them for being somewhat 'limp'. That seemed to be the consensus on President Fillmore.

"THANKS FOR YOUR VALUABLE INSIGHT"

As a bland leader, President Fillmore didn't really show a lot of strong insight. I guess he'd have to jump off the fence to show some leadership or inspirational qualities, and he certainly wasn't prepared to do that. However, he was a very friendly man who always had time for people.

Whenever possible (i.e. pretty much all the time), he deferred power to Congress. They are, after all, the legislative branch of government. Whenever he had to make a decision about something, his manner of handling it was very low-key. For a start, he wouldn't really 'handle it'. As a hands-off manager he'd often delegate the decision and the actions required to his cabinet whenever possible.

And if he had to make a decision about something and either a member of his cabinet or Congress was unhappy about the position taken, President Fillmore would invite them over to discuss the issue, listen intently, thank them for their 'valuable insight' and probably end up compromising the decision he made before. Everything, and I do mean everything, was decided on the middle ground. So sometimes he'd side with the authoritarian-wing of politics, and other times with the more libertarian side. And if – presumably because you'd lost the will to live – you'd care to look back on his (few) political decisions, you'd see that his decisions favoured no one: 50/50 with either side.

BUT THE DOG CAN BITE

Occasionally, President Fillmore did give us a demonstration of backbone.

He was very angry at the way that President Taylor's cabinet seemed to constantly disrespect him, so what did he do when he became their boss? Yes, can you believe it, he actually fired them all! A bit of action for a change!

And then he jumped even further. He signed the Compromise of 1850 into law – the same compromise that Taylor refused to sign. It was in these ways that the docile President Fillmore suddenly seemed to want to flex his muscles and new-found powers.

Of course, if you read the previous chapter on President Taylor, then you know my theories on slavery, that a free society will always reject slavery in the long term. Not by government interference, but because the free market always exposes slavery as inefficient and the capitalist voluntary work system as more productive. Unfortunately, the increasingly authoritarian Millard Fillmore did not share my view. And hang on a minute, where did his authoritarian streak come from all of a sudden? I missed the old Millard!

President Fillmore was totally convinced, despite the evidence to the contrary based on what was going on all over the rest of the world, that removing slavery-enforcement would destroy the economy in the Southern States. At the time, it was true, 60% of US exports came from the cotton industry of the slave-states. But he failed to understand that by letting slavery dwindle and die out as a practice, would increase the economy in the long term.

He felt that, if you can get your head around this, slavery was effectively protected by the Constitution, and by signing the Compromise of 1850, he could settle the debate forever. He couldn't be more wrong. And hadn't he read the 10th Amendment? It's the one that basically says "just because he haven't thought about certain rules and authorities the government might want in the future, doesn't mean the government can automatically take them". Or to put it another way; "just because we haven't thought about it yet, means you can't do it".

The Constitution was quite clear on this issue. Anything not included the founding documents weren't therefore okay for the government to implement. In fact, the Founding Fathers wanted the federal government to have as little power as possible. Go buy a copy of the US Constitution. Count the number of pages. It's really short, and that's the point.

But for a man so keen to compromise on so many things, such a significant change of direction by President Fillmore was taken without any sense of 'middle-ground'. By supporting the compromise, he thought he was appeasing everyone. But in the end, no one, even in his own party, was happy.

So by the time the election of 1852 had descended on America, the Whig Party no longer wanted Millard Fillmore to be their candidate. And the democrats, though many sympathetic to the idea of state-enforced slavery, didn't want anything to do with him either. Their man this time around would be Franklin Pierce.

And with barely a whisper goodbye, the President served out the rest of his predecessors term and went back home. And the Whigs never took Presidential office again.

FOURTEEN
FRANKLIN PIERCE

Took Office: March 4th 1853
Left Office: March 4th 1857
Party: Democratic
Term: 17

AMERICA WAS BURSTING AT the seams. And this was happening despite the fact that drive-thru fast food was still 60-odd years away from becoming a mainstream fixture of the American diet. The Compromise of 1850 was barely holding America together. It was only a matter of time before something gave way – possibly the union itself. The nation needed a leader to guide them in a new direction, and mend the destructive nature of slavery.

As a positive candidate, Franklin Pierce seemed to tick some of the right boxes. Though he was from New Hampshire, he was a member of the Democratic Party and had strong links to the south, which the slave-states appreciated. The northern states were maybe not so enthused by his southern/slave links, but they welcomed him also, as they felt he would finally bring balance, peace and happiness back to the American way of life.

Signs would go up wherever Pierce went on the campaign trail, welcoming the man who "has been faithful to the constitution and true to the union." The likeability factor was huge. He knew all the right people in the Democratic Party, and they all gave him two very strong thumbs up.

THE "BEIGE THEN BLUE" PRESIDENT

Franklin Pierce didn't become the President because of his wonderful oratory skills, or his charming charisma, or his inspirational vision. He became President, with very little fuss, because he was simply considered offensive to no one. Not exactly the best campaign slogan you'll ever hear, but after the in-fighting and trouble with the Whig Party, and America just looking for something pleasing and simple, Franklin Pierce entered stage-left, and had very little competition.

However, as we will find out, by the time he left office, he was disliked by all.

His nickname on the campaign trail was Handsome Frank. Pleasing to the eye, yet with a slightly darker streak. He was known by many as being a bit of a drinker. He was however courteous, polite and chivalrous at all times, (even when intoxicated) so many people at the time didn't read too much into his occasional alcoholic binges. It certainly wasn't going to be used as a handicap against him by his political opponents, of which there were very few.

Looking back on the mid 1800s, many academics refer to the period as the age of the 'alcoholic republic'. Being a candidate for political office usually meant being the guy who'd 'work' the taverns. It was all about buying constituents a drink or two, sharing a laugh and then securing their votes while they thought of you in a favourable manner. So Handsome Frank's excessive penchant for booze had no real damaging effect on his perceived character. In fact, (and this will be hard to comprehend today), if anything, his excessive drinking probably made lots of voters feel more comfortable around Pierce. After all, it proved that he was "one of us". The goal that many a politician try to achieve even today. And many of them are no was near as good at it as Pierce was.

But his time in the oval office was a very different matter. President Pierce handled himself in a considerably more sober manner than he did during the beer-addled lifestyle that preceded his time in high office. And no one can argue that a sober Commander-in-Chief isn't a very good thing indeed.

TRAGEDY

Being sober is one thing. Being emotionally sane is quite another. And it's really something that we can't make a joke of.

Just weeks after being elected into office, horrific tragedy struck the Pierce family. Franklin Pierce was involved in a train crash. His wife Jane was with him, as was his eleven-year-old son Benny. Pierce and his wife were perfectly fine, but they witnessed the awful sight of their son Benny decapitated during the accident.

In a vain hope that Jane wouldn't get a chance to see the full awfulness of the image, Franklin immediately threw his cloak over his sons' body. But of course, she saw the whole thing. It was a truly horrendous event that you'd wish on absolutely no one. And, as anyone can imagine, this had a very significant impact on Franklin Pierce's emotional state.

And to make it worse, (as if it could get worse), Franklin and Jane had already lost their two other sons through disease, which was all too common an occurrence at the time. Benny was their last surviving child. As a result, they doted on him a great deal. To have that taken away from them as well is a tragedy I can barely comprehend.

It was beyond Franklin Pierce's comprehension as well, and he seemed incapable of dealing with the loss. His whole character changed, and he never truly recovered.

But would you?

AND THINGS GOT WORSE

While still coping with the death of his son, President Pierce had yet another death to deal with. His Vice President, William Rufus King, died just six weeks after Pierce took the oath of office.

But even that event paled in comparison to what happened next. Members of the Democratic Party came to visit the President early in 1854. They informed the President Pierce that they were introducing a bill into law called the Kansas Nebraska Act. The Act was designed to essentially repeal the Missouri Compromise Act of 1820. If you remember, this Act banned slavery in all states that were north of the Missouri southern-border. The new Act was simply put in place to allow Kansas and Nebraska, (two newly-formed states that were north of the Southern Missouri border), to decide for themselves whether or not they could be free or slave states.

And the Democrats made it very clear: They would make life very difficult for poor President Pierce if he did not agree to support the new Act.

It is at moments like these that we may be inclined to hope for a President that wouldn't be bullied in such a way. We may yearn for a President who would stand up for himself and lead the executive branch in the direction that he wants, based on his own judgement. However, possibly due to his changed character, Franklin Pierce was not that President.

With very little fight, and hardly any noticeable contempt, President Pierce agreed to give the Kansas Nebraska Act of 1854 his full unconditional support. Whether he had concerns of his own, whether or not he felt that this Act would have opened the door for lots of bullying and misleading, and introduce slavery in areas that overall didn't want it and would have prospered much more without it, we'll probably never know.

All we know is that Pierce was asked to put the party's wishes ahead of the peoples. And he did so.

As a result of having President Pierce's backing, the northern Democrats on Capitol Hill supported the Act. And that, combined with the predictable backing of the southern Democrats, the bill was pushed through Congress and became law.

It was rather unsurprising that the growing anti-slavery groups in the northern states went crazy over the new bill. They did what all good lobbyist groups did when their backs were up: they went straight to the presses.

There was some delightfully-worded pamphlets distributed at the time. They described the Democrats as "kingly tyrants of old", and that we'd all become "slaves of an oligarchy" eventually. Some even when as far as to call the having the Democratic Party in office was "worse than the veriest despotism on earth". I don't even know if 'veriest' is a word, (it doesn't come up on my spell-check), but it doesn't sound favourable, does it? There were calls to remove "that corrupt and ignorant legislature" at once.

Basically, the libertarian-wing of America was not impressed. The Americans who believed deeply in the words of Thomas Jefferson, Madison and the like, were fed up with being cast aside as a 'quant' lunatic fringe of American politics. They wanted change. They wanted the freedom that the Founding Fathers fought so hard to give them. And among this angry pro-freedom movement, was an up-and-coming, (but relatively unknown) Whig politician from Illinois, called Abraham Lincoln.

Lincoln was furious with the increasingly authoritarian stance of the Democratic Party that he decided to establish a new party. A party that would stand for the more pro-freedom principles that America was founded on. He envisaged a political party that wanted limited government, less slavery (leading to an eventual total eradication of the practice) and more individual freedom. He wanted the centralisation of power to be removed from Washington and put back in the hands of the people. He rightly felt that slavery was an ignorant government-enforced tool used to prevent the social mobility and prosperity that would occur if freedom was offered as an alternative.

He understood, as many of the Founding Fathers did, that a truly free society had no need of slavery, and that societies without it prospered much quicker than those who. He could see this for himself. In the northern states, the standard of living was rising for the people in levels that no one had ever seen before in the history of the human race. But in the southern states, the control of government and the authoritarian impulses of those in office seemed to be causing their poverty levels to stagnate, or even get worse.

So, out of a need to win back the ideals of the classical republic that the Founding Fathers dreamed America should be, Abraham Lincoln formed the Republican Party.

Meanwhile, the pro-slavery and abolitionist groups were fighting each other in a series of vicious battles in the Kansas territory. Things were coming to a head. While Lincoln was becoming a significant figurehead in the political scene, President Pierce, the man who had the power and the responsibility to sort the slavery issue out, was becoming more and more irrelevant.

Despite his own feelings that he could have won a second term in office, the Democratic Party refused to let him run under their banner. President Pierce left Washington and returned home to New Hampshire under a cloud. It wasn't so long after, that his wife died.

And poor, poor Franklin Pierce spent his last years intoxicated and alone.

But, regardless of the tragic nature of his presidency, it would soon become clear that Pierce had it really easy in comparison to in successor.

FIFTEEN
JAMES BUCHANAN

Took Office: March 4th 1857
Left Office: March 4th 1861
Party: Democratic
Term: 18

THE TRAGIC NIGHTMARE THAT was Franklin Pierce's presidency is possibly one of the saddest in the history of the American executive branch. President James Buchanan however, was destined to follow very closely in his predecessors footsteps.

Many wonder why Buchanan frequently finds himself at the very bottom of the list of American Presidents, when they are listed in order of positivity and merit. I wouldn't quite put him right at the bottom of the list myself, but he's got to be way down there. Simply put, Buchanan's presidency is the story of the civil war. It is the story of a man whose actions hastened what was probably an unfortunate necessity in the journey of America's maturity. Due to the feelings and influence of many American people and politicians, the civil war between the north and south was almost certainly going to happen. But Buchanan is considered to be the guy who sped the process up to its full bloody conclusion.

Slavery was an old imperialist disease that the free market would have exorcised from American society long ago, had it not been for the strength of the protectionist lobby keeping it a mainstay of the south. Too many Presidents had dawdled on the subject. Too many calls for liberty had been marginalised. War was coming.

QUALIFICATIONS AND LOVE-LIFE

There is no doubt that James Buchanan was one of the most politically accomplished Presidents that the republic had ever seen. His previous political roles included being a congressman, foreign minister, senator and secretary of state. Basically he ticked every 'experience' box going. He was a hard-working chap, and his résumé probably provides all the proof that is needed in that respect. One thing is for certain; James Buchanan got the top job on hard graft and merit. He earned it.

While James Buchanan is often referred to as Americas only bachelor President, (he never married), others go further and suggest that he was Americas first gay President as well. Former Vice-President William Rufus King may well have been Americas first gay VP too. Both men had a very close and personal relationship. Just how close, history will never disclose. But one thing is for certain: William Rufus King and James Buchanan lived together in the same house for sixteen years.

However, this doesn't mean there wasn't a first lady. In fact, the term only came about in general use during President Buchanan's time in office. His niece, Harriet, served the President as 'official White House hostess'. Quite a mouthful to contend with, but because she wasn't the President's wife, what else could you call her? It wasn't long before the term 'first lady' was coined, and used not only during Buchanan's presidency, but it became the official title of every subsequent Presidents wife.

But while Harriet wined, dined, and generally kept White House visitors entertained, less amicable struggles were going on behind the closed doors of the oval office.

TREASON?

President Buchanan was presiding over an increasingly divided America.

He had decided to go along with the pro-slavery constitution that was written by pro-slavery politicians in Kansas. This set him up for a rough time with the predominantly anti-slavery north. It was becoming clear to Americans in the north, that President Buchanan was not going to be much of a friend to them.

Interestingly enough, this was a notion that made politicians from all political walks of life uncomfortable. The very idea that an American President could use his influence to enforce such an anti-libertarian idea such as slavery onto a state made him a traitor in the eyes of the north.

Many politicians were leaving the traditional Whig/Democratic Parties and joining Abe Lincoln's new Republican Party instead. A party that promised to represent what the original founding fathers wanted. The Jeffersonian vision of America: with liberty and justice for all. A return to the classical republic based on limited government, freedom and the rule of law instead of the tyranny of the majority.

This vision of America didn't seem to be what interested President Buchanan at all. His decision to support the pro-slavery Kansas constitution was totally out of step of both a majority of Americans and the vast majority of Senators.

As time went on, President Buchanan pushed through more and more legislation that was pro-southern. Even more than that, most of it was so authoritarian and pro-slavery, that he was acting more like the President of the south, of the forthcoming confederacy.

And this is the real crux of the matter for President Buchanan. Did he or did he not commit treason?

When a President takes the oath of office, they promise, to the best of their ability, to preserve, protect and defend the constitution of the United States. The increasingly non-libertarian stance that President Buchanan was imposing was one thing. But so much of it was aimed at undermining the constitution and the Bill of Rights. The tenth amendment of the constitution effectively states that "just because there are other powers that we haven't yet thought of, doesn't mean that the government is allowed to use them." There are many who feel that this incredibly important amendment, which was significantly the last item of the Bill of Rights, was violated by President Buchanan.

And academics and historians have been arguing over this ever since. In fact, many of the arguments between the scholars get pretty nasty. Watching middle-aged men fight when they're wearing tweed jackets with elbow patches is never a pretty thing to witness.

AMERICA DIVIDED

At this point, there was no doubt in anyone's mind that slavery was going to be the big issue for the election of 1860. With the Whig Party effectively in the dust, it was going to be a strong clash of ideas between the Democrats and Republicans. Would the older increasingly authoritarian, centralised pro-slavery Party get another four years at the head of the executive branch, or could the considerably new, more libertarian, decentralised anti-slavery Party get a shot at the title?

President Buchanan pulled out all the stops, but he could not match the oratory skill nor the general ability of his Republican Party rival, Abraham Lincoln. Lincoln seemed to communicate with so many Americans on a level that many politicians had failed to do for so long. He reminded the American people of the founding fathers, with their lofty ideals, more libertarian streaks, and dreams of a better world.

Think about it this way: Imagine Thomas Jefferson came back from the dead in 1860, and promised to fight to end slavery. And you may be surprised to learn that slavery was an idea that Jefferson was never entirely happy with, despite having slaves himself. Many of his anti-slavery comments were exorcised from his original draft of the Declaration of Independence.

Now even though most Americans would understand the awful difficulty and huge loss of life ahead of them in the wake of this struggle, wouldn't a majority of them still rally around the cause and fight with Jefferson in order to protect the liberty of the Union? Of course they would have. And they'd do so by a reasonable margin. So their 'born again Jefferson', Abraham Lincoln, was duly elected to the office of President of the United States.

After the election of 1860, the south knew full-well that they would soon lose their ally in the White House.

In anticipation of the new anti-slavery President, South Carolina seceded from the Union. The American Confederation was born. And it happened under President Buchanan's watch. The only real question, was what Buchanan was going to do about it before his one and only term in office was up.

President Buchanan made a number of speeches that secession was illegal. But that was it. He refused to go to Congress and demand action. He simply wagged his finger and did nothing. Again, on this point alone, is this example of inaction at such a crucial point simply unacceptable? Surely this was not an example of President Buchanan "protecting and defending the Constitution of the United States" to the "best of his ability" was it? And again, while I don't want to ignite the flames of elbow-patch warfare amongst the academic historians again, could it be interpreted that Buchanan's inaction here constituted a violation of his terms of office? It might not be treasonous, but it sure wasn't playing the game.

Many in Congress were itching to launch action against South Carolina. But they didn't exactly know what kind of action to launch, and what to do if South Carolina stood up and said "get stuffed."

They needed someone who had the talent and the courage to suggest a course of action that they could get behind. In short, they needed Abe Lincoln. But Lincoln would not be President for a number of months, and this situation was already getting out of hand.

Within weeks, six other states in the south joined the Confederacy. Eight other slave-holding states held their breath, refusing to take action to join the Confederation, but also refusing to fully support the union. They became the crucial border states. Alan and Willie Jones, the founding fathers from North Carolina, would have been quite shocked and disturbed at the attitudes their fellow North Carolinians were showing. The Union of liberty that they had fought so hard to create was being put at risk by a backwards-thinking form of bigoted protectionism.

On February 9th 1861, Jefferson Davies was elected the first President of the Confederation. He presided over seven states at that point, and appeared to have more authoritarian power of the people and states he represented.

One month later, with no one more relieved than the man himself, President Buchanan's time in office was over. Abraham Lincoln was the sixteenth President of the United States of America. And the fight for liberty had begun.

SIXTEEN
ABRAHAM LINCOLN

Took Office: March 4th 1861
Left Office: April 15th 1865
Party: Republican
Terms: 19 & 20

NEVER HAD THERE BEEN such an iconic figure as honest Abe. He wasn't exactly blessed with good looks, and that was probably one of his many advantages. Instead, Abraham Lincoln had to rely on his smarts. His raw intelligence and great intellect.

They served him well.

He was an ordinary Illinois-based Whig politician at first. The continued oppression that many were suffering under slavery was the thing that galvanised him. He wanted to represent the people under the banner of a Party that would represent the traditional (and we have to say again, more libertarian) values of the Founding Fathers. The Republican Party was born, and Abraham Lincoln easily beat Democrat President Buchanan to become the first Republican

President.

Also, it's worth mentioning that upon finally leaving office, the relieved President Buchanan told President Lincoln that "If you are as happy to be entering the Presidency as I am to be leaving it, then you are a very happy man." I think I would have preferred to be simply told "good luck."

HONEST ABE, LOG CABINS, AND GOOD OLD-FASHIONED SPIN

Have you ever been to the Lincoln Memorial in Washington D.C.? It's worth a visit, especially when you go at a time that isn't as busy. Maybe it's worth popping up there in a weekday evening, out of the holiday season. Go alone, spend some time with the great man. There's just something about that great statue, sitting restlessly on a large but modest throne.

Anyway the only reason I mention it, is that I think the time you spend with that statue might convey a sense of the man in a way that my words will fail to do. Same goes for the Jefferson Memorial too. And what's great about the Jefferson one, is that it's never that busy, you can always pencil in some personal face-time with the libertarian third President.

And while we're bringing up that great man, it's worth remembering that Thomas Jefferson was probably the most articulate of the founding fathers. He was very much the man who had a vision of an America that was "one nation, indivisible with liberty and justice for all". President Lincoln was another great titan of the political stage, who advanced Jefferson's ideas courageously.

However, this was never really Lincoln's intent. His simple aim was to restore the Union to the way that it was before the creation of the Confederacy. However, in order to do that, one thing was certain: slavery had to be abolished. If the regional governments in the south hadn't used political power to keep slavery in place, it would have almost certainly collapsed of its own accord. But government was keeping it in place. So government needed to remove it.

In this respect, Lincoln did not start out to be the 'great emancipator'. But he certainly became it. As the events of the civil war unfolded, it became clear that without demanding liberty and justice for all, the classical liberal foundations that built America would not last. And it was those foundations that President Lincoln was fighting to protect and restore.

He had a powerful personality and used this to draw people to him. He was a complex man, who always had a joke on tap, or a humorous anecdote ready to make a point. Once, when he was accused by a political opponent of being two-faced, he pointed to his own (rather ugly) face and said "If I were two-faced, would I be wearing this one?!"

But, like so many great thinkers, he would bow down to very deep levels of depression, frustration, sadness and despair.

Due to his compulsion for seeking out the truth, his campaign literature would dub him "Honest Abe". Actually, in Lincoln's campaign strategy, his spin doctors very much wheeled out all the old political chestnuts. He was known as the 'rail-splitter', and they used his hard-graft attitude and his working class roots to the fullest effect. The iconic image of the log cabin was used once again with great results at the working class-rallies. Future Presidential candidates take note: I still think this log cabin thing might work today!

Lincoln was a deeply ambitious hard-working politician. There was no doubt that he was another President who achieved high office through good old-fashioned merit.

GOING TO WORK

President Lincoln did not want to cabinet of 'yes men'. Like all good Presidents, he chose across the Party divide and picked anyone who would have the intellect to give strong and well-reasoned opposing views. That way, Abe thought, he would be able to make the best decisions. Even, as a judicious delegator of authority, if that meant picking political opponents and rivals to take key positions in his government. But of course, he always reserved the ultimate decision for himself.

President Lincoln's main initial aim was to halt the expansion of slavery into the western territories. He was quite clear on this. He felt that if by saving the Union he kept all the slaves in bondage in the south, then that is what he'd do. However, the secession from the Union of so many southern states meant that war was also going to have to be a key component of his term in office. His initial thoughts of slavery, like so many anti-slavery politicians at the time, were that you simply had to contain slavery and it would collapse of its own accord. While that may have been true, the breaking-up of the Union no longer made this a viable option.

Makes you think, doesn't it? If only America had a President Lincoln a few Presidents earlier. Maybe none of this would have had to happen.

IT BEGINS

As soon as President Lincoln sat down at his desk in the oval office, there was a letter waiting for him, from Major Robert Anderson, the Commander of Fort Sumter in the harbour of Charleston, South Carolina. His letter was brief and to the point. He told the new President that without a new shipment of provisions, he would have to surrender to the Confederates.

President Lincoln had a choice to make right off the bat. He could order the men at Fort Sumter to attack, surrender, or he could send provisions. He chose the latter. He told the Confederate President Jefferson Davis that if he allowed the provisions to go in unhindered, then that would show a diplomatic respect that both governments could work on, and maybe, just maybe, the dispute between the north and the south could end peacefully.

But Davis didn't even wait that long. Before the supplies even made it to Fort Sumter, he ordered his men to attack the Fort.

The civil war began with the first shot on Fort Sumter on April 12th, 1861.

Four other states were now pushed by their pro-slavery politicians to enter the Confederacy, including North Carolina. Four more states continued to act as the Border States and 'sit on the fence'.

Fort Sumter was finally captured by the south. But to his credit, Major Robert Anderson managed to leave with the Union flag, and return it to New York intact. It was slightly burned, tattered and torn, but somehow, this flag was important for the Major. It became increasingly more important to all Americans still desperate to preserve the Union at all costs.

As a matter of a fact, some feel that the actions by Major Anderson are probably what gave birth to such patriotic 'flag-waving' in America today. One thing is for sure, the attack and capture of Fort Sumter stirred a passion for liberty in the north. They were not going to take this rise of collectivist, large centralised government, pro-slavery Confederacy any more. The heartbeat of the north started to rise. And cries of "The Union Forever!" rose across the states.

So President Lincoln had very carefully baited the south into starting the war, but neither he nor President Davis could have foreseen what happened next.

A TERM OF WAR
Lincoln's Presidency was the only one to be totally defined by war. The other issues of office were thrown to one side and practically never attended to. The next four years were simple. The north versus

the south. The Union versus the Confederacy.

President Lincoln was the Commander-in-Chief at the helm of the huge effort to preserve the Union and end the Confederacy. Volunteers across the United States signed up to bring an end to the rebellion.

He had no military training or experience for himself – and where is General Eisenhower when you really need him? – So the President got some of the best military minds together and gave himself a beginners course in military strategy, equipment, administration, and everything else relevant. The technology and weaponry used was also important to him. It wasn't long before he was well versed in all aspects of warfare. Who needs Eisenhower after all?

Yet all the military textbooks in the world can't tell you how to deal with the actions of your Generals out in the field of battle. General Fremont had caused controversy by declaring martial law in Missouri, and declaring "all salves of rebels free". This was not the Presidents intention. Lincoln was deeply concerned that this action would insight all the slave owners in the Border States to rise up against the Union and push their states into the Confederacy. So he nullified Fremont's actions, and relieved him of duty.

In February of 1862, President Lincoln's 11-year old son died of typhoid fever. The President had so many high hopes for his son – as so many fathers do – and was struck by a grief that all too many Presidents seem to have had to deal with. After that, he was never the same. Lincoln was always less nimble, less quick to joke and tell anecdotes. Hardly surprising.

In an effort to grieve properly, or whatever reasons they needed to deal with their sons' tragic death, the President and first lady moved from the White House to the Soldiers Home in North Washington. The Soldiers Home was an asylum for the wounded and dying men who had fought in this bitter conflict. They eventually adopted the home as their summer residence, finding piece and, I suppose, a kindred relationship with the men there. Lincoln basically commuted to the White House each day. At least 'rush hour' hadn't really been invented then.

The war was consuming all of President Lincoln's time. He could think of little else. He worked night and day, seven days a week, eighteen hours a day and more.

On April 6th, 1862, nearly one year since the attack on Fort Sumter, the Union Army won a key victory in the Battle of Shiloh, also commonly known as the Battle of Pittsburgh Landing. It was a huge battle in the western theatre of the American Civil War. And though it was a victory for the Union President, it came at a huge cost of American lives. It was clear now that the carnage would not stop until there was a total war. It could no longer be a war about simply preserving the Union. It had to address slavery and its total abolition.

Finally, in July 1862, President Lincoln confided in his cabinet that he intended to abolish slavery in the United States and end slavery forever. He understood that it was the only way to end the war quickly and remove the authority and power that the southern politicians had wielded for too long.

It was on September 22nd, 1862, that President Lincoln issued his Emancipation Proclamation to the world. As with Thomas Jefferson's earth-shaking document before, this was the second Declaration of Independence.

This however, didn't stop the battles. The Union had started to win significant victories in the west, but was being devastated in the east. Virginia was being overrun by Robert E. Lee's rebel army which was advancing on Pennsylvania.

In the first days of July 1863, near the small town of Gettysburg, the conflict would come to a climax. Three horrific days of bloodshed ensued. The early photographers exposed the American people to the horror of war for the first time. President Lincoln himself was emotionally crushed by this. Overcome by the incomprehensible levels of loss.

In September of 1863 Lincoln travelled to Gettysburg to help commemorate the battlefield as a national cemetery. He spoke for two minutes. That's all. In this two minute speech, he was able to galvanise and inspire the Union to continue this tragic but now necessary war. If not, then the Union and liberty itself could be vanquished from the face of the earth. To this day, the Gettysburg Address is considered one of the most important speeches ever given by any politician in history.

RE-ELECTION

Despite the inspirational power of the Gettysburg Address, most Americans were weary of the bloodshed and wanted to see an end to the Civil War. In 1864, Democratic candidate General George B. McClellan stood as the man who would compromise with the south and bring an end to the war, by allowing slavery and centralised government control to continue in the Confederate states.

It was going to be a tough race for Lincoln. Would the American people agree with his difficult libertarian stance, or go the (seemingly) easier route with McClellan?

When Lincoln refused to back down on the Emancipation Proclamation, it appeared that it would cost him his Presidency. He had a Democratic running-mate in the form of Andrew Johnson to balance out the ticket, but that didn't seem to be what was going to swing it. However, President Lincoln came into a bit of luck.

General William Tecumseh Sherman's troops had just captured Atlanta, and Sherman was beginning his infamous 'March to the Sea.' Suddenly the Union Army had momentum. And President Lincoln acquired the momentum with it. In the loyal states, he still received 56% of the vote. The people chose liberty over compromise.

On March 4th, 1865, President Abraham Lincoln took the oath of office one last time.

By now, he was more of a broken man. He was deeply affected and in his second inaugural address, made a very moving statement about his growth as a person over the previous four years. He laid out his road for reconstruction as soon as the war was over. He promised "malice toward none, and charity for all."

On April 9th, 1865, merely weeks after President Lincoln's inaugural address, Robert E. Lee finally surrendered the Confederate Army to Ulysses S. Grant. The war was almost over.

And to his credit, Lincoln spoke of no malice to the south. In his last public speech he talked of how the nation needed to heal itself. He said that the black man must be allowed the vote, and that the south needed to be welcomed with open arms back to the Union, and back to liberty. He spoke like the Founding Fathers, almost a century beforehand.

TRAGEDY

It was April 14th 1865, just a couple of evenings later. To celebrate Good Friday, The President and first lady were at Ford's Theatre in New York, watching the comedy "Our American Cousin".

It was during this play, that President Abraham Lincoln was shot and killed.

The assassin was John Wilkes Booth, an actor and Confederate sympathiser. Booth had also plotted with fellow conspirators Lewis Powell, to kill William H. Seward, (the then Secretary of State) and George Atzerodt to kill Vice President Andrew Johnson. Booth hoped to create chaos and overthrow the Federal government by assassinating Lincoln, Seward, and Johnson. Although Booth succeeded in killing Lincoln, the larger plot failed. Seward was attacked, but recovered from his wounds, and Johnson's would-be assassin fled Washington D.C. upon losing his nerve.

Lincoln left a legacy like no other. He replicated the values of the founding fathers by both saving the Republic and reinforcing the principles of the men who created it. Lincoln understood that no matter who you were, and what your background was, you should be free to pursue the American dream.

SEVENTEEN
ANDREW JOHNSON

Took Office: April 15th 1865
Left Office: March 4th 1869
Party: Democratic-Union
Term: 20

IT'S FAIR TO SUGGEST that most Vice Presidents dream of eventually taking the top job. Some never have that ambition, due to attaining the Vice Presidential office so late in life and so on, but for the most part, winning an election on your own platform is the honour that many strive for.

It is in this instance, that you must feel sorry for Vice President Andrew Johnson. Yet another man destined to take office under a grey national cloud.

On the evening of April 14th, 1865, treachery was in the air. The President was shot and killed and the Secretary of State was stabbed. General Ulysses S. Grant was also targeted, but happened to be away from Washington D.C. at the time. And yes, Vice President Andrew

Johnson was on the hit list too.

In fact, Johnson was invited to the Fords Theatre to see the same play that President Lincoln had gone to see that night. Not being one for the theatre, and having an awful lot of work to catch up on, Vice President Johnson turned the invitation down. Only hindsight would reveal how fortunate an act that was.

John Wilkes Booth, the man who assassinated President Lincoln, knew exactly where Vice President Johnson would be that fateful evening. He sent a co-conspirator to the boarding house where the Vice President was spending the night.

Resting in his suite, the Vice President lit a few candles, read some documents, then prepared for bed, completely unaware of the national tragedy that had just occurred. The plan of the assassin was simple: he was to knock on the Vice Presidents door that night, and when Johnson answered, he would have received a knife in the heart.

However, we can all be thankful for the fact that the man assigned to kill Vice President Johnson that night lost his nerve. He never went through with the attack. Some say that if he had gone ahead with it, with everything that had gone on that night, he would have almost certainly been successful.

So the following morning, on April 15th, 1865, when President Lincoln had finally died from his gunshot wounds, Andrew Johnson became the first man to ascend to the office of President of the United States, due to the bullet of an assassin.

HE'S JUST NOT ABE

And that's where President Johnson's problems began. To many, he was simply a 'pretender to the throne'. In the eyes of many, he wasn't who they really voted for, and was therefore seen with some distain by many swathes of the American people, including (or especially) those who had proudly voted for the Republican Abe Lincoln to take them through a second term of increasing freedom. The idea that a Democrat who could potentially take them back to the old collectivist ways of stagnation and slavery was very troublesome for many. Even if he was not that way inclined at all, many Americans still distrusted this President who got there on a 'technicality'.

But he was not a Democrat in the traditional sense of the word. Otherwise his relationship with President Lincoln wouldn't have been as good as it was. He was very insistent during the civil war that his Party affiliations were with what he called the 'Democrat-Union', which I guess means a Party that believes in the general principles of the Democratic Party, but also in the notion of the American Union. It's kind of the basic standpoint of the Democratic Party today.

It's fair to point out though, that in contrast to his martyred predecessor, he was a Southerner who had at one time, owned slaves of his own. However he was the only Democrat Senator of a seceding Southern State that strongly stayed with the Union. The idea of a Confederacy splitting the nation in two was too repulsive an idea for him. In order to broaden Lincoln's appeal for his second term, Andrew Johnson was a winning strategic component. But no one had foreseen him taking the oath of office for himself so soon, and it worried a number of people who were loyal to Lincoln. In fact, many of the people in charge of organising President Lincoln's campaign for a second term in office, would never have wanted Andrew Johnson to become President in his own right, let alone just days into Lincoln's second term. This was going to be a difficult time for all.

Like his predecessor though, President Johnson had risen up from poverty on his own wit and merit, thus proving to be yet another example of the social mobility that was (and is) abundant in America. However, that's where a great deal of the similarities ended.

I kinda feel sorry for the guy. Here we are, pretty much a quarter-way through the chapter on President Andrew Johnson, and all we're doing is comparing him to the amazing man who was in office just before. How is he supposed to compare to the 'Jefferson-second-coming' that was Abe Lincoln? He can't, and didn't. But these differences are very important if we are to understand the man.

Unlike President Lincoln, who was somehow able to deal with all kinds of different opinions and personalities, Johnson just had a hard time dealing with dissent. Anyone with a different opinion to him was to be avoided if possible, or ignored at a last resort. I bet we've all had to work for bosses like that in the past! Naturally this rubbed members of the cabinet up the wrong way on numerous occasions.

Everyone wanted to know President Lincoln. He was the big personality in the room. Even if you disagreed with him, you could engage with him, and his powers to persuade and shape the direction of things were legendary. It's easy to say this about a great many political leaders in history, but President Lincoln was a man who really did know how to inspire people to follow his vision. In contrast, President Johnson didn't have many friends. He was a bit of a 'Billy-no-mates'. He was often quite miserable, and hated having to listen to people with different opinions than him. It makes you wonder why he ever bothered entering political office in the first place.

And where President Lincoln made his decisions based on logic, circumstance and reason, President Johnson was stubborn, irrational and inflexible. When he made a decision to do something, it was often based on a misunderstanding of the facts. But he was incapable (or unwilling) of changing direction or steering back onto the right path.

THE END OF JACKSON
Johnson looked to President Andrew Jackson for inspiration. They both came from the same state and in many respects, you could say

that he was the last Jacksonian Democrat. He took President Jackson's old saying 'Our Federal Union must be preserved' and used it throughout his time in office as justification of everything he did. It was a case of "Yes, I know that my decision about the budget today was a stupid one that will have damaging effects, but our Federal Union must be preserved!"

He was arbitrary and crude, and saw everything in misguided black-and-white ways. He thought that there was a conspiracy on every corner (which might be understandable, when you consider what had happened to his predecessor), and thought that almost everyone with a different opinion to him in Washington D.C. was out to get him in some way. A precursor to Richard Nixon maybe?

President Johnson was similar to Andrew Jackson in other ways as well. He felt that he too, was the voice of the common man. And how many politicians have used that empty phrase over the years?

The problem was, President Johnson was also as indifferent to the issue of the slavery as Jackson was. In fact, some historians say that Johnson is perhaps the most racist President America has ever seen. Now most of them at this stage (including surprisingly, Abe Lincoln) have said some pretty astonishingly racist things, and I think we really have to be both appalled by this, and look at them in the context of their era. President Lincoln said that the idea of a white man and a black woman having a relationship filled him with disgust. Not really the words of a great emancipator in our eyes is it? But again, it was a consensus opinion that was decidedly uncontroversial at the time and we have to be thankful that most of our attitudes today have evolved to a point where comments like that are no longer the consensus. Some people still have those views, and are welcome to express them. We too, are equally welcome to call them morons.

President Johnson's racist attitude demands special attention though. He constantly referred to black people as 'savages' and 'barbarians'. He simply believed that after all the suffering and fighting between the north and the south, that the blacks should go back and work on the plantations and leave the sphere of public life to the white Americans. Even in the mid-1800s, this was not really what decent people believed any more.

CAN THE TAILOR STITCH THE UNION BACK TOGETHER?

So it was down to the racist President from the South, a man with no formal education who had trained to become a tailor, to stitch the Union back together again.

Thankfully the civil war had all but ended. However, that meant that the real work was still to be done. Reconstruction would be the big item on the agenda of the new President.

And the crisis of reconstruction was second only to the crisis of the American civil war. Sure, the southern states could integrate back into the Union pretty easily, but the big questions were still in the air. Would America continue to grow into what the Founding Fathers promised? Who would get to be a citizen? Could you vote in America regardless of your skin colour? It was rather tragic that President Lincoln wasn't around to find the answers to these questions.

The so-called 'radical Republicans', were the extreme members of Congress who wanted drastic reform. They were the most keen to get a sense of President Johnson's policies. Would he do the right thing? Unlike Lincoln, many of the radical Republicans wanted to see the South punished for what it did. But they had nobler interests as well. They wanted all former slaves protected and made full unconditional citizens.

Initially President Johnson seemed to go along with most of these reforms. Then when Congress retired for the Christmas break, he took the opportunity to come up with his own reconstruction plans. The South was prepared for the worst.

However, they didn't have too much to fear. The Confederates were given full amnesty, and the Southern states were welcomed back into the Union with much haste. So far, so good. Lincoln and many Republicans (though not the radical wing) would be happy with that. But the newly-freed slaves ended up getting little or no protection from the potential tyranny of their former masters.

It's no surprise that many of the former slaves were persecuted during this time. And it's no surprise that eventually the NRA (National Rifle Association) was founded in New York, partially with a significant purpose of making sure that these newly-made American citizens could be armed and protect themselves. It's no coincidence that the same year the Klu Kulx Klan became an illegal organisation, the NRA was formed. The NRA mostly consisted of Union officers who passionately believed that all Americans had the full right to defend themselves and their liberty under the 2nd Amendment, and you can track their success pretty well. In areas of newly-freed slaves where the NRA managed to get to and train them to use firearms, the number of lynching-reports was very low.

Not giving blacks the right to vote and full citizenship as the Republicans had demanded, puts President Johnson on the wrong side of history and morality. He failed to see that America had changed. When Congress got back from the winter break, they were shocked at what the President had done.

The strong Republican Congress put in action President Lincoln's idea of the Freed Man's Bureau to help former slaves transition to citizenship. President Johnson vetoed the bill. That continued back and forth. And every time Congress passed a libertarian bill, President Johnson vetoed it. He made a record-breaking 29 vetoes in total.

But the Founding Fathers had got a system in place that allowed the democratic will of the people to stand up to the President's authoritarianism. When Congress put the Civil Rights Bill of 1866 together, they knew they had the support to override President Johnson's vetoes. They overturned the President's veto a record 15 times. They continued to do good work in Congress, limiting the Presidents power. When they eventually introduced the Tenure of Office Act of 1867, that essentially made sure that the President's power to remove appointees without the Senates consent was greatly limited.

The Lincoln/Jeffersonian wing of the Republican Party was working very hard to limit government and maximise individual freedom. The huge increase in prosperity and living standards across the nation is testament to their hard work. However, this is something that President Johnson will never be able to take the credit for.

Eventually Congress had given the President enough rope to hang himself. He removed the Secretary of War from office, a guy who was appointed back in the day by President Lincoln. By doing this he violated the Tenure of Office Act and was impeached in 1868. Their charges were pretty flimsy, but a trial by the Senate to prove whether or not he had committed any of the 'high crimes and misdemeanours' that the Constitution required to remove him from office, was underway.

Forget O.J. Simpson, this was the trial of the *nineteenth* century! In the end, President Johnson was spared the humiliation of having to leave office by just one vote. After that, he passed his time in office with little fuss.

And the good news for Americans was that it brought about a new age of limited government. A string of Presidents with limited powers came along after, who were more subservient to Congress in the way the libertarian Founders wanted. And, as we shall discover, America blossomed.

EIGHTEEN
ULYSSES SIMPSON GRANT

Took Office: March 4th 1869
Left Office: March 4th 1877
Party: Republican
Terms: 21 & 22

A LITTLE GOVERNMENT AND a little luck are both necessary in life. But only a fool trusts either of those things entirely, and for the same reason. After the inspiration of President Lincoln, and the muddling mess of President Johnson, the American people wanted more of what the Founding Fathers had offered in the first place: limited government. A system where the head of the executive branch's power was greatly reduced, and political orders and laws are made and passed by Congress. A system where the President is merely in charge of executing the will of Congress to the best of their ability.

And the fact that this era also happened to be an era of unprecedented prosperity for America, and was the real reason why America is the superpower that it is today, is of no coincidence.

Something worth remembering: whenever the President does less and has less power, and whenever government in general is smaller, the people have more say over their own lives, and the nation becomes more prosperous. After the departure of the authoritarian President Johnson, the next 30 years worth of Presidents exercised a lot less power, and historians usually look down their noses at these 'mediocre Presidents'. But the nation was infinitely better off as a result.

THE GOLDEN ERA BEGINS

And so enter General Ulysses Grant, stage right.

In his military persona, he was considered the very saviour of the Union. Kids playing 'war' in the streets of the late nineteenth century would always fight over who got to play him and shout "the Union forever!" General Grant's image represented the very embodiment of the American Union. Make no doubt, he was the 1860s/1870s version of a celebrity. And many years before *Hello! Magazine* even existed too.

He was the youngest man ever to win an election. At this point, blacks could vote too, and they played a decisive role. In fact, Grant did not win a majority of the white vote, and had to rely on the votes of the former slaves in the South to gain office. They accounted for a vital 12% of the total vote. Seems like this whole democracy thing works pretty well after all.

You'd think that kind of support would have given President Grant a serious ego-boost. But the 'silent General' as he was often called in his military days, was actually rather humble, loyal and very shy. Not one for significant public speaking, and preferred to run the White House in very much the same way as his military operations; with efficiency, and simple, effective communication.

He was a very talented artist too. Some of his paintings of native

Americans, etc. are still publicly viewable today, and are rather impressive, if you like that sort of thing. There was no way he was ever going to win a 'best dressed' award, being as scruffy and 'rumpled' as he often looked, and many today would turn their noses up at the fact he usually seemed to carry with him the stench of cigar smoke. He actually smoked about twenty a day!

This was a short, dumpy, ungallant and dishevelled-looking guy. But there was real character about him. He was an adrenaline junkie, but because fast cars and bungee-jumping hadn't been invented yet, he had to rely on horse-power to satisfy his needs. In 1866, he had an impromptu horse & coach drag-race through Central Park in New York City. And he won. Incidentally, the coach he was racing against was carrying President Andrew Johnson. Why don't politicians do this anymore? Wouldn't have been more fun if President Obama said to Vice President Biden after his inauguration "Yo, Joe: I'll race you to the White House!"?

RUN IT GRANT-STYLE

President Grant had an unfortunate tendency for nepotism. He would appoint cronies, such as relatives of his wife. And when these guys got top jobs and cabinet positions, unfortunately they started to abuse their roles.

He felt that his appointment to President was simply a continuation of resolving the civil war. His campaign slogan, now etched in stone in several places in Washington DC and beyond, was "Let us have peace." However, his time in office was anything but peaceful. But, as we shall learn, we can't really blame the eighteenth President for that.

By the time Grant took high office, things had gone pretty well. Due to their newly-granted rights to vote, blacks had overwhelmingly voted for Republican politicians in the Southern States. A trend that would continue, on and off. From Texas to Florida, the former Confederacies were suddenly Republican strongholds. But the after effects of war were still strongly felt. There were still grievances on both sides. Many from the Republican North still wanted to punish the South for its 'un-American' actions in creating the Confederacy. And many from the Democratic South were keen to take their anger out on the blacks.

It's still uncomfortable to say in this day and age, but the Klu Klux Klan were essentially the terrorist wing of the Democratic Party at the time. And in this capacity, there was almost another civil war commencing. And the purpose of these horrific acts of lynching, murder, whippings, cross-burning (never quite understood what that was about) and other such terrorist acts was simple: the KKK and the Democratic Party simply wanted to undermine the predominantly Republican government.

Over a century before President George W. Bush coined the phrase for himself, President Grant launched a war on terrorism. The Klan had to be stopped at all costs. As I mentioned in the previous chapter, in the same year that the KKK was declared an illegal terrorist organisation, the National Rifle Association was formed. In the Michael Moore documentary 'Bowling for Columbine', Moore insinuates that the NRA is somehow linked to the KKK, which is kind of true, but for the complete opposite reasons that he tries to insinuate in his polemic. The NRA is a pro-Union organisation, that went into the deep south and tried to train the newly freed slaves how to use firearms to protect themselves and their families. After all, the 2nd Amendment rights were guaranteed to these people as well as those in the north.

History is very clear and there's no doubt about it: the KKK and NRA are total enemies, right on the opposite sides of the battlefield. The Republicans and the NRA were fighting to protect the blacks and their civil rights, the Democrats and the KKK were fighting to take those rights away. It's no surprise that after his time in office, President Grant becomes a significant figurehead for the NRA, which consistently had noteworthy Union officers as its presidents. Oh yeah, and Charlton Heston.

PEACE, SCANDAL AND VIOLENCE

Thanks to the anti-Klan laws passed in Congress, President Grant succeeded in crushing them in the south. 1872 was the most peaceful year in the southern states since the start of the civil war. Phew. Let's take a breather.

But the peace was to be replaced by good old-fashioned scandal. The friends and family that he put in place in his cabinet and other positions, were being exposed as corrupt. They would do all sorts of dodgy deals behind his back and many started to link him with the corruption of his subordinates.

Now President Grant didn't really know that any of these dodgy scandals were going on, and there's certainly no evidence that he profited from any of it. But he was defiantly tainted with the disgrace of his subordinates lining their pockets with public money. Some figured that this would all but guarantee that he would become a one-term President.

However, that wasn't to be the case. He won a decisive victory in 1872. However, his second term in office was marred with yet more unpleasant newspaper coverage. The coverage was mostly on the violence in the south. Slowly but surely, the Democrats were taking over again, and an escalation in violence was on the rise as a result.

Previously, President Grant had used the powers granted by Congress to crush this upsurge in violence, but with more Democrats in Congress, the political map was looking a little more diluted than it once was. In 1873, a mild economic depression in the north made people less enthusiastic about spending so much time and money on the reconstruction of the south.

The northern public's taste for the occupation in the south was waning. And President Grant's ability or desire to continue the occupation was waning also. And when the Governor of Mississippi called upon the Federal government to send soldiers to dampen down the rise of electoral violence there in 1875, Grant did nothing.

As a result of his inaction, terrorist groups such as the KKK and its variants, continued to take over the Southern states and overthrow the democratically elected governments there. Once again, the political landscape in the south was changing for the worse.

Another of President Grant's difficulties was with the Native Americans. He said that he wanted unconditional peace with the Indians. Since the age of Jackson and before, there had been too much strife and too much grievance. He wanted that to end once and for all.

But again, he failed. There was even more war. Well into President Grant's second term, the infamous battle of Little Big Horn commenced. General Custer and his men were totally annihilated by Indian fighters. Many battles, usually involving the overwhelming victory of American soldiers, took place over this time. Peace between the Natives and the Republic seemed like a distant hope.

FAILURE AND SUCCESS

Despite fighting adamantly for a policy of peace, there can be no doubt that President Grant failed. His use of force did no good, and attempting to make a peace-deal with others seemed fruitless as well.

However, we have to remember was else was going on at the time, that the history books (usually) don't talk about. It's very easy to record tangible events like wars and so on, but during President Grant's time in office, social mobility was on the rise for most Americans, and even the northern states' minor economic downturn in 1873 didn't stop the overall rise in the standard of living. If we were getting these sorts of standards increases today, it'd be the equivalent of us almost doubling our incomes every 10-15 years!

So the success of President Grant's time in office really has nothing to do with the man himself. By allowing Congress to do its thing, and by government letting the people do their thing, prosperity was the overwhelming direction that America continued to move in.

Also in recent years, historians have been kinder to Grant. After all, on his watch, we saw a man willing to fight the good fight and defend all Americans, regardless of the colour of their skin. That's a pretty significant effort on his part, and well worth us all being thankful for.

But the scandals surrounding President Grant's cronies were getting too much for some to bear. The Republican Party knew they needed someone more clean cut, who could rise above these smears. The man they chose as their Parties nominee was just that: the 'incorruptible' Rutherford B. Hayes.

NINETEEN
RUTHERFORD BIRCHARD HAYES

Took Office: March 4th 1877
Left Office: March 4th 1881
Party: Republican
Term: 23

THE SUCCESSION OF REPUBLICAN Presidents was set to continue. The majority of Americans still didn't support the pro-slavery positions of the Democratic Party, and yearned for the promise of limited government. Americas prosperity was to continue with Rutherford B. Hayes. But what kind of man was he, and what type of President was he to become? Funny you should ask...

In many ways, he was the perfect antidote to the scandals that plagued the Grant years, and (unfairly) tarnished Grants name in certain circles. There were valid reasons for this. Hayes was the kind of man who would appoint people on the basis of merit rather than the fact that they were in his 'circle of friends and family.' There was certainly going to be no charges of nepotism in the Hayes administration.

There is a downside to all of this though. He was considered rather bland. One political commentator at the time described him as "a third-rate nonentity, who's only recommendation is that he is obnoxious to no one". However, as American history has so far proved, it is better to have a small-scale limited-government 'bland' President, than a fiery authoritarian/dictatorial 'colourful' one.

THE LAST BATTLE OF THE CIVIL WAR

Hayes was fortunate to even be alive for the Presidential campaign of 1876. His stint in the Union army had been a pretty tough one. He was wounded five times, and had four horses shot out from under him.

With that kind of record, I don't know whether that means he was very lucky or very unlucky.

Some would later call the election of 1876 between Hayes and New York Governor Samuel J. Tilden as the last battle of the civil war. The last big fight between the Republicans who stood on a ticket of anti-slavery, pro individual freedom, and pro liberty, and the Democrats who wanted a return to the ways before the civil war, and possibly the growth of a Confederacy of sorts yet again. As with previous elections based on the same platforms, the Republican candidate barely made it.

The legendary election night of 2000, between Governor George W. Bush and Vice President Al Gore, didn't have anything on the one in 1876. On election night, it looked like Tilden had won.

Tilden was something in the region of 260,000 votes ahead towards the end of election night. This is the equivalent of a big margin today. Upon receiving this news, Hayes decided to go to bed. Would you blame the guy? Why stay up just to confirm your defeat? And it's true – Hayes did lose the popular vote. However the tally in the

Electoral College painted a slightly different picture. It seemed to favour Tilden still, but it was a close thing.

However, just like in 2000, results from a number of states were in dispute from both sides. This didn't stop Hayes from talking to the local papers in his state of Ohio about the fact that he had 'lost'. He was gracious to his opponent, despite the pretty bitter campaign that was fought.

But word from his campaign staff soon got to him – "Hayes, stop telling everyone you've lost; you could win this thing!" And that's when the lawyers stepped in.

After many recounts, compromises and disputes, both groups agreed to allow a specially appointed group of men to make the final decision. This electoral commission would settle the matter once and for all. And they did. Barely.

They voted 8 to 7 strictly along Party lines, in favour of Hayes. All three disputed states were given to him. The election was over. Well, almost.

The last stepping stone that Hayes needed to conquer was getting the final confirmation from the House of Representatives. This was going to be tricky, because many Democrats in the House were not best pleased that their man lost by such a slim margin. I'm beginning to see why so many of the Founding Fathers didn't like the idea of political parties, don't you?

Democrats threatened a filibuster in the House. That old tactic of yore, used to great effect in the brilliant classic Jimmy Stewart movie '*Mr. Smith Goes to Washington.*' However, the opposition to Hayes' appointment very quickly evaporated. It would not be until much later, that scraps of evidence here and there, would point to there being a great compromise reached.

It seemed that Hayes made concessions in exchange for the keys to the White House. While it seems clear that some background deal was made, it's not clear what was promised to whom. We can speculate all we like, but I've got a feeling that we shall never truly know. But who cares, unqualified speculation is fun!

For Hayes, this was not the greatest of ways for him to start his Presidency. The air of dodgy-dealings lingered over him. Many called him names, like "His Fraudulency", "RutherFraud Hayes", or "The Great Usurper". I think "RutherFraud Hayes" was my personal favourite. But regardless, the image of him being the whiter-than-white candidate was well and truly gone.

But regardless of some people's apprehension, Hayes was sworn in as the nineteenth President. He was the first to do so actually in the White House itself. They then took a public 'ceremonial' oath of office on the steps of the Capitol Building a couple of days later. Go figure.

THE HAYES OUTLOOK

Before we get onto the important stuff, let's point out some of the (minor) cool additions brought in by the Hayes administration. He was the first President to have a telephone installed in the Executive Mansion (but his internet connection didn't arrive until over a hundred years later – something to do with that being the only time the telecom engineers could get there, which sounds familiar).

Also both he and his wife did a very impressive job of adding to the White House paintings. They bought tons of the things, which is a shame because it left very little room for President Ronald Reagan to put up his cool 50s movie posters when he became Commander-in-Chief. Hayes commissioned now infamous portraits of former Presidents Jefferson, John Adams, and Jackson. Very good portraits for sure, but Jackson's hair looks a little too bouffant for my liking in his painting.

Despite President Hayes' (suspected) backroom dealings made in order for him to attain high office, he had an otherwise fairly noble reputation for honesty. Despite all the pictures of him looking like he's had a sense of humour transplant, he was in fact a very jolly fellow, with a rather sunny disposition. He had an optimistic streak in him and was always keen to govern by compromise, and meeting his opponents in the middle.

This optimism took a bit of a blow once he entered office though. He was rather crushed at the pettiness of office in many ways. He had to spend a little bit of time with snivelling, paltry little people. He didn't seem to understand that a big part of being President meant that you had to deal with mundane, day-to-day human shortcomings and disputes.

The Hayes White House was a rather passive one. Little was done, which, as I've often stated, was a fairly good thing for the American People. They were left alone to prosper and grow. And government didn't grow at the same speed or faster (for a change). If anything, it probably shrank a little. More and more people around the country were rising up the social ladder, and more immigrants were coming into the country in search of the American dream. And many were getting it. We can look on the late 19th Century with snobbish contemporary eyes if we wish, but if you look past the lack of social and technological advances, it really was a time of real globalisation, real liberty, real freedom, and real prosperity.

President Hayes' wife Lucy was very much the Queen of Quiet. Which is not surprising for a woman who gave birth to eight children. You'd be too tired to talk, wouldn't you? They called her Lemonade Lucy, which, apart from sounding like a lame rapper, was a nickname given to her to describe her intolerance towards alcohol in the White House. Yep, the executive mansion was a teetotal place under the Hayes Administration. President Hayes wasn't exactly over the moon about this idea, but he went along with his wife regardless. Now there's a well-trained husband.

This became something of a laughing matter in Washington D.C. The line that many a White House staffer would joke about, was that in the Hayes White House, water flowed like wine. Cute.

And the way President Hayes conducted the various affairs of his office, was frankly boring. But boring in a very good way indeed. He would recognise a problem or issue, consult the proper experts on the matter, weigh up the evidence, seek further advice if needed, then make a decision based on reason and evidence. So like I say; dull, but, well... good.

He was adamant that Congress was the place that made and passed the laws, and that the Supreme Court was the place that interpreted the laws, and that his role was simply to execute the laws, to the best of his ability.

Funny, that's kind of what the Founding Fathers had in mind. And put simply, it worked. It worked well.

MOVING ON FROM THE CIVIL WAR

When President Hayes took office, the country was still very much dealing with the reconstruction effort, and all of the division and strife that went with it. The real test was could such a rational man finally resolve such a difficult task? Not in a way you're going to like.

He had Federal troops stationed in Louisiana and South Carolina, in order to protect the Republican governments there from being taken over by the Democrats and their terrorist friends. In the most controversial move of his Presidency, he actually decided to remove the troops from the statehouses, where they were protecting the state governments. It was pretty much his one and only decision that wasn't taken with the calm and rational analysis that he was becoming famous for.

This move, somewhat inevitably, lead to the hostile takeover of the states by the Democrats. In many ways, this was the final, symbolic end of reconstruction. But in many ways, reconstruction was over way before President Hayes took the oath of office anyway.

Some say that maybe this uncharacteristically irrational decision was the result of the 'back-room deal' that Hayes made in order to become President. The idea being that by letting the Democrats control all of the south, they would allow Hayes the White House, and in return, would promise to exercise a modest policy towards the blacks and respect their rights to citizenship. How much of that they actually did, is very much in dispute.

Hayes has been vilified for his actions, and you can kind of see why. But look at it a little closer. Is this compromise, this "dodgy-deal", all that it seems?

Hayes was convinced that the return of civilian rule in the south, would bring about a return in civility itself. Maybe in some respects, Hayes' decision actually finally united the states, and brought about an end to the bitterness of the north/south divide. I don't know if it's totally accurate, but based on the rational stance that Hayes continually made, I'd be foolish not to throw that idea out there.

However, to his bitter disappointment, President Hayes' idea that the 'southern gentlemen' would treat blacks with respect, was washed away pretty quickly. And as a result, the segregation of blacks in the south continued for many, many years. The changes would come, but it would only do so in the next century. And many believe that the equality and respect that the African-Americans deserved, is a component still missing from the psyche of increasingly small sections of the south.

Some Americans in the Republican Party felt that with the window on the civil war closed, they could turn their reforming agenda onto a different issue. That of civil service. Some felt that reform of the civil service would be as important as the anti-slavery movement was. They were concerned that people who had attained roles of importance in the civil service were in worrying positions. These people were often very corrupt, and could skim a great deal off the top of most taxes. They also had a lot of power and wielded it for their own gain. And none of these people were democratically elected.

If they were working in the private sector, no one would have worried. But because they were working in the public sector, they could use their power to alter the rules to favour them and their special interests, and pervert the natural system of a free market, where good rational decisions get rewarded, and bad decisions get punished.

A lot of the civil service fraud manifested itself in New York's corrupt political machine. These people in the machine were usually Republican stalwarts. Hayes removed the Chief Collector of the New York Custom House and replaced him with someone of merit and integrity.

What was the name of this corrupt head of the New York Custom House? A certain Chester A. Arthur. And his real story will show up a little later on in this book.

In the final year of his time in office, President Hayes travelled by train to the West Coast – the first President to do so. He hoped the symbolic gesture would bring unity to the country.

Many were impressed by his time in office, as a man who used reason and classical liberalism where he could. They asked him to run again, and there would have been a good chance that he would have won, too.

However, honest to the last, he upheld his campaign pledge to be a one-term President. And that wasn't a tough decision to make. He said many times after leaving office, of how little he liked being the head of the executive branch. Yet again, a little reluctance goes a long way it seems.

President Hayes retired to Ohio and spend his twilight years working tirelessly for education reform, and became an important figure in the libertarian fight for blacks' civil rights. In doing so, he set a standard for future ex-Presidents, who went on to win Nobel Prizes and all sorts.

TWENTY
JAMES ABRAM GARFIELD

Took Office: March 4th 1881
Left Office: September 19th 1881
Party: Republican
Term: 24

AFTER FOUR WILDERNESS YEARS, Ulyssess S. Granted wanted another shot at the Presidential title again. The idea being, that the old tarnish of corruption had been put to bed, and most people by then had realised that he was not responsible for that corruption. The voters had seemed to forgive him. So could he put enough pressure on the Republican Party to secure their nomination?

Also, in the four years since he left he'd become something of an international celebrity, going all over the world and shaking hands and doing photo-ops (yes they had photos at this point) with every foreign mover-and-shaker he could. His image was not only intact, but rather strong and dignified. The consensus amongst the chattering classes in Washington D.C. was that Grant would be a shoe-in for the Republican nomination. However neither they, nor Grant reckoned on the emergence of another General from Ohio. James Abram Garfield.

MAKING HIS MARK

Most people discovered General Garfield for the first time during the Republican convention of 1880. Like so many politicians before or since, his speech there made people finally stand up and take notice.

Grant did a noble job of putting his case for nomination across, but just couldn't seem to match General Garfield's ability to engage on the stage. So Garfield got the nomination, and on a continued promise of limited government and yet more liberty, he won the Presidency pretty easily too.

President Garfield was the only preacher to ever hold the office. He had however, promised to maintain the separation of church and state, which reassured voters that they were not sleep-walking their way into a theocracy. He was also the first President to be a former college professor. Oh, and he also had a much bigger, bushier beard that President Grant, which I'm sure probably swayed a number of the undecided voters!

He was a member of the House of Representatives and moved from Capitol Hill directly to the White House – one of the few Presidents to directly leave that chamber of the House in order to become the head of the executive branch.

His style and popularity won the day outright. He was quite a warm, friendly and outgoing gentleman, who seemed to keep a smile on him despite having to deal with seven children. He was also a big baseball fan, and had an eye for the minutiae of public policy. In fact, whereas most Presidents find the intricacies of policymaking a rather tiresome task, President Garfield seemed to relish the chance to have a good old dig around, dotting the 'i's and crossing the 't's.

And how does sometime marry up their love for both baseball and policymaking? It's an interesting balance, and one that Garfield made carefully during his time in the House of Representatives. He would often bury himself in notes about trade tariffs, and how certain taxations affect certain industries. He worked tirelessly on the precision of how government could influence the economy and society for good or ill. It was through this that he understood, as many did before him and do still, that the more 'hands-off' government was, the more prosperous the people became.

But then of course, there was the 'baseball' side of Garfield. And on numerous occasions, he would discreetly slip off out of the House of Representatives chamber and catch the odd baseball game. No one seemed to mind all that much, as he was clearly doing such a good job overall. And why not let him have a little fun every now and then? He certainly seemed to deserve it!

President Garfield was a man known to waffle an awful lot. His dedication to getting things right, meant that he needed to frequently trawl through the details and search of accuracy. This meant, in the eyes of many, that he was prone to drone on and on. He'd make a great filibuster in the House if the time ever arose.

Also, his unwillingness to just throw an opinion in the air sometimes meant that he was seen to be quite an appeaser. He was known as a man who liked to sit on the fence. This isn't really fair or accurate. He simply liked having the facts on his side, and making judgements based on those facts. This meant that an awful lot of the time, if he wasn't 100% sure about something, he'd just seek the middle ground and play it safe. That may have won him a majority of votes most of the time, but also frustrated some people.

And the big problem with frequently trying to make everyone happy, is that often you end up upsetting a great deal more than you appease.

President Garfield's first job as Commander-in-Chief, was to dole out the political appointments. In recent years, this had become a notoriously corrupt process. However, thanks, in part, to President Grant's 'crony-based' appointments of a few years ago, the public were getting pretty sick of the nepotism and 'sleight of hand' going on in Washington. There was a national outcry for appointments based on merit, and not friendship.

After President Hayes had done a decent job at tackling certain areas of civil service reform, the bulk of the issue was sitting on President Garfield's in-tray as soon as he sat down in the Oval Office for the first time. The real question was how much of a civil service reformer was he going to be?

It seemed that Garfield was up for a fight. He was ready to take on the big boys and win. He believed in limited government and despised the increase in centralised power he had seen. He wanted to take on New York Senator Roscoe Conkling over who should be the person who gets to appoint the Chief Collector of the port of New York.

In the past, the New York Senator had filled this post with one of his own cronies. We many never know just how much money was skimmed off the top during this time. Because the tariff collected in the port of New York was the principle tax for all of the United States, something really had to be done about this.

President Garfield, after seeking legal advice to make sure he was allowed, took it upon himself to appoint a Chief Collector of the port of New York. And in order to make the point, he appointed a rival to Senator Conkling. And despite lots of people being angry about it, (many of whom had their snouts in the trough), the President held firm. Senator Conkling even resigned in protest.

Victory belonged to President Garfield. He had taken on the New

York cronies and won. He knew full well that now the other corrupt areas of government would fall and be replaced by something much more transparent and honest. However, the President would not live long enough see the fruits of his labour.

MORE TRAGEDY FOR AMERICA

The seeds that led up to the tragic death of President Garfield were sown not long after he took office. The White House was a very free place. Anyone, barring minimal security, could simply walk up and enter. It was an open forum for the people. While things weren't quite as open in the days of President Jefferson, where you could walk in, meet with the President and discuss whatever was on your mind, it was still a pretty public place.

Every day after President Garfield took office, he spent his time talking to potential office-seekers. Many wanted in on cabinet positions, and many more wanted posts lower down the food-chain. This was an awful lot for a President to handle, especially as he was taking on the corruption in New York at the time. He tried to only deal with the important roles and delegate the others to different people in his cabinet. The protests about corruption meant that the American people preferred to see most roles fulfilled by the President himself. This was an awful burden, and meant the President had to personally make 'face time' with a great number of job-seekers.

One such man, seeking an appointment, was named Charles J. Guiteau. There was no doubt that there was something not right about this gentleman. He spent the election summer of 1880 hanging around the Republican Party headquarters, but had no job or real reason to be there. But for some reason, he got it into his head that by being there and supporting the President, he was owed a job. He identified himself as a part of the Republican Party known as 'the Stalwarts', which included the disgraced New York Senator Conkling, as well as Garfield's Vice President, Chester A. Arthur.

He had been around these men in the past, but didn't do anything that noteworthy. He had shaken Vice President Arthur's hand one time, and had once managed to make his way into the Presidential waiting room of the White House, just off from the Oval Office. But his link with the other 'Stalwarts' was tenuous to say the least. Many regarded him as a bit of a joke.

So Guiteau was pushed into a level of mental instability. He was angry that President Garfield had ignored his requests for a political appointment (the very cronyism that Garfield had fought to abandon). He was also apparently furious that Garfield had essentially run Senator Conkling out of political office. Added to that, he felt that he had a calling from god to remove the President from office. His descent into lunacy was pretty much complete.

On July 2nd, 1881, Guiteau stalked President Garfield to the Baltimore & Potomac railroad station in Washington D.C. He shot the President twice.

One bullet grazed the Presidents arm. The other was lodged in his torso.

As Guiteau was taken away by the police, he shouted: "I did it! I will go to jail! I am a Stalwart and Arthur will be President!" They were four things he was certainly right about. Guiteau is often labelled in the history books as a disgruntled office-seeker getting revenge. But he truly was insane. A very disturbed individual who was pushed over the edge.

President Garfield didn't die right away. As he lay bedridden with a bullet still lodged in his torso, updates of his medical condition were telegrammed across the country, in the same way the news would travel by internet now. Americans all over the country showed their support. Ironically, President Garfield was more popular after he was shot than before.

Our understanding today of the medical procedures practiced on President Garfield in the last few days of his life, show that these were what probably killed him. They just didn't know enough about what they were doing back then. But actually, the quality of medical care given to the President was awful, even for that era.

In August, Garfield wrote a letter to his mother back in Ohio, telling her not to worry. He wrote "It is true I am still weak and on my back. But I am gaining every day, and need only time and patience bring me through."

But on September 19th, 1881, President Garfield died. He had only been in office for some six months.

TWENTY-ONE
CHESTER ALAN ARTHUR

Took Office: September 19th 1881
Left Office: March 4th 1885
Party: Republican
Term: 24

THE INEVITABLE HAD FINALLY happened. For a while, it had seemed as if President Garfield might just pull through. But eventually, it was considered only a matter of time. Though the circumstances were far from perfect, this did give Garfield's Vice President time to comprehend the duties of office that would eventually fall on his lap. And arguably, that made him a much better man than many people thought he would be.

On September 9th, 1881, Chester A. Arthur became not only the twenty-first President of the United States, but he was also the third man to hold that position in that same year. 1881 was the year of the Presidential hat-trick, for reasons that no one was all that happy about.

There is, however, one thing worth noting if you're an advocate for limited government. During the two months that President Garfield lay dying from his gunshot wounds, Congress remained out of session. By all records and accounts, it is patently clear that the country ran very smoothly and the standards of living for many Americans continued to soar, nonetheless.

TAKING IT EASY

It was common knowledge that Chester A. Arthur was a product of the corrupt New York political machine. He was appointed to the role of Chief Collector of the New York Customs House under President Grant's term, and was one of the men swept away in the reforms of Rutherford B. Hayes. Many Americans were therefore, highly sceptical of Arthur's ability to continue the reforms that President Garfield had so diligently (and effectively) pursued in his all-too-short time in office. In the end, Arthur would surprise a great many people.

So here he was, by virtue of assassination. President Arthur. Just three years after having to leave his role in the New York Customs House under such a wave of scandal and disgrace. Some were shocked. And to put it mildly, people's expectations were low.

While President Arthur originally hailed from Vermont, there was no doubt he was a through-and-through New Yorker. As such, he had high-class New York tastes. He had a wardrobe that rivalled many Princesses in the old country, and loved the finest food from the most extravagant restaurants.

He considered the required move to the White House as (incredibly) something of a social demotion. Used to living in such luxury that most couldn't comprehend, President Arthur insisted that major renovation be carried out on the executive mansion.

It was all about the look for Arthur, which is curious for a man so fat that he had no chin. He was a real peacock, very keen on looking his finest in all occasions. He was concerned about his appearance in the way that too many contemporary politicians are.

We can't talk about President Arthur's look, without talking about those sideburns. Many men had big, full-on beards back then. Many went clean-shaven. Arthur was something else. He had a modest moustache, but that was offset by this enormously large sideburns. They went down beyond his chin (that he didn't really possess) and stuck out in a way that made his face look incredibly wide. In the farcical facial-hair stakes, very few could beat the twenty-first President.

As his wife died in the previous year, it fell on President Arthur's sister to take on the role of social hostess. Drinkers will be pleased to hear that she was nothing like 'Lemonade Lucy' of President Hayes' administration! The wine flowed, and the Washington party-scene elevated by several notches.

President Arthur spent a great deal of his time with the (also disgraced) now former New York Senator, Roscoe Conkling. They enjoyed long fishing trips together and were very much the best of friends. How could anyone have assumed that anything but base cronyism and corruption would pour out of every orifice of the Arthur administration?

And it was easy to see how the corruption could be allowed to spread. There's no sensitive way of wording this, so if you forgive me, I'll resort to bluntness. President Arthur was basically a man who didn't like to work very much. I guess he thought life was too short, and why not spend as much of it as possible, having fun?

Was it a 'lazy-mans' Presidency? Arthur would stroll into the oval office at around 10am, sign papers and attend meetings, have an extended lunch-break, and go for a pleasant walk at the end of his working day, at around 4pm. However, it's fair to point out that he did in fact get quite a lot done in his working day. So he wasn't so much a lazy President, as he was a very efficient one.

One member of White House staff later recalled that President Arthur would "never do today what he could put off until tomorrow." We've all had bosses like that before.

TAKING ON THE MACHINE

The only way for the President to have any credibility, would be for him to continue the path towards greater transparency. He had to tackle the corruption of the New York political machine. And that involved, amongst many things, isolating his dear friend, Roscoe Conkling.

And amazingly he succeeded. By the time his term was up, President Arthur was seen as one of the great reformers. The American people really did respect him and the open and honest way he took a sweeping brush to the corrupt cronies who were once his friends. In fact, some of them still were, but he took all the necessary steps to make sure they could not wield their power and influence for illicit personal gain again. I wonder how many of them actually stayed friends with him as a result? In fact, I often wonder what President Garfield's assassin, Charles J. Guiteau, would have made of Arthur's grand reforms?

After all, it was Guiteau who shot President Garfield, hoping that the Presidents death would bring about a return to office of the 'stalwarts' and, through President Arthurs cronyism, allow the likes of Roscoe Conkling to return to power. Thankfully for everyone else, President Arthur took a dramatically different route.

In many ways, it can be seen in retrospect as rather obvious. Because Arthur was a product of the corrupt system, that meant he was in the best possible position to change that system. Those who profited from the old ways were more inclined to listen to a man who was 'like them'. Some would go even further and pose the question: would President Garfield have actually been as effective at rooting out the dishonesty and scandal that plagued American politics as President Arthur? A tough question to pose, and an even tougher one to answer.

All we know, is that it was President Arthur, and not Garfield, who signed into law one of the strongest pieces of civil service reform legislation ever passed. It all but insured a level of honesty and transparency that had never before been seen in the public sector, and lead to reforms that many thought would never have been possible. But why this change in attitude? Why did the king of cronyism make such a u-turn in his mind-set? Perhaps the best summary came from one of President Arthur's New York friends, who once simply noted, "He's no longer Chet Arthur, he's the President."

And that was exactly it. Something transformed 'Chet' when he finally took the oath of office. Maybe he thought of Thomas Jefferson, or James Monroe. Maybe the weight of these important figures of liberty and justice made him pause to think and reflect on what exactly a President should be like. Maybe he was very aware of the hands of history that lay on his shoulders. Maybe he knew that his three years in office would be what history would judge him for. Or maybe he just wanted to guarantee another term in office. We may never really know, but America can be very thankful for the great turn-around.

AN IMPORTANT UPGRADE

One area of Federal expenditure that had been lacking for some time, was the American Navy. It had become rather neglected, and if the United States suddenly needed to call upon it's naval battleships, she'd have been left rather wanting. It was President Arthur who ignited the passion for supporting this wing of the American armed forces. He encouraged Congress to pass a series of bills, allowing for significant Federal investing in the Navy to occur once more.

Before these bills were passed, the American Navy was something of an international joke. There were maybe three ships in the entire fleet that could stand up to the other warships of other nations. Not exactly what John Paul Jones, the real father of the American Navy, would have approved of.

This upgrade to the Navy also sent out a strong message to the rest of the world: don't try it on with America. The prosperity of the United States was the envy of the world at this time, and it was fitting that a significant force could be called upon to defend the republic if needed. America still had a Jeffersonian non-interventionist policy at the time, which was rather simple: no nation-building, or policing of the world. The armed forces role was simply to protect the country.

And when these steel beasts of the sea were complete, America finally had a navy that could take on any other and win. This would prove to become useful in the years ahead.

NEVER IN HIS OWN RIGHT
It must be said, there would have been a significant chance that President Arthur would have been able to win a Presidential term in his own right. His popularity was quite high, and the American people had really appreciated the surprising steps he took to stamp out corruption. His party however, didn't see it that way.

They plumped for James G. Blaine of Maine as their candidate against Democratic hopeful Grover Cleveland. Who knows why? Maybe they thought that because 'Blaine' and 'Maine' rhymed, they could do some clever things on the posters and election slogans. But that's just more of my daft speculation.

However, with hindsight, it was rather academic anyway. Two

years after leaving office, President Arthur died of a kidney disorder that he secretly fought throughout his Presidency.

At a time where basic competency was all that many expected from a President, it's certain that the Americans got more than they bargained for between 1881 and 1885. In the end, President Chester A. Arthur did something that very few Presidents have ever been able to achieve: he entered high office with very low approval ratings, and left with them rather high.

TWENTY-TWO
GROVER CLEVELAND

Took Office: March 4th 1885
Left Office: March 4th 1889
Party: Democratic
Term: 25

THINGS HAD BEEN FANTASTIC for America. A number of Presidents had come and gone, and none of them had interfered in any significant way with the free decisions that Americans were allowed to make for themselves. The American people were free to pursue their own dreams and ambitions. And as a result, prosperity reigned. It was the golden age of the American dream.

Many felt at this time that the Presidency didn't really matter that much. As the Founding Fathers intended, the role of head of the executive branch was a pretty limited one. And most of the serious Federal decision-making was conducted in both houses on Capitol Hill. Congress was the central hub that truly made the rules, and even they were fairly hands-off.

However, it was clear to many people in the political scene at the time, that things were not always going to stay that way.

CHANGING TIMES

Finally the significant upheavals from the civil war were over. And the momentous freedom that Americans were living under at the time brought forth a new revolution. One of industry.

And some believed that the men of industry were the real powers. However, they too, were subservient to the rule of law. And in the game of capitalism, everyone was allowed to play.

The real excitement was that most would prosper from this growth of industry, and you never quite knew who was going to see incredible success next. It was an era where the rich got richer, sure. But the poor got richer too. And proportionally, if you care to measure it properly, the poor's wealth was increasing at a faster rate. This very 'American' idea of free enterprise really was working.

However, the truth doesn't always mirror up to people's feelings. Many Americans started to buy into a disenfranchisement about the way things were going. Men with greedy ambitions of political office, would frequently sow the seeds of discontent in a population who were living better than any population of people in history.

These men nourished what many would today call the politics of envy. The politics of envy are manifest in the idea of spreading an untrue rumour. The rumour being that you (the working man) are lower down the economic ladder than him (the employer) and that he got there by climbing all over you. It was a narrative that appealed to many, but was simply untrue.

DIRTY TRICKS

By the time the election of 1884 was underway, it was clear that the gloves would be off. This would be a significant fight, between two men who both seemed quite at home getting in the mud and firing scandal cannon-balls at each other. This, rather entertainingly for us, would be one of the dirtiest elections in American history. Roll up your sleeves and let's get stuck in!

In the blue corner, for the Democrats, weighing far-too much and sporting a moustache so small you wonder why he bothered: Grover Cleveland. Cleveland was known as 'Grover the Good', due to his reputation for cleaning out corruption during his time in politics. Quite admirable actually, for a New York Governor.

And in the red corner, for the Republicans, weighing significantly less and sporting no moustache at all: James G. Blaine of the state of Maine. As we mentioned in the previous chapter, it had appeared that the Republicans could have secured a second term had they stuck with their man President Arthur, but Blaine had won a few admirers and had beaten the Commander-in-Chief to the Republican nomination.

The first of the two men to strike a blow was undoubtedly Blaine. It turned out, that Grover Cleveland had a rather interesting skeleton in his closet. The crux of the scandal: Cleveland had, it seemed, an illegitimate child. The shame! How could Cleveland get out of this? As it turned out, he did so quite simply, and rather brilliantly.

Stunning all the chattering hacks in Washington D.C., Grover Cleveland simply owned up to it. He took full responsibility for what he did. The public were very impressed. Not only did they forgive him, they praised him for his frank honesty. Politicians of today, please re-read this paragraph. Please.

But as I said, the Democrats were far from shy about slugging this one out. They made a series of sweeping attacks against Blaine, making him out to be a far from 'clean man' in politics. Very rarely would they use his name without mentioning 'corruption' in there somewhere. They even had a poem they wrote about him: "Blaine,

Blaine, James G. Blaine, continental liar from the State of Maine." It's not exactly John Donne, but it's pretty good by politicians standards.

In the end, you could have almost flipped a coin. There was an average turnout, some arguing that the dirty tactics on both sides put some voters off, (again, politicians of today, please re-read that last bit), but in the end, Grover Cleveland managed to stick his neck out for a photo-finish, and became the next President of the United States.

CLEVELAND, HE SAY 'NO'

President Cleveland had a slightly different take on the limited-government positions of previous heads of the executive branch. Like the last few in his position, he believed that Presidents should be a bit more hands-off. However, unlike them he felt that his main role was simply to stop bad things from happening. And what did he think was the best way to implement this? The veto.

It would take until the power-hungry President Franklin D. Roosevelt got into office before anyone could match the number of vetoes President Cleveland made. How many are we talking? Four-hundred and fourteen. Yes, President Cleveland, who we only see in office for one term, exercised his veto power more than twice as much as every other President before him combined.

I'm beginning to see why people like Thomas Jefferson weren't so happy about the President having this power in the first place. It was regarded by some as a rather significant abuse of power, and one which rocked many of the American people.

President Cleveland refused to see his high office as a place where someone could instigate positive change. He simply felt that it was a place where you could stop Congress from changing things all the time. In many ways, that's almost commendable, but he seemed to veto everything. Even the stuff that seemed to give government less power and the people more power. It was a very bizarre thing for Congress to witness. The general idea has always been that if Congress (who are a representation of the people), have voted for a particular thing to go through, then you have to let it happen. You can't just say 'no' because you're the President and you don't like it. If you don't like it, then you need to fight the corner, use your influence and respect (assuming you have any) to change Congresses mind – heck, maybe even to change the people's mind. That way, you win some, loose some, but democracy and freedom remain intact.

But at least he never skulked around and tried to be deceptive. He was, in fairness, as honest as his campaign slogans said he was. He just pushed his power in this regard too far. He was a hard-working type, and after what I've told you about his veto-power addiction, it wouldn't surprise you to learn that his management style was rather hands-on and inflexible. If someone in his cabinet wasn't happy about a course of action, then he'd simply do it himself.

And 'doing it himself' was really his style. He didn't make proper use of a Presidential secretary. He would answer the phone himself. In fact, in a funny link to Thomas Jefferson, he'd even answer the doorbell to the White House on occasion. But you have to see the real difference here: President Jefferson would answer the doorbell because he was a man of the people, and saw the executive mansion as a place that effectively belonged to the people and he was merely their servant. President Cleveland answered the doorbell because he was a bit of a control freak.

And his obsessive controlling nature didn't stop at the menial stuff. We know now about his veto-fetish, but this desire to govern every aspect of the Presidency manifested itself in a number of different ways. He would write pretty much all of his own speeches. Sometimes they would turn out better because of this. Other times, not so good.

He would stay up till all hours, studying every little aspect of legislation personally. Chester A. Arthur, he was not.

ROOM FOR LOVE

Unusually for Presidents, Cleveland was a bachelor when he was elected, and didn't seem to have any space (or time) in his life for love. And how could he? The demands that he put upon himself in office were so great, that there was surely no time to look for someone to fall in love with? But that's the funny thing about relationships, the best ones sometimes happen when you're just not looking for them.

However, there was more to President Cleveland than met the eye. Out for respect for her, he had kept her out of the public eye when he was running for office, and surprisingly the Republicans had not gotten wind of it. Grover Cleveland was in fact in a relationship with a 20 year-old college girl called Frances Folsom. As soon as Frances left college, Cleveland got down on one knee and proposed. And in fairness, this was a pretty big guy, so that must have been pretty difficult. I don't know if she had to help him back up again afterwards.

Thankfully, the arduous task of going down on one knee wasn't in vein. Frances agreed and as a result, on June 2nd, 1886, Cleveland became the first President to actually marry in the White House. Aww, shucks.

The nation not only celebrated the wedding, but they took the new First Lady into their hearts. She was a very pretty girl, and was loved by many.

And this was quite convenient for President Cleveland, as the media attention his new wife received, allowed him to step away a little from the spotlight and get on doing what he liked to do best; pour over legislation, and exercise his veto power.

He considered many bills that passed under his snout as 'unwanted drains on the Treasury.' In fairness, he was probably right in most cases.

However, one of the problems with saying 'no' all the time, is the voters tend to get a bit put off. History always seems to favour the politicians who were seen to 'do something', even if that 'something' wasn't so great. And some of the bills President Cleveland vetoed were just plain unpopular. One of which being the bill concerning the pensions for Civil War veterans.

And without the veterans vote, President Cleveland lost the election in 1888. It's as simple as that. Cleveland was not a veteran of the war himself, and standing up against a Republican candidate who had served, and <u>did</u> want to pass the pension bill through, signalled the end of Cleveland's Presidency.

Neither President Cleveland nor his new wife were happy to be leaving the White House. They both felt there was more 'good work' to be done that they hadn't finished. As a matter of a fact, just before leaving, the outgoing First Lady asked some of the White House staff to "take good care of the place. We'll be back."

TWENTY-THREE
BENJAMIN HARRISON

Took Office: March 4th 1889
Left Office: March 4th 1893
Party: Republican
Term: 26

THE MANY TRANSITIONS THAT the Republican Party have taken make it a rather extraordinary political institution. From the libertarian instilment of the Democratic-Republican Party, to the affirmation of those principles when Abe Lincoln established the Republicans onto the American stage, to the more protectionist policies of the later nineteenth century, to the revival of the free market in the 1920s and 80s, to the increasing hawkish neoconservative outlook by the end of the twentieth and early twenty-first centuries. Quite a roller coaster.

What will they do next?

For the election race of 1888, the Republicans were growing increasingly protectionist. They were moving away from some of the ideals of Jefferson and Lincoln. And in their new guise, the found an attractive candidate for high office, in the form of a lawyer called Benjamin Harrison.

Not only was Harrison a veteran of the civil war, he was very sympathetic to the plight of the (now much older) civil war vets who were not receiving any state pension.

Like all men who run under a big government ticket, he received a lot of backing from certain special interests, and appeared very happy to serve those special interests once he had got into power. He was the big money candidate. So big in fact, that it's surprising you can't find any pictures of him smiling…

PROTECT AS WELL AS SERVE?

When it came to the election of 1888, the big political hot potato of the day was protectionism. The most significant piece of legislation that everyone was talking about was the Republican-backed 'Protective Tariff', which was levied on most foreign goods.

The Republicans had been a Party of protectionism in some respects for the duration of their existence. When they were founded by Lincoln, he felt that this was a necessary evil in order to allow the American economy to grow and prosper. In terms of the industrial revolution, America pre-Republican Party, was a falling behind similar nations.

However, it is fair to note that most of the time from Presidents Lincoln to Arthur, America didn't really encounter any significant protectionist legislation that favoured American goods over foreign ones. That's not to say that such legislation didn't exist, it's just that it wasn't significant. In many ways, the mid/late nineteenth century Americans had seen real globalisation, the likes of which had never been seen before or possibly since.

As a result, America was very unsure of any promise to increase this protectionism to the significant levels that Harrison was promising. The country was truly divided. Some felt that the free markets had brought about unprecedented levels of prosperity and freedom, and were rightly worried that putting up international barriers to trade could damage America's ability to continue breaking the prosperity mould. Others incorrectly thought that giving protectionism a shot could be a good thing for the country, because the loss of prosperity would be negligible, and the job security that it might bring about would offset the loss of earnings and lower prices that free trade brings.

So when it came to the Presidential election itself, many held their breaths. And it turned out to be awkwardly close. It became clear that President Cleveland, the man promising to continue to limit government and not support the tariff, actually won the popular vote. So the people wanted another term with Grover the Good.

However, by the Electoral College points system that is used to elect a President under the constitution, it was Benjamin Harrison who won. So on March 4th, 1889, the protectionist Benjamin Harrison became the twenty-third President of the United States.

WHAT A CONTRAST

From George Washington's election in 1789, to Benjamin Harrison's election in 1889. America had seen one hundred years of Presidents. It was to be something of a thorn in President Harrison's side – after all, how can you live up to such a contrast?

Many Americans, especially upset that the majority of them had voted for the 'other guy', felt rather disillusioned. From Washington to Harrison in just a century. Rather disappointing really. However, that didn't stop them wanting a proper knees-up, and to celebrate the centennial Presidency, Harrison performed his inauguration in New York City, just as George Washington did. His speech was reasonably well-made for the period, but it was not on a par with the quality of the first Presidents inaugural address.

Of course, he wasn't totally removed from the bond of the Founding Fathers. One of the signers of the declaration of independence was a relative. And of course, Harrison's own grandfather, William Henry Harrison, had been the ninth Commander-in-Chief. However, as you may remember, the previous President Harrison's time in high office was quite short lived, one month in fact. Most of his achievements were before he got the top job. Obviously President Benjamin Harrison didn't want the same thing to happen to him.

And unlike his fairly well-respected grandfather, President Harrison the younger wasn't so warm. His personality was as mild as an iceberg. Usually when someone becomes the President, they start getting calls from friends they never knew they had and so on, but Harrison seemed to be the total opposite.

No sooner did he become the President, and people stopped returning his calls, and took great steps to distance themselves from him and his administration.

Some even called him 'the human icicle'. You're not going to win any friends with a nickname like that are you?

But hang on one second. Surely I'm going a little far here. Okay, so he had a bit of a frosty personality. So what? He was the President of the greatest nation on earth. Most people must have been able to look past his bad attitude and work with him to get things done? Well, no. Not really.

By the time that Benjamin Harrison was inaugurated as the twenty-third President of the United States, he had pretty much alienated every major boss in the Republican Party. People just simply didn't want to deal with him, all just because of his icy personality.

You know what? Being able to produce that kind of alienation takes real talent, and clearly the second President Harrison had that 'talent' in spades. So we have to understand that a great deal of the isolationism that the twenty-third President faced was very much self-imposed.

KEEPING PROMISES

Once in office, President Harrison did exactly what he had promised to do during the election. And that's the problem. He created a pension scheme for the civil war veterans. However, as with so many increases in the size of the governmental reach, this new ruling created a number of devastating unintended consequences. Consequences that Grover Cleveland was right about after all.

His administration presided over America's first billion-dollar Congressional budget. Funny how they always seem to go up isn't it? As soon as the comprehensive civil war veterans' pension bill was passed in 1890, thousands of young girls across the nation realised that they could strike gold. In their droves they went out and married 70 year-old veterans from the war, knowing full-well that they could cash in when their new husbands kicked the bucket. It was a disaster and almost bankrupted the federal government.

And his other protectionist promises were being fulfilled as well. President Harrison signed into law the highest protective tariff America had ever seen: the McKinley Tariff of 1890, named after the congressman William McKinley. Remember that guy's name, it'll come up later.

This tariff set the rate of imports of goods into America at 48.4% and had legislation in place to protect American manufacturing. Needless to say, the law of unintended consequences reared its ugly head yet again.

The tariff was devastating to the American farmers. Since wages and imported components were more expensive, it massively drove up the price of farm equipment, and failed to halt sliding agricultural prices. The reason why the price of farmers produce was falling was because there wasn't much competition with imported goods in the first place: American agricultural produce was already cheaper than imports.

So Farmers were forced to buy high-priced, frequently inferior protected equipment from American manufacturers, but had to sell their own products into highly competitive, unprotected free world markets. When protectionism fights the free market, the free market always wins. Feel free to look it up for yourself; when a trade embargo of some kind or other is initiated by one country over another, and the other country keeps its trade free, the country imposing the embargo is actually the one that suffers. No one had thought (or been able) to point this out to President Harrison or the Republican heavyweights who continued to push for more protectionism in Congress.

Suddenly an era of increased corporatism reigned in some sectors of American industry. Certain businesses in the States became effective monopolies, imposing a price for their products, knowing full well that Americans would have to either buy it or go without, since they couldn't look to the rest of the world for a cheaper and better alternative. It's still laughable to me that this kind of thinking is still lauded as 'fair trade' by many. But history has taught us one thing on this: free trade feeds. And fair trade starves.

NO ROUND TWO

The slight minority of Americans, who supported President Harrison's protectionist policies, had all but evaporated. The people were hit with wave after wave of expensive prices as the cost of being an end consumer just went up and up. The constant attacks on the free market from politicians on the hill and in the White House was on the verge of undoing all the good that limited governments with free markets had been producing for so many previous administrations.

There was no chance that President Harrison could win a second term.

And in the background to all this misery was one man saying "I told you so." Yep, the 'Mr. Smug Award' in all this had to go to the previous incumbent to the White House, President Grover Cleveland. And his reward for such observations, was to be another shot at the big job.

TWENTY-FOUR
GROVER CLEVELAND

Took Office: March 4th 1893
Left Office: March 4th 1897
Party: Democratic
Term: 27

THE GRAND PROTECTIONIST BUBBLE had well and truly burst. Increasing the size of government and protecting special interest groups, had made most of America suffer. And irrespective of who would become the next President, a great deal of the damage had already been done.

The one man who was the most vocal critic of President Benjamin Harrison's protectionism was, as we've already established, his predecessor, Grover Cleveland. As such, it came as little surprise to most people that Cleveland was the Democratic Party's nomination to run for office again. This time around, he won the Electoral College vote as well as the popular vote, and became the only man to ever win two non-consecutive terms as President.

It's always an odd thing to understand. Even Presidents get it wrong. In his 2009 inauguration speech, President Barack Obama incorrectly made a reference to the "forty-three men" who had stood there before him over the years. But of course, there were only forty-two men before him. He was counting Grover Cleveland twice.

Forty-three Presidencies, but only forty-two Presidents. Yeah, a little confusing, and maybe a little pedantic, but this is a book on the American Presidents, so I have to get this sort of thing right.

GC'S ROUND TWO

President Cleveland had campaigned on a platform to reduce the oppressive McKinley Tariff, and his idea worked perfectly. He didn't just win a decent victory against President Harrison. He was voted back in to the White House on a landslide victory.

As with today, image was beginning to matter significantly. Photographs of the President were available for all to see in the newspapers, and Cleveland's family unit really helped his election. It wasn't just him and his beautiful wife this time around. In the four years since he left the White House, they had a new addition to the family unit. And, just as they did with President Cleveland's wife, America fell in love with the adorable baby Ruth.

It was fair to say that the Cleveland family was more popular than ever before. There was a real sense that this term in office was going to be much more significant than the last. However fate, it seemed, was not interested in playing ball.

ECONOMIC CALAMITY

The honeymoon period for President Cleveland did not last long. Four years of increased protectionism, bigger government, more 'social-engineering' and the law of unintended consequences were all about to take their toll. The economy had taken a battering, and needed to a bit of a lie-down, to put it mildly.

Just one month after President Cleveland took office, the Panic of 1893 hit. Of course, this had absolutely nothing to do with any action Cleveland had taken. But it was occurring on his watch, and he was the one America turned to, hopeful that he could somehow 'fix' it. Many years of steady, strong and dependable economic growth in the nineteenth century had been replaced with four years of protectionism and interference in what would otherwise be free markets.

Growth still continued under President Benjamin Harrison's watch, but it was artificial growth, not built on any strong, genuine wealth-creating foundations – a bubble if you will. And finally, even inevitably, the bubble had burst.

This wasn't just a decline in the rate of growth. It wasn't even merely a drop in productivity or a recession. This was a full-blown economic depression. The worst America had ever seen up to that point.

The effects were immediate to many Americans. In 1893, tens of thousands of people suddenly found themselves out of work. The 'artificial' growth that so many had depended on for the last few years had gone, and reality had set in, replacing the pseudo-wealth creation with a vacuum.

The worst, in many respects, was still to come.

As we have already seen and shall learn more about later, a number of White House residents learnt that increasing prosperity, or combating tough economic times, could only be done in a meaningful way, by limiting the one element of life that sucks wealth away from the individuals and those who create or acquire it: government.

If, in tough economic conditions, government shrinks, it lowers the burden of cost for the unproductive sector, and allows the productive sector more 'breathing-space' to flourish and grow its way out of decline.

However, most of the Americans who suddenly found themselves out of work, were not ready to calmly sit down and take a social studies lesson in supply-side economics. Thousands of them took to the streets of America's capital, demanding that the government spend more money and provide a bigger social safety net.

Ironically, many who voted President Cleveland into office on his mandate of limiting protectionism and increasing freedom, had suddenly done a u-turn on their opinions in just over a month. It was a crazy time.

The only really big question here, was could the President use his powers of communication to get the American people to understand the long-term difficulties that would arise, by him instigating short-term fixes in social welfare?

Unfortunately, both his oratory and interpersonal skills were left rather wanting. Instead, he chose to use force. A large number of the protestors were arrested for trespassing. That didn't really help them understand what needed to be done politically.

Now President Cleveland was not an uncompassionate man. He very much cared about the plight of the poorest people who were suffering. He just understood that if America was to prosper and grow again, and get out of this economic mess quickly and in a meaningful way, the Federal government could not be the ones bailing out and subsidising people with extra layers of bureaucracy and welfare. That way led to social and economic decline. It also would put America on a path for long term stagnation.

In other words, Cleveland understood that you had to take a hit in extra poverty and tougher times now, in order to make longer-term gains and prosperity later.

MONEY TALKS
Adding more complications to the mix was the growing debate over

America's monetary system.

The gold-standard had been the basis of American economic stability and prosperity for years. But what exactly was the gold-standard?

Basically, back then, the money that you had in the bank was backed by gold. In the American Constitution, the only job the Federal government has in this area is to declare how much a dollar was worth. So just for a made-up example, let's say a certain purity level of 15 grams of gold, equalled one dollar. So a single dollar bill, issued by a private bank, could be redeemed anywhere for a 15 gram gold coin of that purity level. Banks could only print bills that equalled the amount of gold being held in their vaults.

This was the gold standard, or 'commodity money standard', and was one of the driving reasons for American having the best currency system in the world. You've heard of the expression "as good as gold", right? Well, that's where it came from.

A five dollar bill was as good as its number in gold. As we shall learn much later on in this book, moving away from that standard, has caused nothing but problems for America and the rest of the world.

There was an increasingly agitated number of Americans who were not happy with a simple and effective gold standard. Headed by a grassroots political group known as the Populists, a number of Americans wanted to change things. They wanted a system called bimetallism. Sounds like a spinoff form of progressive rock, but I'm afraid it's merely an economic monetary system.

Now the bimetallism that the Populists wanted to see used, was not so different from the gold standard. It just simply involved silver as well.

In many respects, this wasn't a big deal. After all, silver was a precious metal, and by simply finding the commodity differences between silver and gold, it was very easy to add this to the standard. So if say, silver is only worth half the like-for-like value of gold, then using my earlier example, a dollar would also be redeemed for a 30 gram silver dollar coin. You could do the same with diamonds, platinum, and other such 'liquid' commodities. Simple.

However, the debate was about something more than that. A number of people in the political scene secretly wanted to change America from the libertarian nation that it was, into something with a lot more governmental force. Government would have to dictate the market differences between silver and gold which, in financial terms, set a very dangerous precedent.

They wanted a central bank that determined policy, a fiat currency, and a redistribution of wealth. And with so many Americans suddenly finding their economic situation in tatters, this argument was beginning to hold a lot of weight.

President Cleveland correctly pointed out that the sound nature of the gold-standard would help end the depression. He knew that adding silver in its own right could undermine the power of the gold-standard, and he also understood the veiled agenda of those wanting to move to bimetallism. For those people trying to push the bimetallism agenda, it was merely stage one in a plan to go further.

If Cleveland didn't act to stop this transition of the monetary system now, it could have disastrous consequences for America decades later.

Unfortunately, President Cleveland's ability to explain this in a persuasive or meaningful way was rather poor. He was beginning to lose the argument and the faith of the American people. He was right on this issue, but it really didn't seem to matter anymore. The aptly-named Populists were rallying more people to their way of thinking, and were the driving force of policy in Congress.

The Populists used every tactic and suggestive trick they could, and in the end, successfully (but incorrectly) made President Cleveland look like a rather flaky pawn of the industrialists.

NO THIRD TERM

Despite the wave of popularity that brought him back to the White House, and despite fundamentally being correct on the chief issues of the day, it was over for President Cleveland. He was simply labelled as being out of touch with the impulses of the American people.

He was a man who achieved the impossible. He brought the Democratic Party back into the mainstream and brought it back in line with the Constitutional Moderates. But he did this at a time when more and more Americans looked to the government for handouts and safety nets. And, in the long term, more fool America for not seeing what Grover Cleveland had to offer.

He was dropped from the Democratic Parties ticket for the election of 1896. The Democrats understood that to stay popular, they had to out-do the Republicans' new devotion to bigger and bolder promises about what the politicians would promise if elected.

There was a black cloud on the horizon. An era of bigger government felt like it was getting increasingly near.

TWENTY-FIVE
WILLIAM MCKINLEY

Took Office: March 4th 1897
Left Office: September 14th 1901
Party: Republican
Terms: 28 & 29

THE GOLDEN AGE OF free American prosperity was, in so many respects, over. The strongly-held ideals of liberty, limited government
and individual freedom that the Founding Fathers spoke about so
often, was being labelled as 'weak' and 'insignificant'. It didn't seem
to matter much that this libertarian way of thinking had turned
America from a third-world republic into the most successful nation
in human history.

The fact that poverty had drastically fallen, and prosperity had so
significantly risen during this time, didn't seem to register any more.
The first one hundred years or so of America had been the greatest
years of affluence, freedom and poverty-alleviation that the human
race had ever seen, yet with the spectre of economic depression over-

hanging everything, these facts just seemed somehow inconvenient to many Americans. Politicians who resisted increases in the size of government or the welfare state were ignored in Congress. Suddenly the weakest arguments for anything being debated in government were if you made either a moral or a constitutional argument. If they were around to see it, the likes of Presidents Washington, Jefferson, Madison, and even Lincoln would bury their heads in their hands in bewilderment.

The truth, facts and reason didn't seem to matter anymore. The fact that the economic depression was caused by increased government interference didn't faze most Americans of the time. The fact that increased interference would prolong the depression and plunge America (and the world) into cycles of economic booms and busts didn't seem to bother most Americans either.

The country wanted a change in how things were done. They wanted bigger government. And many men were around at the time to give it to them. It didn't matter whether the Americans voted for a Republican or a Democrat for President. Either way, it seemed like they would be lumbered with a 'statist' who craved more and more centralised power.

WHOEVER WINS, WE LOOSE

The Presidential election of 1896 consisted of two men, both pleading the case for bigger government. William McKinley, the man behind the McKinley Tariff of 1890 was the Republican front-runner. Remember the anti-free trade McKinley Tariff of 1890? It was implemented in President Benjamin Harrison's term and was responsible for the economic mess that America found itself in. Ironically, because he seemed the most 'statist' out of the candidates, the American people gave him their vote. He was inaugurated on March 4th, 1897.

This Ohio-born President, rather like President George W. Bush who came into office in 2001, instigated a kind of Republican-socialist style of neo-conservative attitudes in his administration. Despite being funded by big-money, he seized on the idea many Americans had at the time that corporate America, (the wealth-creating industries that had been the single biggest factor in increasing mean-average wealth while lowering poverty), was getting 'out of hand.'

He successfully spread a lot of fear in the minds of many Americans about private business being somehow less moral than the more 'noble' public sector. It was nonsense then, and it is nonsense now. But people still buy it.

He was rather puritanical in his attitudes, and presented himself as the righteous character, and that 'all these others' (such as his political opponents, or captains of industry) were shady and not to be as trusted. He had a vision for America in the world. And it was not what the Founding Fathers had in mind at all.

His tranquil demeanour caused many to underestimate him. Many Americans had previously, for better or for worse, voted for Presidents with the skills to get the job done. By now at the end of the nineteenth century, it was much more of a personality/popularity contest.

Despite attacking many of the foundations of capitalism, he was very much in the camp that some incorrectly link with capitalism: corporatism. Corporatism is a very different beast. The big businesses that financially supported his campaign, started to receive favourable policies. This really took away the 'level playing field' idea of capitalism. The notion that everyone is allowed to do what they want, subject to the equal rule of law was deeply undermined. Also, learning from his corporatist allies, McKinley applied a corporate efficiency and sensibility to the White House. Many big businesses know that image is all important. President McKinley knew this too and applied a very modern approach to how he dealt with the press.

It was the McKinley administration that figured out how to use the press as a propaganda tool. They learnt how to feed the press news stories, and how to persuade newspapers to publish a favourable article on the promise of a juicy story later on down the line.

CUBAN FREEDOM

The one thing that President McKinley couldn't do anything about in his 'media management', was the sensationalist stories about Cuba that were flooding the papers. It was pretty clear to most Americans. The Cubans were suffering a great deal under the rather brutal and unpleasant regime of the Spanish Empire.

The Cubans had been fighting for their independence for a number of years. The rebellion had been spluttering on for some time. It wasn't exactly on a par with the American minutemen, but you could see where their heart was. The sickening fact was, the Spanish had a particularly vicious way of dealing with it. Most of the dissenters (and their families) were put into concentration camps.

President McKinley was not totally opposed with the idea of going to war. But his experience in the American civil war had rightly taught him to use it as a last resort.

Depressingly, his lack of enthusiasm for war was not down to an adherence to Thomas Jefferson's wise and noble promotion of a non-interventionist foreign policy: peace, *friendship and commerce with all nations, entangling alliances with none*. Any remaining politician in Federal government trying to make the case for Jefferson's ideals was being literally laughed off the stage. This attitude, as we shall see in the politicians to come, brought about a series of dangerous times for America and the world.

Many Americans felt that war was inevitable. The tales (sometimes inaccurately told) of suffering in Cuba was understandably shocking to so many people. In Washington DC, there seemed to be a real contest on for which politician could 'posture' about war and be seen to be 'doing something' the most.

Also, Americans had another fear. The size of the empires of Britain, France, Spain and others, were growing. In a total reversal of the overall idea of the American experiment, many started to say, with no apparent awareness that this violated the very principles of the free nation the Founders had bequeathed, that America needed to take colonies also, in order to stay a world power. Evidently the fact that America had become a significant world power precisely because it had stayed out of such matters, never seemed to register.

Many in both the Republican and Democratic Parties, had been looking for an excuse to go to war. They wanted to see a new form of imperialism, and a world where American bases were to be found all over the globe. They wanted American power and force to expand wherever it could. Finally they had gotten the power to do just that, and with the Cuban crisis, they had, at last, the excuse they needed too.

Many power-hungry, anti-libertarian men had risen up the political ranks. A certain Theodore Roosevelt, in the Navy Department (at the time) would spend his time studying maps of the world, seeing what pieces it would be 'tactically advantageous' for America to take over. Under President McKinley, the dark clouds of interventionism were beginning to appear above America.

Theodore Roosevelt was President McKinley's assistant secretary of the Navy. He was a rather vicious bully-boy. Seeing the potential for American imperialism that it promised, he hungered for war with Spain. His great oratory skills and powers behind the scenes had made him America's number one influence for the direction of the nation's foreign policy. Theodore Roosevelt single-handedly pushed the United States of America into war with Spain. In rather chilling Hitler-style of tone, Teddy Roosevelt once commented that it is typical that "master races" always end up having to fight "other races."

President McKinley was still wary of sending America immediately down the warpath. He sent one ship, the USS Maine to Cuba to 'protect American interests.' On February 15th, 1898, the USS Maine mysteriously exploded. Desperate to capitalise on the sensationalism, one newspaper's headline read "Maine Explosion Caused By Bomb Or Torpedo?" Neither, as it turned out, but that didn't stop the increased demands for war.

President McKinley could no longer stop what so many were demanding. On the 20th April, 1898, America declared war on Spain.

Roosevelt, desperate to dive into war himself and restore his families name, (he was always ashamed that his father managed to avoid the draft in the civil war), resigned his executive position, and put together a regiment known as the 'Rough Riders' to fight in the war. Roosevelt did engage in one battle, and by all accounts, was exceptionally bloodthirsty. He was very angry that he didn't receive a congressional medal of honour, but at the time, just fighting for one day wasn't considered enough to earn that medal. President Bill Clinton gave him a medal posthumously many years later.

Americas fight with Spain had suddenly turned this free republic into an Imperial power. America took control not only of Cuba, but Guam, the Philippines, and Puerto Rico. By the time America had taken possession of these territories, it was eventually revealed that, incredibly, the USS Maine was almost certainly destroyed by an accidental engine room explosion. But by then, the damage was done.

MORE TRAGEDY

By the time of a new election-cycle, the Republicans wanted to remain in power. President McKinley agreed to have Theodore Roosevelt as his running mate. Some who disliked Roosevelt's unpleasant attitudes and 'un-American' imperialist postures were quite happy to see him as the Vice-President. After all, they though, that would effectively neutralised his power. Boy were they ever wrong.

The McKinley/Roosevelt ticket won, and President McKinley was elected to a second term. But it was not long before tragedy struck America again.

In September 1901, just six months into his second term, President McKinley went to the Pan-American Exposition in Buffalo, N.Y. to give a speech and see the parades. Amidst the crowds, excited to see the President, was Leon Frank Czolgosz, a troubled man who was an anti-libertarian, and deeply concerned with the gap between the rich and the poor. Like so many, he had bought into the lie that government was the fountain of all knowledge and wisdom, and that it was the only source of real power. He was a self-described anarchist, and a deeply disturbed individual. Like something out of the Martin Scorsese movie 'Taxi Driver', Czolgosz had bandaged his hand up, as if it was injured. Secretly though, he had a gun up there. When, in line with a number of selected well-wishers, it was his turn to shake the Presidents hand, he shot him. President McKinley died instantly.

Americans couldn't comprehend the sheer horror of a third Presidential assassination. The nation went into a period of both shock and mourning.

And more damage to the nation was yet to come. Though he was considered a hero by many and a maniac by many more, the pro-imperialist, anti-libertarian, authoritarian Theodore Roosevelt had just automatically ascended to the head of the executive branch of government. And there was no way that Teddy Roosevelt was going to act in a humble and reserved manor.

TWENTY-SIX
THEODORE ROOSEVELT

Took Office: September 14th 1901
Left Office: March 4th 1909
Party: Republican
Terms: 29 & 30

IT TOOK JUST ABOUT one-hundred years of American Presidents for the very ideals of the executive branch to be turned almost entirely upside down. If you want to get into the mindset of the war-mongering imperialists of today's political scene, and want to understand just how different they were from the moral, decent freedom-loving Founders of America, then read on. Theodore Roosevelt is the very embodiment of the imperialist anti-libertarian attitude that has infused so much of the western political scene.

Please let me issue a word or two of caution. Take a deep breath before you dive into this one. As we shall discover, the real story of Teddy Roosevelt is not the usual story that certain historians have allowed us to learn about. There's no two ways about it. The real truth about the twenty-sixth American President is not going to be all that pretty.

THE MINDSET OF THE MAN

President Roosevelt was morbidly fascinated with killing and war. I'm serious, there was something unusually bloodthirsty about him. The man who would go on to become the biggest Presidential bully-boy America had ever seen was fond of shouting "bully bully bully!" at the top of his lungs during the day he killed many Spanish troops in the war he so desperately forced President McKinley to instigate. When questioned about his imperialist war-mongering, he would, as I mentioned in the previous chapter, simply point out the fact that (as he saw it) going to war was a necessary and inevitable function of human beings.

He justified his actions by simply saying that throughout history "all the great masterful races have been fighting other races." Ironically, Teddy's fifth cousin, the thirty-second American President, would eventually have to go to war against an evil individual who believed exactly what Theodore Roosevelt implied in that line.

The great friend of freedom, Mark Twain, met Teddy twice and concluded in no uncertain terms that he was "clearly insane." Hidden away in the many biographies on the twenty-sixth President, we learn that as a young man, Teddy once, after an argument with his girlfriend, went home and shot his neighbour's dog.

After becoming President, Roosevelt would take morning rides through Rock Creek Park, randomly shooting at tree branches with a pistol like a crazed maniac, clearly oblivious to the harm he might do to the nearby private homes and citizens in the District of Columbia. He once strung a wire across the Potomac River so that he could hang on it because, he said, his wrists needed strengthening. No, I'm not making any of this up.

THE 'MENACE OF PEACE'

And just how far gone do you have to be, to regard peace as a 'menace'? That is precisely the opinion of Teddy Roosevelt. He was adamant that peacetime was a dangerous period. This was a man, by the way, who was eventually awarded the Nobel Peace Prize.

It was this rhetoric that invigorated great chunks of the Republican Party. He felt that the noninterventionist foreign policy of George Washington and Thomas Jefferson, ('peace, friendship and commerce with all nations, entangling alliances with none'), was antiquated. Funny, it was doing pretty well until Teddy showed up.

The peace and free trade that a noninterventionist foreign policy had permitted had brought about, gave America untold levels of social and economic prosperity. It cannot be said often or loudly enough: America was THE beacon of hope for the world. Its libertarian principles were the reason for that. But Teddy didn't seem to know or care about this.

He labelled Jefferson, Twain and other great men of freedom as 'anti-imperialist'. And yes, unbelievably, he meant it as a form of slander. Interestingly enough, a group of these more libertarian people of the time, such as Grover Cleveland, Mark Twain, Andrew Carnegie, and William Graham Sumner, all retaliated by forming the "Anti-Imperialist League". A political organisation against President Roosevelt's foreign policy of violence and intimidation. But Teddy ignored them. Or worse, he used intimidation to shut them up.

We can see Theodore Roosevelt's lust for war clearly in the writings of his first book, which was about the war of 1812. Biographer H. W. Brands remarked that this book was "a story of war by one who obviously had never witnessed or experienced the real thing."

Teddy's basic summary for the 1812 war was just a silly polemic against Thomas Jefferson. Ignorantly Teddy believed that the war occurred because of Thomas Jefferson's failure to build an adequate navy. Before the American civil war, you couldn't say a thing against Jefferson. There was no doubt he was a great man – the facts were clear. If you have any heart at all, you can't read the beautiful elegance of the Declaration of Independence without feeling the hairs on the back of your neck rise. Those masterful words that sum up a commitment to freedom are just breathtaking. Roosevelt however, did everything he could to undermine this. And unfortunately, for the most part, he succeeded.

Once he was in power as the President, he proceeded to ignore the rules laid out in the American Constitution. The supreme law of the land in America is pretty clear: the President cannot, under any circumstances, go to war without the approval of Congress. It's one of the most important checks and balances of power that there is. Teddy just didn't care. His only significant lament after his time in political office would be that he never had a serious war to make his Presidency 'great'. While he was Vice President, he wanted to instigate what he thought was the strategic importance of war against the Philippines.

But how could he get the Americans on board with this plan? By dehumanising the people who he wanted to fight. In a series of speeches that have all the hallmarks of a Nazi rally, Theodore Roosevelt would describe the Filipinos as people who "must be made to realize... that we are the masters." He would go on to call them "savages, barbarians" and "wild ignorant people" who were nothing more than "Chinese half-breeds." This strategy, I'm sad to say, worked. The US army would go on to murder almost a quarter of a million Filipinos before the 'war' (i.e. slaughter) was over.

The sad fact is, this sort of bullying and intimidation seemed to always work. How else could he have managed to install a puppet government in Panama and get the Panama Canal built?

HATRED OF FREE TRADE

Not only was the twenty-sixth President a hater of the libertarian brand of foreign policy, he hated their economic principles as well. He gained quite a reputation very early on as a 'trust-buster'. He's been praised for it too, mostly by people who don't know the first thing about economics or free trade, which, it seems, is true of most historians. Roosevelt used his increased governmental power to apply the blunt force of the state to punish and intimidate many of the most competitive businesses and industries in America.

And who benefited from this? The consumer? Nope, they got a raw deal out of it in the form of higher prices and less competition. The larger businesses Roosevelt went after suffered with layoffs, etc. so the workers suffered too. So that's both of those myths blown very easily out of the water. But it leaves a very significant question: Who did benefit from the 'trust-busting'? Simple: the less efficient competitors who had sour grapes about the better business practises of the successful businesses. Roosevelt's economic interference promoted protectionism, and special interest corporatism, not healthy competition.

America was sliding down a path away from capitalism and the free market, (which had produced so much prosperity and social mobility to all Americans), and instead moved to a more socialist system of corporatism and government interference, which, the more it has been enforced, has slowed down both the rate of wealth-creation and socio-economic mobility.

The bizarre thing was that Roosevelt was allowed for all this time to continue his insane propaganda that he was the big champion of the consumer. Nothing could have been further from the truth. He supported the Republican Party's hyper-protectionist tariff policy, which inflicted even further harm on defenceless American consumers, who were unaware of the cause and effect of these insane anti-capitalist policies.

And if that wasn't enough, his macho trust-busting also led him to sign the Hepburn Act, which crippled the U.S. railroad industry by allowing the Interstate Commerce Commission to impose price controls on the railroads. Before Teddy Roosevelt interfered with this, the American railroads were a private enterprise, and they criss-crossed the entire country. In practically every conceivable town and borough, you could find one, two or even more private railroads and train-services. That competition was the main driver behind cheaper priced tickets, and better service. The reason why this doesn't happen anymore, and the reason why there's so many thousands of miles of unused track all over America, is President Theodore Roosevelt.

He thought it was 'unfair' that those railroad companies (or at least, the ones who weren't forming special interest groups to cosy up to him), should not be allowed to charge more on lines where there was only one private service catering to a certain town, etc. But if there was a great need for a cheaper service, the free market would have catered for it. If the government wanted to speed that along, it could lower taxes and incentivise businesses to cater to that market. But all Roosevelt's interference did was put these companies out of business and deeply hurt the mobility for millions of the poorest Americans.

And the power he gave to the Interstate Commerce Commission didn't just stop with price controls. He all but outlawed volume discounts to large freight customers, and 'socially engineered' most other aspects of the railroad marketplace through regulation. What happened as a result? Tons of capital was no longer delivered using the tools of the railroad industry, and, because it would be a long time before something better came along (some intelligently argue that nothing never has as yet), there was a serious drag on the entire economy that still negatively affects American business and consumers today.

He also fabricated a food crisis. Many believe that there was a real problem with the availability of food during this time. Utter nonsense. I mean, sure, the negative effects of his regulations on the railroad industry and business in general made it harder for things to get where they were going, but that wasn't the food crisis Roosevelt dreamed up.

The food crisis he invented was all about the quality of different foods. Why invent such a thing? Because then he could heroically 'save' America from this crisis, and win another election. Outrageously, this strategy was a success. Before winning his second election, he promised the American people that it would be his last term. Thankfully, despite his wishing that he hadn't have said it, he was true to his word in the end and didn't seek a third term.

But this food crisis that so many people praise him for even today, needs real examination. I've done a lot of the leg work for you, but you're welcome to check it out for yourselves. Without wasting tons of extra pages here, simply put, there was NO food safety crisis. There were no epidemics related to commercial food processing. Roosevelt just made most of it up.

Again, these so-called 'pure food laws' were just another example of the corporatism of Roosevelt's administration. These laws didn't protect consumers from harmful products at all. These laws were simply aimed at protecting certain producers. A great number of these early laws set exceptionally high regulatory standards on imported foods from other countries. Think about it, that's just a veiled form of protectionism. Food inspection laws during the Roosevelt era were usually pushed into being by larger corporations who understood that the laws would disproportionately harm their smaller competitors. The 1906 'Pure Food and Drugs Act' gave a disproportionately large amount of power to one man; the Agriculture Department's notorious quack, Harvey Washington Wiley. Wiley was a strange one. He conducted insane crusades against foods and businesses that were competing with the interest groups that he served. Again, this had nothing to do with protecting 'the little guy.' This was all about holding the little guy down and giving him a damn hard kicking.

BUT AT LEAST HE WAS A GREAT CONSERVATIONIST, RIGHT?

Wrong. Sorry, but this is the last bubble we have to burst of Teddy Roosevelt. The ideas that the Grand Canyon and other such places would have been 'removed' were it not for the twenty-sixth President are frankly, daft. There is no evidence to suggest this at all.

Furthermore, the active 'conservation' policies he enacted were an utter disaster, nearly always having the opposite effect than they were supposed to. Theodore Roosevelt's Presidency is an embodiment of the 'law of unintended consequences', and the conservationism that he promoted is a startling example of that. He misspent obscene amounts of taxpayers' money and degraded much of the natural environment in America.

Roosevelt launched a federal dam-building program. Nowadays, many people hold him in high regard for this. Well this move by the 'champion of the environment' caused many canyons to be flooded, and you can guess what that did to the ecosystems in those areas. These dams also disrupted the natural water flows, and didn't even work well as dams. Many lost huge amounts of water through evaporation, because they were placed in areas where it wasn't very sensible to install a dam because of the heat. Why were they placed in those areas? Because the Governors of those states usually were able to use their political influence and get the dams built in their states instead. Yet again, instead of resources being rationally distributed by the cool-minded, intelligent and calculated allocation of the free market, the bumbling crude mess that was created was solely the fault of government – and Teddy Roosevelt in particular.

The dams also increased the salinity of irrigated soil so much that very little could grow on it. I bet the farmers loved that. Everything that Roosevelt touched was a mess. And yet people still demanded more without seeing the consequences, and he continued to blindly provide them.

As for Roosevelt's national forest policies, well, they only achieved two things: the overgrazing of grasslands and the arrival of forest fires, the likes of which had never been seen before. So more disaster.

Roosevelt strongly opposed the privatisation of all government-controlled land. What he failed to understand, and what so many fail to see today, is that private individuals always take care of their own land much better than the state does of public land. Private voluntary initiatives to protect land and areas of natural beauty always achieve their goals much better than when governments do it, and usually with a lot less negative unintended consequences.

In reality, the so-called conservationist policies of Roosevelt were just another form of nasty big state socialism/corporatism. All the special interest groups used their knowledge of the federal governments 'secret handshakes' to advance the goodies in their favour at the expense of other groups of people. It was crude, nasty, deeply unfair, and decidedly un-American.

GOOD RIDDANCE

Though many Americans were sad to see him go, (and those still married to the propaganda of his 'achievements' today still miss him), Theodore Roosevelt did agree to stick by his promise and so stood down after his second term. He would end up regretting it later in life, but I for one do not.

His re-assertion of the Federal income tax into the mainstream of debate started a dependency of government, that truly free and prosperous societies can always do without. His interference in the marketplace, and his isolationist policies of interventionism started a chain of events that helped lead the planet into the disastrous and horrific First World War. And so many of the bad things we've been coping with ever since, can be traced back to these moments.

So it was goodbye to Teddy. And for this writer at least, it was good riddance too. Unfortunately it seemed like it was not to be good riddance to his policies though. For Theodore Roosevelt had hand-picked his successor…

TWENTY-SEVEN
WILLIAM HOWARD TAFT

Took Office: March 4th 1909
Left Office: March 4th 1913
Party: Republican
Term: 31

EVEN THOUGH HE HAD promised the American people that he would not take on a third term, President Theodore Roosevelt wanted to find a way of having one, nonetheless. He did not want his lust for power to end when he left the executive mansion. There was, in his mind, only one solution to his problem. He needed the next President to be a carbon-copy of himself.

T.R.'s hand-picked successor was William Howard Taft. And there was no doubt in Teddy's mind, that Taft was the perfect candidate for the continuation of his policies. Taft, he felt, would do all of his bidding. Roosevelt would simply be a power behind the throne. To put it mildly, that's not a very 'American' position to take, but, as we've already established, Teddy didn't much care for the 'American' way of doing things.

After the horrific imperialistic escapades into the Philippines, Taft was given the title of Governor General of that nation. He had therefore been placed in the civil service originally by President McKinley, and had built up quite a reputation as a government yes-man.

THE RELUCTANT PRESIDENT

Many supporters of Roosevelt considered Taft to be what we would now call a 'go-to guy'. If you wanted something done, if you wanted some force applied, then Bill Taft was your man. And as President Roosevelt's right-hand man, Taft seemed very happy. He never had any real personal desire to be the Commander-in-Chief. He was in many respects, disinclined to run for the top job.

In so many respects, he wasn't really a natural politician. It was not a vocation that he was that up for. This might beg you to ask why did he get into the dirty art of politics in the first place? The answer is simple: his wife.

Taft's wife, Nelly, had always dreamt of living in the White House. Some say that the day of her husbands' inauguration was the best day of her life. Finally her dreams had come true. Sadly for her, very soon after the inauguration, she suffered a severe stroke. The opportunity for her to enjoy the first lady lifestyle that she had wished and hoped for was cruelly snatched from her.

And President Taft had dreams too. His did not extend to the White House though. A lawyer by trade, Taft had always dreamed of becoming a Supreme Court Justice. So as a President, I guess you could say that he was working in the right city, but in the wrong big white building.

Taft once stated that a good judge "is our model in our minds of what god is like". Sounded to me like another guy hungering for governmental power. Taft yearned for the ability to have god-like power over the administration of justice. Luckily for us, the Founding Fathers gave the President no such power. However, the powers of the executive branch were increasing all the time.

But before we lay into Taft too much, we should really understand the meaning of his 'god' phrase. He wasn't suggesting that judges should have any divine power. He was merely saying that a good judge should have the highest morality possible. That's not too bad an attitude for a good judge to have. After all, the law is supposed to be a moral institution is it not? Though judging by some lawyers, maybe that's something worth questioning occasionally.

With his heart in the Supreme Court, it comes as no real surprise therefore, to learn that President Taft took a very narrow, legal attitude to the Presidency. He wanted to make his decisions on the straight basis of law, which actually set him apart quite a bit from Teddy Roosevelt's authoritative attitude to executive power.

President Roosevelt was a dynamic sort – always riding on his horse, getting into real and metaphorical fights, where as President Taft was a lot more laid back and relaxed. And as Roosevelt moved around and was always on the go, the rather portly Taft lumbered at a more sedate pace.

As we've mentioned before, Abraham Lincoln was always able to chime as a friendly sort with voters – and one of his tricks was the use of light-hearted self-deprecation about his looks. President Taft possessed a very similar knack. He was a bit fat guy, no doubt. But he'd laugh about it all the time. One of my favourite examples: he once spoke of his natural generosity, saying that once when he was riding the streetcar, he got up and offered his seat to three ladies!

Unfortunately, once he got to work in the White House, a great deal of his sense of humour began to falter. He hated being under the intense scrutiny and glare of the media spotlight. He wanted to just get on with it. But in a country blessed with the first amendment, being held to account for his actions was always inevitable. And, let us not forget, it was also very right that he was held to account.

A lot of bigger people eat when they're unhappy. And unfortunately this was true of President Taft. The trauma of the stroke his wife incurred, and the general level of scrutiny he found himself under, really got him down. During his one term in office, he gained an incredible 100 pounds in weight. And look at the pictures and old stock footage of the guy. Towards the end, he looked like a small planet, big round belly and all. If one of the White House interns had shined his shoes for him, he'd have to have taken their word for it.

And in the most humiliating experience of his Presidency, Taft had such trouble with his weight that he once had to be prised out of his bathtub in the Presidential bathroom. The physics that must have been involved for such a task are mind-boggling. The images it conjures up are terrifying.

FAILING TO DECIDE

As well as the physical condition of his wife, and the 'intrusive' level of scrutiny he faced, another reason for President Taft's unhappiness was in his inability to lead the nation in the way he wanted. Many criticised his weak leadership, not least of all Teddy Roosevelt.

Taft would delegate responsibility wherever possible. Now, decentralising the power of the Presidency is a noble thing. It keeps that branch of Federal government more honest. And it's fair to say that throughout the nineteenth century, the Presidents who had given lots of their power to their cabinet members had seen, on the whole, a fairly successful term in office as a result. Unfortunately, this was the twentieth century, and most of the men in politics wanted to be seen to 'do' things and increase their power and use the state as a tool to control society. Giving these guys more power isn't quite as good a thing. And Taft was beginning to see it. And the American people couldn't help but notice it too.

In order to solve some of the dilemmas of the day, President Taft needed to sit in the driver's seat, and make decisions. But instead, he would procrastinate. Now stopping and thinking about what to do (and taking the better option, do nothing at all), is a very good thing. But Taft would never come to any conclusions about anything, resulting in so many of the big questions of the day hanging in limbo.

Taft saw, in many respects, the Presidents job as upholding the Constitution. Again, he's spot on. But you still have to make decisions about things. Many of the great Presidents in the previous century before Taft felt that upholding the Constitution was the main job of the executive branch. But in order to perform that function correctly, you had to actually make decisions. Contrary to popular belief about President Taft, it was his lack of decision-making, and not his constitutionality that was the reason why his Presidency was so unpopular at the end.

I've already mentioned Teddy Roosevelt's opinion of all this. He was furious. Because Taft wasn't making any decisions, a lot of the 'bigger-state' initiatives that Roosevelt had set in motion were beginning to recede. In many ways, this was an unexpected bonus of Taft's lack of leadership abilities. But Roosevelt wanted to extort revenge on his hand-picked successor. President Taft, however, was not going to let himself be bullied.

SPLIT THE VOTE

By the end of his first term, Taft was pretty much done. He didn't really want to continue the job. His real dream, as we mentioned, had always been to become a Supreme Court Justice. And that dream was slipping through his fingers the longer he stayed at the White House. At the time, he felt that his chances of being one of the Judges on the Supreme Court were basically dead in the water.

And, oddly, this had changed his attitude. He felt more like a man with nothing to lose, and was getting tired of having to defend himself from the criticism of Teddy Roosevelt.

In 1912, the former best friends, William Taft and Theodore Roosevelt, battled it out for the nomination of the Republican Party. This was an exceptionally bitter contest. Teddy's attacks on Taft got more and more hateful and vicious. But would you have expected anything less nasty from the imperialist bully-boy T.R.?

At one point in the election contest, it is reported that President Taft broke down in tears. He couldn't get over the sheer unpleasantness of his opponents assaults. I'm almost inclined to say that Taft should have just sat on Teddy Roosevelt and ended the matter. But then that would have been a nasty attack on Taft in a similar manner to the ones T.R. performed. So I'll keep my big mouth shut on that one.

In keeping with the high intellectual level of debate that Theodore Roosevelt was used to, his campaign against President Taft consisted of him calling the President things like 'fat head', 'puzzle wit', 'dimwit', and so on. Unsurprisingly, this didn't with either man much support overall in America. I will say though, my favourite piece of name-calling by T.R. had to have been when he accused President Taft of having "a brain of three guinea pig power." How delightfully Shakespearean.

You have to give the Republican Party some credit here. They were becoming increasingly uncomfortable with Roosevelt's hatred. I only wish they had gotten uncomfortable with it some twenty years earlier, then maybe less damage would have been done. Enough, they felt, was enough. They nominated Taft for their candidate. Unsurprisingly, T.R. was furious.

As a way of defeating any chance that President Taft might have had for winning a second term, Roosevelt join a progressive political organisation called the 'Bull Moose Party'. If nothing else, this Party wins my vote for best name.

Unsurprisingly, this move by Roosevelt caused a big split in the Republican vote, causing Taft to come third, and a sweep-in victory for the Democratic candidate. That candidate was Woodrow Wilson. The Republican in-fighting meant that Wilson had become the twenty-eighth President of the United States.

But one final vital footnote before this brief history of William Howard Taft comes to a close. After stepping down from the Presidency, Taft lost weight, put his 'game face' back on and eventually fulfilled his true lifelong ambition: to become the Chief Justice of the Supreme Court of the United Sates. And by most accounts, we was easily one of the greatest Chief Justices America had ever seen.

TWENTY-EIGHT
WOODROW WILSON

Took Office: March 4th 1913
Left Office: March 4th 1921
Party: Democratic
Terms: 32 & 33

THE HILLBILLIES WERE OVERJOYED at the news. The South was back in the White House. And they had gotten there, due to the huge rift in the Republican vote that Theodore Roosevelt and William Taft had caused. Outside of the South, Woodrow Wilson received a majority of votes in only one other state – Arizona. It was clear that the vast majority of Americans elsewhere had voted for someone other than Wilson. But Woodrow was not going to let that get in the way of his radical (and in many ways, deeply unpleasant) reign.

Teddy Roosevelt declared in his campaign rhetoric that he stood "at Armageddon to do battle for the Lord." He made it clear that the 1912 election race was one of fierce urgency and without him back in office, America would literally crumble. However, there is no doubt that he felt relieved when Wilson was victorious. Roosevelt really just wanted anyone other than Taft. And, it seemed, Wilson shared a lot of things in common with the twenty-sixth Commander-in-Chief.

PUTTING THE 'WHITE' IN WHITE HOUSE

Even though both main Parties had been lurching into this direction, it was the Democrats who were traditionally the party of government intervention, social engineering and limiting the freedom that the American people had as a birthright. They were the party of racism, segregation and collectivism. It isn't said often these days, but shouldn't be ignored: President Wilson was very much a man of his Parties original values.

But under the Democratic President Grover Cleveland, the progress in liberty of African-Americans was on the rise. However, and again, I apologise for mentioning Theodore Roosevelt once more, but it was Teddy who reignited this idea of blacks being somehow inferior. He opposed voting rights for Africa-American men, despite the infinitely more libertarian Abraham Lincoln making that right inalienable in the 15th Amendment.

T.R. simply felt that the 'black race were still in their adolescence and couldn't be trusted with a vote.' There can be no doubt that President Wilson felt exactly the same way.

Despite all the progressive changes to the attitudes of many Americans in Washington D.C., President Wilson seemed to try and reverse the trend of freedom and liberty for the former slaves. As well as having male and female bathrooms in the White House and other public government buildings, he added extra ones for 'people of colour'. Why this stupid 'backwards-hick' form of segregation? Because Wilson thought that African-Americans were more likely to carry venereal diseases and so shouldn't be trusted using the same toilets as whites. And if reading that last line is making you feel as uncomfortable as I am writing it, then that's sort of my point. What a truly horrible attitude for a twentieth-century President to take.

Many would (and have) defended President Wilson for his attitudes by saying he was simply a 'product of his time'. I can usually understand that argument with people in history, except Wilson wasn't really espousing a huge amount of mainstream attitudes. He was in fact, rather behind his own times. Compare someone like President Wilson, going back to the old racist ways that still pervaded many aspects of the South, to say, Thomas Jefferson, a man who despised slavery, agonised over its existence, spoke with hope about a free America that would one day no longer have slavery, and penned his aversion to it in the early drafts of the Declaration of Independence, and yet, like many men in a similar position to him in that time, was a slave-holder for almost all of his life. Now the slave-holding aspect of Jefferson is an example of him being a 'product of his time'. But pondering over how to eradicate slavery and how a free society can, should, must and will end the business was how he was a forward-thinker. With that understanding in mind, in every respect contrasted to Jefferson's attitude, President Wilson was deeply backward.

Wilson's position as a racist retrograde was apparent way before he was President of the United States. As president of Princeton, he turned away black applicants, refusing them the social mobility that he afforded to whites. His main reasons and justifications were simply to do with him seeing blacks getting an education as an 'unwarranted' measure.

Under the Wilsonian Presidential leadership, black workers were getting a raw deal across every aspect of the federal government. And the fed was controlling more and more aspects of American life. To continue the segregationist attitudes, many federal officials built separate housing structures for the black workers to live in. The growing numbers of black diplomats were virtually all replaced by whites. A significant amount of highly competent and talented black federal officials were being removed from their posts for no reason other than the colour of their skin. Back in D.C., the local fire departments and police force stopped hiring blacks.

To continue the collectivist irrationality of racism further, President Wilson considered all this segregation and discrimination an act of kindness towards the African-Americans. I'm not kidding. A protesting black delegation, who were disgusted by the ugly racist turn his government was taking, was told in no uncertain terms by Wilson that "segregation is not a humiliation but a benefit, and ought to be regarded [as such] by you gentlemen." When they protested this claim further, using (to their infinite credit) reason and rational argument, the President ordered them out of the White House, telling them "your manner offends me."

He didn't care at all for the increasing plight of the blacks in America. They were victims of the inherent dangers of too much democracy that the Founding Fathers warned of. They were confounded by the tyranny of the majority. President Wilson once bluntly claimed, "if the coloured people made a mistake voting for me, they ought to correct it." But they couldn't. They were the minority who wouldn't be able to sway an election 'their way', and their freedoms were being once again taken away by a collective majority.

The point of America's independence was not that it was a democracy, but that it was a republic. The African-Americans should have been left alone to pursue their own happiness in freedom. The Presidential interference in this matter prevented that freedom. The Founding Fathers understood that the most important minority is an individual and that giving each individual law-based freedom over the majority was vital for the growth of liberty and prosperity. President Wilson believed instead, in a despotic democracy. But ask yourself this question: if 51% of the population wants to take your rights away, should they be allowed to? The Founders of the United States of America thought absolutely not. And the practical application of their way of doing things blossomed the most free and successful nation on earth. By this point in history, so many of those freedoms were fading.

THE NEW FREEDOM = SAME OLD TYRANNY

President Wilson's growing desire for power could be seen in many things that he did. He was the first President since John Adams to deliver his State of the Union addresses to Congress in person. George Washington had done so, and was very keen to never give a hint of legislative bias in his address. The first President once described "motives of delicacy" as deterring him from "introducing any topic which relates to legislative matters, less it be suspected that [I] wished to influence the question" before Congress.

The great libertarian Thomas Jefferson, who we have already mentioned in this chapter, went the whole hog and stopped delivering the addresses in person altogether. His commitment to freedom and an executive branch with limited powers went hand in hand with this policy. A policy which stood firm for 112 years. President Wilson broke that tradition, in order to use his great oratory skills to exert ever more power over the legislative branch. The Founders would have been quite disgusted with this idea.

The progressive agenda that President Wilson pushed forward in his first term, was referred (by him) as 'The New Freedom'. Across the board, this pretty much meant what I like to call the 'New Restrictions on Freedom and Greater Governmental Authority'. Less catchy but much more accurate.

Government had been interfering more and more with the free market banking industry. They were scared that certain 'captains' of finance like J.P. Morgan held too much power over the leading of money. But there was not much regulation, and competition was rife. As Bob Dylan sings in *The Times They Are A-Changin'*, "the first one now will later be last." In the free-market system (which I'm sure Bob Dylan wasn't referring to at all), the people at the top of the tree are usually not there for long. Someone always builds a better mouse-trap, and takes market share from the frontrunners, even if the front-runner continues to do better than they have before. Sure enough, with the gift of hindsight, we can see that J.P. Morgan's banking empire would have grown but lost market share had the government not gotten involved. And everybody playing the game would have won – especially consumers. But President Wilson didn't want to see the game played. He wanted power for himself.

The President created the Federal Reserve System. He sold the public on the Federal Reserve, based on the idea that one bank could otherwise get too much power. Think about the lack of logic in this. If there's a free market banking system, comprising of big and little banking businesses, then what happens when one of them, (like J.P. Morgan's), gets bigger? Well, it got there by doing a better job than other banking businesses. And someone will eventually come along and do a better job later (the better mousetrap idea). What happens if one of the smaller banks fail in this system? Well, that had happened before, and there was usually regional and/or minor fluctuations in the marketplace, but healthy banks would buy up the bad ones and we'd all benefit. And if, as President Wilson was getting everyone worried about, a really big bank failed, then the same would happen. The negative effects would be short and minor, and the 'better' banks that did a better job at self-regulating (i.e. more sensible interest rates, better implementation of reserve banking based on what's in their vaults, etc), would quickly pick up the pieces and things would go on as successfully as before.

The idea of a Federal Reserve therefore, was (and still is), utter nonsense. Why replace a free system that naturally punishes failure and rewards success for the betterment of everyone, with a system that replaces this freedom with one central bank, whose policies affect every other bank because they have to conform by force? If the danger that President Wilson claimed is true, (and he's right), that there can be negative repercussions for some people when a bank makes a stupid business decision, then that danger is significantly worse when there's just one bank that dictates these terms. And if that one bank, the Federal Reserve, makes one stupid move, it goes on to have devastating effects for the entire banking industry and the people as a whole.

And it's also worth remembering: the free market banking system was self-governed by the rational decisions made in the marketplace. Whenever someone made a bad move, then the market would very quickly be able to correct it. Because the decisions were made based on genuine wealth-creation through profit-motives, the chances of those mistakes being repeated or being serious were very low. When a government bureaucracy takes over, its motives are not for profit but for the electioneering of those in charge in government, and for the desires of those in power to socially engineer. This system is not only more likely to make mistakes; the mistakes, as we shall find out further into this book, are more likely to be devastating.

Many like to point out that certain aspects of the free-market banking system were failing before President Wilson set up the Federal Reserve. But again, all these main failures were happening simply because of increased government social-engineering and interference from the late 1800s, and certainly not because of the free market.

Rules preventing certain banks in certain states becoming chains and franchises were limiting the growth of successful banks and encouraging less successful ones to grow more than they should have done. It can't be said enough – that happened because of government interference, not despite it.

THE GREAT WAR

By the second decade of the twentieth century, across the western world, many had adopted rules governing greater authority over the people. America was no exception, and President Wilson was a total embodiment of this increased authority.

Tariffs, trade embargoes, higher taxes and the like had breed isolationism and resentment. Isolationism breeds greater desire of interventionism. Interventionism leads to violence, suffering and war. It's far out of the scope of this book to describe how governments moving away from libertarian ideals caused the First World War. So let's just simply say that it did, and by 1914, the guns of Europe were firing on full-steam.

President Wilson also suffered a personal tragedy at this point. The first lady had died of a kidney ailment. Rather unsurprisingly, he was devastated. However, his much-needed grieving would have to be put on hold to deal with the very real prospect of war.

Most Americans didn't want anything to do with the war in Europe. Greater tariffs, taxes and import restrictions on both sides of the Atlantic, had caused many Americans to resent the continent from which many had originally come from. Why should they help out certain groups of them? President Wilson, instead of helping the war come to an end by removing the embargoes and freeing up global trade (we've already established he's not a libertarian, right?), decided instead, to pledge neutrality.

By refusing the policy of non-interventionism (i.e. allowing more free trade and ultimately peace), President Wilson's isolationist neutrality didn't last long. The Germans were sinking many British civilian ships with their submarines, which often carried Americans and their imports. In one instance, a ship called the Lusitania, was sunk by German torpedoes, and resulted in the death of 128 Americans.

But still the American people wanted nothing to do with the war. They felt that Europe had gotten itself into a real mess. And though a significant part of the population wanted America to free up the trade routes and try and bring an end to the conflict, President Wilson was resolute in making sure that this didn't happen.

Wilson kept his head down, and carried on his high levels of domestic government control. He remarried to a fellow widower named Edith Galt, just seventeen months after his wife died. The following year, he was narrowly re-elected as President. The victory was slight, mostly due to the poorer conditions Americans were finding themselves in. By increasing the size of the government, President Wilson was sucking the wealth of ordinary Americans and channelling it into the state.

And this bigger-government policy was affecting the war, which still raged in Europe. By Wilson refusing to free up trade and possibly end the conflict, Germany finally declared that all American ships would now be targeted. It was clear that America was now sucked into this war, whether they liked it or not. President Wilson did not want to be led by foreign affairs, but his isolationism and desire for control over freedom had all but guaranteed that America would have to fight.

On April 2nd, 1917, President Wilson asked Congress for a declaration of war against Germany. He declared that "the world must be made safe for democracy." As inevitable with isolationist policymakers, the President had finally demanded a new world order. Had he pursed non-interventionism and freedom, then maybe none of this would have been necessary. Nonetheless, Congress approved the declaration. This was finally a war on a global scale. The Great War.

Wilson's desire for power and big-state mentality called for a single authoritative governing body, the League of Nations. The idea was that this group could settle disputes without bloodshed. The United Nations would later on attempt to achieve the same goals. So far, this idea of global governance has resulted in failure. Seems that a policy of "peace, commerce and friendship with all nations, entangling alliances with none" has been the only one that's really worked, but so many have long-since abandoned that Jeffersonian concept.

President Wilson did handle the war correctly however. He set goals of his military generals to achieve, and gave them the freedom to do so. However, his lack of respect for freedom at home was becoming ever more ugly. A piece of legislation that was passed in Congress, was the Sedition and Espionage Acts of 1917. President Wilson, as the head of the executive branch of government, used this act to instigate the most brutal campaign against dissent in the history of America. If you've never heard of these rules before, then stand back: these acts meant, quite simply, that it was now a crime to criticise the American government. Anti war protestors were the initial main targets, but after that, who would be the next offenders? Who would be next to be marginalised or suppressed?

Overseas, the American heroes fighting in the trenches were winning. Just 19 months after declaring war, the allied forces were victorious and Germany surrendered. To help decide the terms of the peace, President Wilson became the first sitting President ever to go to Europe. He arrived in Paris for the Treaty of Versailles. Again, instead of setting in place a framework of free trade, increased globalisation and limited government, the allied forces placed protectionist restrictions on social and economic freedom on the German people. Despite the heroic welcome that many in Europe gave to the President, the obvious resentment the Germans made of these policies would come to a deadly conclusion in the decades ahead.

In order to bypass Congress' understandable opposition to his global-governance embodied in the League of Nations, President Wilson decided to go on a large campaign trail across the United States, whipping the Americans up into a (fairly irrational) frenzy in support of the idea. It was a success, but he over-exerted himself. He ended up suffering from a stroke. For the most part, he spent the last eighteen months and more of his Presidency unable to really perform the duties of the chief executive. By accident, America suddenly had something of a limited government again. It is of no coincidence whatsoever, that the social mobility for many Americans rose slightly during this time. Unfortunately, the growing government interference of the economic freedom of the people, was commencing a storm on the horizon.

Eventually, President Wilson was informed that the idea of America taking part in the League of Nations was dropped. Congress had not approved it. Wilson simply remarked that Congress had "shamed us, in the eyes of the world". By 'us', I think it's fair to say that he meant 'himself'.

The American people were becoming increasingly uncomfortable with President Wilson's rhetoric. They were beginning to see that the limitations on freedom and the increase in government were having negative effects to most aspects of their lives. There seemed to be enough Americans who wanted a change. They wanted a return to freedom, and limited government. Thankfully, they were about to get it.

TWENTY-NINE
WARREN GAMALIEL HARDING

Took Office: March 4th 1921
Left Office: August 2nd 1923
Party: Republican
Term: 34

WHAT PRIORITIES DO HISTORIANS have when they 'rate' Presidents? It's always been a most peculiar set of standards. And the embodiment of this strange rating-system is most clearly manifested in the form of the twenty-ninth President, Warren G. Harding.

President Harding is frequently rated as the worst President. They say that he was corrupt, but only a minor bit of digging into the history shows that there's no real substance to this claim. In fact, when he discovered that some of his subordinates had been up to something they shouldn't have been, he rebuked them so severely that two of them committed suicide. You've got to wonder what he said to them haven't you?!

Historians also say that he had an affair and had loose morals, but that's completely unfounded. And besides, even if it were true, and it were the reason for President Harding receiving a big thumbs down, wouldn't someone like Bill Clinton be right down the list in relative comparison?

To summarise and explain why the attacks are so bizarre, allow me to briefly condense this chapter in one paragraph: Warren Harding, often rated as the worst President in history, won an incredible 60% of the vote, successfully promoted economic prosperity, delivered a balanced budget, cut taxes while reducing the national debt, released all of President Wilson's political prisoners, supported anti-lynching legislation, and instituted the most substantial naval arms reduction agreement in world history. If this man was the worst President, then please help me out here; on what criteria do you pick the best?

DEPRESSION NUMBER ONE

An economic recession had unsurprisingly occurred on Woodrow Wilson's watch. By the time President Harding had taken over, it had already long since been 'upgraded' to an outright depression. Production had fallen by 21%. American GDP had seen a fall of 24% and very quickly unemployment had risen from 4% up to 12%. These figures are only here to make one thing clear: this was a mess that President Harding inherited, and the economic crash was actually worse in all three of these areas than the crash that resulted in the Great Depression a decade or so later.

But by limiting the size of government down drastically, President Harding had turned the situation around. America was beginning to see significant improvement by the summer of 1921. It would go on to lead into a period of economic success that's forever known as the roaring twenties.

How did this economic crash occur? Two words: Federal Reserve.

Woodrow Wilson's 'baby', the Federal Reserve, had been playing with the numbers. They had altered the interest rates in such a way, as to make the economy of America think that it was more prosperous than it really was. This is the constant danger of the government setting interest rates in what would otherwise be a free market decision.

I once heard this great analogy for the dangers of government-set interest rates: It's like a builder wanting to build a house. Instead of being able to count his own bricks and work out that he's got enough to build a two-bedroom house, he's told by the government that he has thousands more bricks than he actually has, so he decides to start building a three-bedroom house based on what he's told. Now all the time that he's building this three bedroom house, he's mistakenly misallocating his capital, and the 'boom' that's being built up, is an artificial credit-based one.

By the time he's completed 70% of his house and goes to get another brick from the government, it suddenly turns out that there's no more bricks left. Devastated, the builder has to knock the house down so he can start again. This is the economic crash that occurs when the market finally realises that it has been led down an unsustainable path. President Wilson's system allowed this to happen. President Harding wanted to end it.

As we've already discussed, Wilson's stroke meant that he did very little in the last eighteen months of his Presidency. Also Congress, many of whom were taking the Presidents lead, was similarly handicapped, and produced only a fraction of the legislation that it had been doing. That was a good thing. That meant that the realisation of the economic crash could (and did) occur sooner, so that less capital was misallocated. And the economy was given the freedom and breathing space by government to adjust and recover. There were tiny little green shoots of recovery for the final six months of

President Wilson's 'accidentally hands-off' administration.

But that wasn't enough to get America back onto the road of prosperity and social mobility. For that, it would take President Harding. Harding knew that government, the wealth-sapping element of society must be curbed in order to deal with the economic problems. The night that he was nominated as the Republican Party candidate for the Presidency, he said simply that the bringing of economic freedom back to the American people and the reigning in of the governments' inflation and social-engineering "ought to have begun the day after the armistice, but plans were lacking or courage failed. We shall attempt intelligent and courageous deflation, and strike at government borrowing which enlarges the evil, and we will attack high cost of government with every energy and facility which attend Republican capacity." Let there be no doubt. President Warren G. Harding was the right man at the right place, in the right job, at the right time.

Harding rightly saw that shrinking the power and size of government was the solution. When he was in a ponderous mood, President Thomas Jefferson once hoped that as America grew wealthier and more powerful, it would grow increasingly wiser too, and wise enough to know that it should only use its power when absolutely necessary. If America had elected a string of Warren G. Harding's into office throughout its history, I doubt Jefferson would have ever had any reason to worry.

The new President did not waste any time. He forced the Federal Reserve to be passive – he wanted to deal with them in a second term. Then he took an axe to the Federal budget. It had reached the dizzying heights of $6.3 billion by the time President Harding was in office. He had slashed it to $5 billion by the end of 1921. Twelve months later, at the end of 1922, he had cut it to $3 billion. By then, the good economic times were back. It worked. Simple as that.

Some suggest that this was irresponsible and that also cutting taxes could not possibly help with the problem of debt. American debt was indeed very high thanks to the last few of Harding's predecessors. But between President's Harding and Coolidge, the supply-side economic boom that resulted from the policies of freedom they enacted caused national debt to be cut by a third. A significant proportion of this boom came out by the top rate of tax being cut from the 70%-area, to 25%. There was real wealth being created. Social mobility was back on the increase. America was becoming everything that the Founding Fathers had promised once again.

And as government continued to shrink, and the American dream continued to grow, it's unsurprising that Harding was able to remark that "the world needs to be reminded that all human ills are not curable by legislation and that quantity of statutory enactment and excess of government offer no substitute for quality of citizenship." Basically, give these people freedom and watch what amazing things they can do.

His refusal to get the government to intervene in the marketplace led to the quickest recovery of the worst economic collapse in history. And many Presidents have been refusing to learn from his success every since.

AGGRESSION TAKE-DOWN

This new, very different President was certainly no Theodore Roosevelt. He signed the peace treaties that led to the formal end of the Great War. However, reading between the lines, I get the feeling that he felt there was something wrong about the Treaty of Versailles, and the way it left things. Reading a great deal of President Harding's speeches can leave you with the impression that he was quite concerned with the way Germany was treated, and that their lack of social/economic freedom in the treaty could lead to the rise of an even worse tyranny than the one that caused the world war in the first place.

It would be less than a couple of decades before we could begin to understand just how right he was on this.

President Harding knew that his first term could not be about changing the world in this way though. There were other promotions of freedom to fight for first. He set his sights on world naval disarmament. He knew that the horrors of war must be stopped at all costs. The Washington Naval Conference of 1921-22 allowed him to achieve a great deal of the disarmament he desired. This can't be emphasised enough. This was a truly remarkable thing to accomplish, considering the war that the world had just fought.

Countless missiles were decommissioned and the tensions that had mounted in the world were beginning to ease off. The world could finally get off of the war footing, and go and have a bit of a well deserved lie-down.

But Harding was not done. He knew that the economic liberties and freedom from war would not be worth anything without civil liberties. The acts in Congress against free speech and freedom to protest could not be tolerated any longer. He not only had them removed, but he also freed those who had been imprisoned by the instigation of those acts.

The freeing of political prisoners was a big part of President Harding's campaign promise of a 'return to normalcy'. Today, this slogan is laughed at – even jeered at. Many see it as a boring idea, returning to the dull old conservative ways. What Harding was really calling for though, was a return to the radical days of libertarianism, of true freedom.

Harding's version of 'normalcy' consisted not only of an end to the imprisonment of political dissenters (such as Wilson's notorious "Palmer Raids"), but also the abolition of wage and price controls, and the reversal of the previous Presidents numerous illegal seizures of private property. Just think of the image of a 'conservative' President, Warren Harding, very soon into his first term, signing the order to free the socialist candidate Eugene Debs, who had been jailed for opposing the war draft. That's what we're talking about here.

And to make sure these freedoms could be kept in check long after he had gone, President Harding appointed the legendary libertarian George Sutherland to the Supreme Court.

THE BEST SECOND TERM WE NEVER HAD

I've often described Warren G. Harding as the best second-term President America never had. Sadly, less than three-quarters of the way through his first term, in 1923, Harding passed away.

This tragic event has often led me to daydream and ponder on what might have been if he had lived. Based on the opinion polls of the time, there would have been little doubt that he would have secured a second term with a sizable majority – possibly even greater than the one that got him elected in the first place.

There would have been the emergence of the Teapot Dome affair, an oil scandal. In 1922, Albert B. Fall, (the U.S. Secretary of the Interior), leased, without competitive bidding, the Teapot Dome fields to Harry F. Sinclair, an oil operator. These transactions became the subject of a Senate investigation conducted by Sen. Thomas J. Walsh. However, the President was never directly connected to this scandal and did not profit in any way. And judging by the ferocity which he had dealt with previous corrupt subordinates, I can only assume he would do the same in this instance, which would have endeared him further to the American people.

As I have already mentioned, his possible concerns regarding the Treaty of Versailles would have quite possibly led to an increase in trade and defiance of the treaty as it stood. Other nations would have followed suit and Germany would have been able to use the competitive force of capitalism properly again, in order to recover socially and economically. As a result, that nation would have certainly never turned to Adolf Hitler to 'sort out' their problems. So President Harding, in a second term, could have been the one man capable of preventing the Second World War. We'll just never know.

Finally, judging him on his extraordinarily successful economic policies, I am positive that a second term for Harding would have resulted in him either removing the teeth from the Federal Reserve, (i.e. taking away its ability to set the interest rate by edict rather than the free market doing that itself), or closing it down entirely and putting America back on a strong track of proper sound 'commodity' money. I think he would have done the latter. And it's a real shame that he didn't, because I have no doubt that if he did, there would not have been a great depression in the years to come.

Sadly, his death gave the Federal Reserve the breathing space to slightly manoeuvre in the markets again. And Harding's Vice President, Calvin Coolidge, was fairly unaware of the operating mechanisms of such a complicated system.

But, as word spread about Harding's death and the inauguration of Coolidge, the more immediate question most Americans wanted of the new President was simple: would he continue the main policies of economic and social freedom? Their wishes would be answered. The continuation of freedom was precisely what they were going to get.

THIRTY
CALVIN COOLIDGE

Took Office: August 2nd 1923
Left Office: March 4th 1929
Party: Republican
Terms: 34 & 35

IMAGINE HOW BEWILDERING IT must have been for Calvin Coolidge to suddenly find himself at the head of the executive branch of American government. The scene is a poetic one. Coolidge was on vacation, helping his father on the family farm. Unlike most other Vice Presidents in history who felt that a bit of manual labour was beneath them, Cal thought nothing of driving the two-horse hitch, bringing in the hay with his pitchfork, and swinging the scythe wherever his father directed.

The farmhouse had no phones or electricity, so the Coolidge's had to find out about Calvin's ascendency late at night. There was a knock on the door from a Post Office messenger. He delivered Vice President Coolidge two telegrams. The first was from President

Harding's secretary, giving official notification of the Presidents death. The second, more hastily composed, was from the Attorney-General. He advised Coolidge to take the oath of office as soon as possible, in order to qualify for the role of President. Upon being asked by his family if he was ready for such an important new role, he simply remarked, after taking a moment, "I believe I can swing it". The oath was written out by hand, and was administered by Coolidge's father. The thirtieth President was inaugurated by the light of an old kerosene lamp.

CONTINUING THE ART OF FREEDOM

There is no doubt that President Coolidge was kind of like a 'Warren G. Harding Lite'. Coolidge believed in most of the same things that Harding did, but instigated a little less disassembling of government authority. Only a little less though.

The big changes that a second-term Harding administration would have commenced, (such as freer trade with Germany, and the castration or downright dismantling of the Federal Reserve), were certainly (and unfortunately) not going to happen on President Coolidge's watch. But the general idea in other areas was pretty much the same. And with the prosperity that came directly from Coolidge's tax cuts and limited government, is it any wonder that America called this period 'The Roaring Twenties'? Furthermore, is it at all surprising that many Americans at the time called it the era of 'Coolidge Prosperity'?

He understood that the real promise of the Founding Fathers lay in self-reliance. People's voluntary actions, of trade, charity, freedom, and of rational self-interest. He knew that America had gone increasingly in the other direction in too many ways, and far too often. He would do what he could to correct this. He once simply said that the American public "cannot look to legislation generally for success".

He knew that real progress needed to come from their own private efforts. It was precisely what America needed to hear, and they voted for him outright with a very sizable majority to finally give him his own full term in 1925.

Instead of using government as an increasingly oppressive tool for social engineering and authoritarianism, President Coolidge chose to limit government interference. He allowed businesses from new and emerging enterprises to grow without new rules and regulations. And as for older businesses, he persuaded Congress to strip away a great deal of the bureaucracy and special-interest favouring legislation. Sometimes he'd manage to remove everything he wanted, other times, just a little bit of it. And, it has to be noted, occasionally he'd be incorrectly persuaded to increase governmental interference. But those mistakes aside, the overall direction was clear. The federal government was getting smaller, and the American people were all the better for it.

Congress would still try and sneak in more and more rules that favoured their special 'friends' over the competition, but President Coolidge was usually able to block these anticompetitive pieces of legislation. Unlike most of Washington, who were trying to exercise their powers for greater gains, President Coolidge was not a man to be bought. He once said, early on in his political career, that it was always "much more important to kill bad bills than pass new ones".

Of the many taxes and regulations that President Coolidge cut or removed outright to increase freedom and prosperity, his continued assault on income tax was one of the most notable. He was very keen to relieve the tax burden on the wealthier in America. He understood that most of these people had not inherited their wealth, they had earned it. And if their taxes were too high, then they would take their industries and entrepreneurial spirit elsewhere, and America's poorest would suffer for it. He understood that simple truth from the science of economics that so many politicians fail to understand: that if you free the entrepreneurs capital up, they will invest it in their businesses and/or banks, and the ordinary workers will benefit from more job opportunities, greater pay from increased competition for their labour and talent, and cheaper/better goods and services, leading to greater wealth and higher standards of living for all.

And President Coolidge put it in terms as blunt as that as well. In his 1924 State of the Union address, he expressed simply that he was "convinced that the larger incomes of the country would actually yield more revenue to the government if the basis of taxation were scientifically revised downward". He couldn't have been more correct. Though taxes continued to plummet, government receipts stayed at around the $3.9 billion dollar a year mark. Considering that federal government was now only costing the taxpayer less than $3 billion a year, it's not surprising that the President was able to pay off so much of the national debt.

SILENT (BUT WISE) CAL

Unlike someone like myself, who has a tendency to waffle, (but you've noticed that yourself by now, right?), President Coolidge was a fairly plain spoken, to-the-point kind of guy. They called him "Silent Cal", and mocked his lack of oratory. He actually spoke quite well, but preferred using a sentence when a normal politician believed ten paragraphs would suffice.

In the blunt, minimal words of the thirtieth President, we hear very wise philosophy. Many of his political rivals joked that Coolidge could be "silent in five languages". One legend of President Coolidge, concerns a woman who told the President that she had a bet with her friend, that she could get him to say at least three words. Without missing a beat, Coolidge simply turned to the woman and said "you lose."

Most of the time though, the lighted-hearted and very personable Calvin Coolidge was not trying to make people laugh. He was a very friendly guy, and had a real knack for making people feel good about themselves. But some of his most simple oratory was also the most important. His reputation of honest brevity could be most keenly heard back when he was re-elected as President of the Massachusetts State Senate. Here is his inauguration speech in its entirety: "Conserve the firm foundations of our institutions. Do your work with the spirit of a soldier in the public service. Be loyal to the Commonwealth, and to yourselves. And be brief – above all things, be brief." Simple, elegant truth.

In 1924, President Coolidge addressed the nation, saying simply, that "one of the greatest favours that can be bestowed upon the American people, is economy in government." The idea was a simple one. Keep government small, and you'll keep the people free.

HIS ONE BIG MISTAKE

There were some in the Republican Party, and indeed, in the cabinet, that did not like this limited-government approach of Harding/Coolidge. President Harding had appointed Herbert Hoover to the position of Secretary of Commerce in the cabinet. Hoover constantly tried to pressure Harding into expanding government when he inherited the economic crash of 1920. To his eternal credit, President Harding refused to give in to most of Hoover's demands. As a result, America had fully recovered from the depression within eighteen months.

During the boom-time of Coolidge's Presidency, Hoover continued to push for government to have a greater role in society. Allowing Hoover and the Federal Reserve a little more control over setting interest rates again from around about 1927, (i.e. by loosening the reigns that Warren G. Harding had tightened), President Coolidge would end up making the first part of his one mistake. Coolidge once said of Herbert Hoover that "that man has given me nothing but advice and all of it bad." If only he had acted upon that quote by removing Hoover from the cabinet.

Coolidge admitted to his ignorance about the Federal Reserve openly. He explained in 1928 that he "wouldn't happen to know anything about" how the Fed set its interest rates. If only he did know. Maybe he would have stopped the crash that led to the great depression. Had he carried out his philosophy of limited government interference and applied it to the Federal Reserve, then the false economic credit-boom that rode on top of the genuine wealth-based economic boom in the late '20s would never had occurred. And that credit-boom, which was administered by the government, would not have been able to fuel the speculative investment boom that would go on to lead to the stock market crash of 1929.

The simple truth is that the changes to interest rates, and the easy-money policies that the Federal Reserve were administering, were too slight for President Coolidge to even notice. And, like most of America, but unlike his predecessor, he couldn't see the damage that the Fed was doing long-term to the economy.

And his big mistake finally is sealed in his last big (and honourable) decision. President Coolidge believed, as did many of the Founding Fathers, that the President should have only limited powers, and should only exercise them for short periods. He had ran and won a term in his own right in 1924, but, after taking the oath for that term in 1925, decided that he should not run again.

The opinion polls were quite clear. The American people would have voted for Calvin Coolidge in a landslide in 1928. But this man of such uncommon moral character, decided that one full term was enough.

I describe this notion as being his one big mistake. Usually, I'd praise an American President for making that kind of decision, and not submitting to an increased lust for power. And I must emphasise that I'm very impressed by the decision to stand down that President Coolidge made. But had he stayed for a second term, the Republican Party would not have elected Herbert Hoover as their candidate for 1928. Hoover would not have won, and he would not have been the man whose bigger-government 'statist' policies dragged America down after the crash of 1929. Instead, President Coolidge would have increasingly lowered the tax burden, removed the interest-rate powers of the Federal Reserve, and would have prevented the greatest depression in American history.

But unfortunately, the brilliantly honourable Calvin Coolidge chose to take the principled route and leave the White House after just one full term. It would be a noble decision that would cost the American public dearly.

THIRTY-ONE
HERBERT HOOVER

Took Office: March 4th 1929
Left Office: March 4th 1933
Party: Republican
Term: 36

UNDER THE LAST TWO Presidents, Herbert Hoover had been involved at the very heart of the major discussions of the day. He was frustrated however, by the lack of respect and power that he had been given. This time, as the head of the executive branch, President Hoover could finally instigate his statist policies in full. This is the story of Herbert Hoover, the thirty-first President. It is the story of a loner with too much power and a penchant for using it. It is the story of a millionaire business man who, despite achieving his own financial success in a free market, wanted to control the way everyone else did business. And ultimately it is the story of how the Great Depression came to be.

While President Coolidge was in office, the Federal Reserve had been getting ever so slightly more powerful again. President Harding kept the Fed under a tight check, but Coolidge, who openly said that he didn't really understand how the Fed worked or how it came up with the (arbitrary) interest rates that the country had to conform to, had allowed the Federal Reserve to quietly expand and gain more power and influence again, under the radar. This had started an economic bubble, an artificial increase in the perceived wealth creation and prosperity America was witnessing at the time.

It is very true that America had indeed been getting more wealthy and better off under the roaring '20s thanks to the limited government policies of Presidents Harding and Coolidge. But from about 1927 in Coolidge's Presidency, thanks to the Federal Reserve's easy-money policies and the like, the additional artificial bubble of wealth had been growing too. And that bubble was set to burst.

THE '29 CRASH

Say what you like about libertarian economists, but they always seem to be right. And when it comes to predicting the economic future, these guys make Nostradamus seem like a fraudulent hack. Okay, so Nostradamus actually *WAS* a fraudulent hack, but you know what I mean.

One such economist from the libertarian, free-market Jeffersonian-style economic thinking which is commonly called the Austrian School, was the Nobel Prize-winner Friedrich Hayek. Hayek was from the Ludwig von Mises School of economic theory. These guys always see economic crashes coming, and for some reason politicians ignore them more than any other group. Maybe they're just less fun at parties than the Keynesians.

Very early in 1929, Hayek spoke out about the forthcoming economic problems. The likes of Herbert Hoover and Franklin D. Roosevelt thought that Hayek was just being silly. Hayek predicted that there was going to be a large recession and, if government and the Federal Reserve didn't change their ways, a significant depression.

When asked about his 1929 forecast in an interview in 1975, Hayek was as to-the-point and spot on as ever. He said simply that he "was one of the only ones to predict what was going to happen. In early 1929, when I made this forecast…I said there [would be] no hope of a recovery in Europe until interest rates fell, and interest rates would not fall until the American boom collapses, which I said was likely to happen within the next few months."

Turns out, he was dead right. Just a few months after giving that exact warning, in October 1929, the 'American boom' collapsed. He really should have placed a large bet on it – he would have made a fortune.

But he doesn't just rest on his laurels. In the 1975 interview, he actually reminded the world of why he knew the collapse would happen. In Hayek's own words: "What made me expect this, of course, is one of my main theoretical [economic] beliefs that you cannot indefinitely maintain an economic boom. Such a boom creates all kinds of artificial jobs that might keep going for a fairly long time but sooner or later must collapse. Also, I was convinced that after 1927, when the Federal Reserve made an attempt to stave off a collapse by credit expansion, the boom had become a typically inflationary one."

So President Hoover had a simple choice to make. He could simply allow the 'artificial' assets and jobs to liquidate and bring America back on track very quickly, or he could interfere with the process, expand the size of government intervention and slow the whole recovery right down. He made the wrong choice.

As soon as the crash happened, President Hoover cut income tax rates by one percentage point (just one measly point – great help Herb, thanks), and began boosting federal spending, increasing it by 42% between the fiscal years of 1930 to 1932.

MAKING THE DEPRESSION 'GREAT'

The economic collapse of the artificial boom that occurred early on in President Hoover's first term was not really that big a deal. As a percentage of GDP, and as a proportion of the population that suddenly found themselves out of work, it was not nearly as bad as the collapse that Harding had inherited from Wilson. Harding shrunk the size of government and minimised its levels of interference and solved the main aspects of the problem within about 18 months. Hoover did the mirror opposite, and, by the time his first (and only) term was up, left the country in a true mess.

By keeping government limited, President Coolidge had run a budget surplus in every single year of his Presidency. He significantly lowered taxes, but the roaring prosperity and surging tax receipts that came from that decision meant that he was able to hold the federal budget roughly constant throughout. President Hoover managed to turn the $700 million he inherited from Coolidge as a surplus, and turned it into a $2.6 billion deficit by 1932. The depression that had occurred soon into his watch wasn't so bad. But by the time he left, it was unprecedented. There was no recovery in sight after three and a half years. Unemployment was at the shockingly high rate of 25%. There is only one word for this: failure.

Now let's be clear. Everyone links President Hoover with failure. He was the man who failed to bring an end to the Great Depression. Some even say, as I do, that Hoover turned a recession that was born out of an economic collapse and created a great depression out of it. But the problem is with the 'how' in this argument. Most people think President Hoover is to blame for the depression, but most people also think that his big fault was that he sat back and didn't do anything about it. That he wasn't in fact a man who liked to interfere with business, and his laissez-faire attitude allowed capitalism to run riot and lead to the depression.

That argument is utter nonsense. Let's look at the facts and find out why.

THE HOOVER NEW DEAL

The quick recovery from the 1920-21 depression has been described by Dr. Benjamin M. Anderson (an expert in such matters) as "our last natural recovery to full employment." Most people think that Franklin. D. Roosevelt was the real creator of the New Deal. Well, he may have coined the phrase, but the principles of the New Deal were actually enacted under President Hoover.

What is the New Deal? Well, in its basic terms, the New Deal is an anti-depression program marked by extensive governmental economic planning and intervention. This intervention can take many forms, but its main ones are things like the bolstering of government spending, (like public works, or subsidies to unemployment). These sorts of policies are precisely what President Hoover instigated. What occurred cannot be seen as a failure of the free market. As Hayek saw, it is simply a failure of government planning.

Though he wasn't so enthusiastic about it, President Hoover supported the enactment of the Smoot-Hawley tariff, a protectionist measure intended to strengthen American business by shielding them from foreign competition. Of course, this didn't work. As we've already seen in America history, when you build up a wall against trade like that, it is only the country imposing the draconian measures that really suffers. Americans were forced to buy higher-priced, lower-quality goods. And as so many couldn't afford it, they stopped buying as much. Because American businesses could not buy certain raw materials and services from abroad at better prices, they produced less, leading to more businesses going bust that otherwise wouldn't have. More American workers lost their jobs.

Directly because of the Smoot-Hawley tariff, a number of American entrepreneurs left the country, searching for countries with freer trade policies that allowed them to grow and prosper. The whole tariff was a disaster. But that didn't stop President Hoover.

He decided to 'stimulate' the economy by increasing federal funding for public works though the *Emergency Relief and Construction Act*. A great deal of American labour was sucked into this programme of 'make-work'. Again, businesses, who had great products to produce, couldn't get access to quite so much labour because it was taken away from them by the government. Instead of allowing the good businesses to grow and slowly start to hire more people, the President Hoover's policies stifled this progress.

Hoover decided that instead of allowing the free market to reallocate capital intelligently based on the rational decisions of the marketplace, he would insist that businesses conform to his arbitrary rules. He demanded that big businesses must not cut wage rates in response to the economic collapse. Part of the reason for the collapse was that people were being paid too much, an artificial increase over what the market could bare. But Hoover didn't care. He had a faulty notion, not based in the realities of economic science at all, that workers' purchasing power was the main source of economic strength. He was wrong. The correct and rational allocation of capital (machines, staff, services) are actually the main sources of economic strength.

Adam Smith, the author of the legendary 'Wealth of Nations' had penned down the truth perfectly back in 1776. The main source of prosperity can be found in three simple things: The pursuit of individual rational self-interest, specialisation of labour, and freedom of trade. This was a truth that President Hoover just didn't seem to understand.

During the 'cruel' liquidationist era before President Hoover, the recessions, depressions, or market 'panics' were almost always over within two years. Hoover saw to it that this would be no ordinary depression. And the large-scale governmental interference he instigated caused an economic crisis that had never been seen in the history of the republic.

WE MUST 'DO SOMETHING'

During his campaign to be re-elected as President in 1932, Hoover reaffirmed his commitment to 'doing something', (i.e. interfering with the free market). He stated "We might have done nothing. That would have been utter ruin." Unfortunately, the accurate analysis of the economic facts tells us the total opposite.

President Hoover has gone down in history, for many people, as a man who stood by and did nothing. This couldn't be any further from the truth if you tried. He interfered in so many aspects of the free market, that by the end of his Presidency, it must have felt like there was almost no free market left. Hoover failed to realise that only when the government doesn't interfere with prices, wage-rates and business liquidation, can the necessary adjustments take place to fix a depression. That is his real legacy of failure.

His adversary on the campaign trail was Franklin D. Roosevelt. Despite campaigning on a platform of criticism for Hoover's 'reckless spending', it would seem that FDR wanted to expand the very ideas that Hoover had laid down. Despite the rhetoric, it seemed that FDR simply, in large part, wanted to elaborate on President Hoover's policies.

America was torn between two evils in this regard in 1932. The terrible choice they were faced with was either the continuation of Herbert Clark Hoover's big-government failure or Franklin Delano Roosevelt's policy of "Hoover on steroids". In the end, FDR's propaganda defeated the propaganda of Hoover. But either choice was not going to be pretty for America's economic futures.

THIRTY-TWO
FRANKLIN DELANO ROOSEVELT

Took Office: March 4th 1933
Left Office: April 12th 1945
Party: Democratic
Terms: 37, 38, 39 & 40

IT REMAINS IMPOSSIBLE TO analyse which would have been the lesser of the two evils. The false choice between big government under Hoover or bigger government under Roosevelt was not a choice many Americans wanted to make. But that was all they got.

To understand the perspective of many Americans at the time of the 1932 election campaign, you can split them into three broad categories. There was a very small number of Americans who got it. They understood that the depression was significant *ONLY* because of President Hoover's big-government policies. They were also savvy enough to see that FDR's policies took them down a route of even bigger government, and even more prolonged failure.

Other Americans also disliked Hoover's big-government policies, but they bought into the rhetoric of FDR. On the campaign trail in 1932, Franklin Roosevelt described the Hoover Administration as having "the most reckless and extravagant past that I have been able to discover in the statistical record of any peacetime government anywhere, any time."

They believed in his criticism and genuinely hoped that he would go down a different path. Their hopes, it would transpire, ended up being shattered.

And finally there was another bunch of Americans who believed in the general consensus that we have today: that President Hoover was a laissez-faire capitalist who basically didn't do anything to 'solve' the Great Depression, and that they needed FDR to 'fix' this.

They were able to read between the lines and realised that Roosevelt would expand the government and solve the crisis. Again, while they were right to understand that FDR would expand government, they were wrong to think that Hoover had done the opposite, and were dead wrong to assume that this statist attitude would 'fix' anything.

GOLD STANDARD GONE

As it became more and more certain that Franklin Delano Roosevelt would win the election, an increasing number of Americans feared for their gold. The Federal Reserve had caused so many problems in the American economy, and many Americans who had lived under the true free-market banking system, were still alive by the 1933 election. They remember what it was like when the gold standard was allowed to hold sway, and allocate capital based on the rational decisions of the marketplace, rather than resources being positioned by governmental edict.

For most of America's existence, the idea of some type of 'commodity money' was set in place. Under the constitution, the federal governments' job was simple. They had to decide what defined a dollar. So a certain weight of gold, of a certain purity, equalled one dollar. That's it. Under the constitution, that's where the government's role ends. If you care to read their notes on the subject, the Founding Fathers were very clear that tyranny, poverty, market collapse, war, and all these other awful things would emerge in greater number, if the government interfered with the money supply in any other way.

So banks could hold the gold of private individuals. They would promise to generate interest on that gold by 'loaning' it out to businesses who promised to pay it back with interest. The bank would keep a bit of the interest, and the rest went back to the person who deposited their gold in the first place.

Now because it's impractical to carry bars (or shards) of gold around, they would issue bank notes. These notes were a guarantee of gold being held in a certain bank. Because of this, banknotes printed in one bank were 100% interchangeable with notes printed elsewhere. You could hand in a $10 note of the Bank of X into the Bank of Y, and they would give you $10 of gold. They were happy to do this, because they could give the X banknote back to the Bank of X at any time and redeem the $10 of gold back. As I have said before, when referring to these old banknotes, this is where the expression 'as good as gold' comes from.

There were problems with this system, sure. But compared to the alternative system slowly imposed upon the American people by the likes of Presidents Wilson and FDR, these problems were pretty much insignificant.

Think about it; if any one bank, (say, Bank Z), made a lousy job of printing money, it could (and sometimes did) have minor ramifications and generally regional, limited disruptions for the overall banking system. The better banks (X and Y) would quickly buy up the good assets, and the bad banking decisions of Bank Z would be liquidated. So even people who had invested their gold into Bank Z with realistic expectations, and those who had gotten 'good' loans with Bank Z, would find that their investments and loans were safe. This was the best, freest, most rational and secure financial system ever invented.

Yet a frightening rumour about Franklin Roosevelt was being spread.

The rumour was that FDR, if elected as President, was going to commit a very anti-American, anti-freedom measure. He was going to confiscate everyone's gold. The people reacted by exacerbating the depression. In order to protect their gold, they would instigate runs on banks to get their money out. And this didn't just hurt the banking system, the whole economy suffered.

The reasons for this are quite obvious. If your gold is now stuffed under your mattress, then it's not in the secure banking system, being used to make good solid loans for reputable businesses.

The evidence, if evidence were needed, that this rumour was damaging, can be seen in the data. Economists have been able to track, practically on a one-to-one basis, the rumours of FDR confiscating gold and runs on banks.

And finally, very soon after his election victory on March 4th 1933, President Franklin Delano Roosevelt did exactly what so many people feared. He stole all of their gold. He horded it into the Federal Reserve. He made it (and I can still hardly get my head around this) illegal for Americans to hold gold!

He literally got Federal agents to storm their way into people's properties and take their gold by force. The gold standard was over. It would never fully return again. America was set for an economic nightmare.

SPENDING SPREE

Much is made of the second President Roosevelt, and his first one hundred days in the White House. The rhetoric of putting an end to President Hoover's 'reckless spending' suddenly went flying out of the window, as soon as FDR had taken the oath of office.

The size of government expanded rapidly overnight. And FDR controlled everything. He started 'make-work' projects, just to put people into work. These are the infamous 'bridges to nowhere' and so on that you hear about. The problem with all of these projects is that they had only one impact, which was to slow down the rate at which the private market could consolidate and liquidate its misallocated capital. Because the government had suddenly become the big force in business, business couldn't compete. And the rational capital distribution of the free market was prevented from growing against the irrational (i.e. politically convenient) provision of capital that the state provides.

Instead of allowing a year or two of significant pain before the free market could complete its adjustment back to genuine wealth-creation, FDR put in place a gigantic system of long, slow, drawn-out economic pain. It was finally clear, that FDR was Herbert Hoover times ten. Americans were in for the long-haul of economic suffering. The recession had unwittingly started under President Coolidge. President Hoover had turned it into a significant all-out depression. It would take FDR to turn it into a great depression. Everything, and I do mean everything, that FDR did to increase government intervention and 'combat' the depression made it deeper and worse.

MR. MESMERISATION

There's a good chance that right now you're thinking "here we go again, Andy Jones has lost the plot once more. How could it be possible that FDR set the stage for such a mess? He can't have really been this bad on the economy, because the man won four Presidential elections." While you'd usually be right about me loosing the plot, that doesn't really answer why FDR was able to win the hearts (if not the minds) of so many voters time and time again. Allow me to explain why they did embark upon this love affair with the thirty-second President.

FDR was described by many as intelligent, but not brilliant. At Harvard, he was very much a "C"-grade student. He was the fifth cousin of the twenty-sixth President, Theodore Roosevelt. Being the only child of a very well-off aristocratic family, he was both a loner and had led quite a pampered existence. Yet one of his more admirable qualities, was his ability to put aside his personal suffering, and despite coming from such upper-class stock, suffering was something he knew all-too-well.

Franklin Roosevelt was crippled with polo from the age of 39. You may think that the image of a physically handicapped President is another strike against his chances of winning an election. However, is ability to get into high office, and to stay there for so long, came from one important element: charisma. FDR was a man of great charm. He was the ultimate political baby-kisser. The 'common man' found themselves in-tune with him. They felt he was 'one of them' deep down.

So despite having the policies and will of a sneering collectivist, who wanted to control increasingly more aspects of the people's lives, he simply was able to stand up in front of the nation and the world on his inauguration and declare that he would pledge "a New Deal for the American people". The nuts and bolts of the deal they would not like, and it would unnecessarily prolong their misery, but hearing him say those words, brought the American people comfort. Even if the comfort was false.

THE NEW (RAW) DEAL

Amid all the massive government spending projects, new top-down rules, and other intrusions into the freedoms of Americans under the banner of 'The New Deal', one of the worst was the significant increase in taxation.

FDR didn't seem to understand at all that the rich in America were not on the whole, as we have said before, people who had inherited their wealth. They were entrepreneurs, searching for the American dream. They were the creators of wealth in America, not the ones who were sucking wealth out of the country. If they were overly taxed and regulated, then their ability to create wealth was limited, and their ability to generate prosperity for everyone else was greatly diminished.

Income tax, particularly for the wealthy, skyrocketed under FDR. This was one of the biggest problems for workers on lower incomes. Why? Because the rich weren't able to buy as much, and were discouraged from working more (which generates extra jobs), saving more and investing in their own businesses.

Though the depression had come about because of global protectionism, FDR felt the way the curb the problems was yet <u>more</u> protectionism. Unsurprisingly, it just didn't work. Americas neighbour to the north, Canada, had just the same economic problems, but got themselves out of it quicker by limiting government intervention in many of the areas that FDR expanded in the USA.

And FDR's ability to misunderstand how punishing the wealth-creators damages prosperity for everyone, can be seen in his rather ignorant questioning of his budget director. FDR proposed a 99.5% tax rate on all income over $100,000. When his budget director nearly choked on this idea and told FDR that it would be unwise (putting it mildly) to implement it, the President simply asked "Why not? None of us is ever going to make $100,000 a year?!"

Unfortunately FDR's ignorance did not end there. The man who was controlling increasingly more of the decisions for businesses in America also happened to be pretty bad at business himself.

FDR had a long string of embarrassing business failures, and he wasn't the kind of man who learned from his mistakes. Franklin Lane, FDR's secretary of the interior, once ominously warned that "Roosevelt doesn't know anything about finance, but he doesn't KNOW that he doesn't know."

There was a great deal of administrative chaos in FDR's Administration. He would pit different cabinet members against each other, and this wasn't done so that logic would win the day. It was done to see how FDR could persuade people of his point of view. This chaos is probably how many of the New Deal policies were drafted. Produced in chaos, concluded in disaster. And, it must be said, instigated in force.

During his second term in 1937, (after winning a landslide victory against another Republican who, like Hoover, failed to make the case for social and economic freedom), FDR continued his violation of the American freedoms that the Founding Fathers set in stone many years earlier.

The Founders understood that to keep a government as honest as possible, you needed three very separate branches: legislative (Congress), executive (President), and judicial (Supreme Court).

FDR felt that, because so many of his policies were unconstitutional, the Supreme Court would (rightly) nullify them. So he threatened to 'pack the Court', that is to say, fill the Supreme Court with 'yes-men' who would do as FDR wished. This bullying of the Supreme Court, sadly, turned out to work in part. He never had any significant complaints from them ever again. Thankfully, however, quite a bit of his legislation did manage to get a little bogged down in gridlock.

It's funny to think of it now, but there were a number of people who were worried that FDR would become a dictator. I know we can laugh about it after the fact, but think about it one moment. Here was a guy who was turning everything upside down, and taking away so many of the rights and freedoms of the American people. And he was happy to break the rules, ignore the constitution and bully people to get his way.

Franklin Roosevelt won four terms, but had he not died in office, would he have ever stood down? It's food for thought, that's for sure.

One of the huge bureaucracies that was intended to fight the depression was the creation of the National Recovery Act, or the NRA. I can imagine that the National Rifle Association must have been rather bemused (and smug) seeing posters about 'The NRA Saving America' all over the place.

FDR simply said that "history will probably record the National Recovery Act as the most important and far-reaching legislation ever enacted by the American Congress." He was right. It was important. And it was big. But that certainly doesn't mean it was the good thing or the right thing to do.

The NRA provided the framework that allowed all the big boys in each major industry to create a "Code of Fair Competition". As per usual, this was a special-interest series of rules that kept the corporatist special interests at the top, and prevented the free market capitalists from rising above them by creating better products and services at better prices. The NRA was government enforced anti-capitalism and government enforced corporatism.

FDR signed into power the Social Security Act which provided a guaranteed pension for everyone and support for those out of work. I understand how noble that all seemed, but if the government just stopped thinking it could control everyone, then private savings, investment, philanthropy and charity would have been able to solve this. Instead, more of the money that would have (and was) being spent on such goodhearted measures privately, just dried up. 'Why bother helping people now that the state does it?' This taxable burden placed America permanently in an increasing spiral of debt.

Some in FDR's cabinet understood the failure of the New Deal. The secretary of the treasury, Henry Morgenthau Jr. simply pointed out that the governmental departments were "spending more than we have ever spent before and it does not work." He bravely spoke out and declared that the FDR Administration (including himself) had not succeeded in making even one of their main promises a reality. He said that "after eight years of this Administration we have just as much unemployment as when we started...and an enormous debt to boot!" What a shame that most of the others (including the President himself) didn't have the courage to be as honest.

The biggest myth that continues to pervade in the history textbooks, is that the Second World War ended the depression. While it's true that FDR's social policies and expansive government intervention didn't end the depression, that accolade cannot be given to the act of war either. During the war, millions of brave Americans put their lives on the line. They got paid for it, and that lowered the levels of unemployment. But again, that was yet another form of government make-work.

The bravery and heroism of those fighting is undeniable. To consider this as a convenient rational for the end of the depression is outrageous, and for those of us who have family who fought in that war, rather offensive. I'd rather the free market had been allowed to function around the globe, so that war was not needed, and the Great Depression could never transpire (or at least that it could end quickly) than see millions of heroes be sent to their death.

The Great Depression only truly came to an end after the Second

World War. But for many Americans, that time of a return to prosperity would be a long way away. And many of them would not live to see it.

THE SECOND GREAT WAR

As we have already mentioned, had President Harding lived to see a second term in office, the global free trade he may very well have instigated with Germany and everywhere else would have put the German economy back on the road to prosperity very quickly after the First World War. But Harding did not live long enough to make this dream a reality.

Every subsequent President after Harding; Coolidge, Hoover and Roosevelt, did nothing to alter the unfair social-economic situation of Germany. As such, almost with a tragic inevitability, the German people turned to extremism to get what they wanted. Extremism came in the form of National Socialism (Nazism) and the rise of one of history's most evil leaders; Adolf Hitler. Hitler had promised the German people a New Deal too. And like FDR, his New Deal would be brought about through force. But unlike FDR, the main crux of Hitler's Deal would be based on irrational racial hatred, as well as an irrational understanding of the marketplace.

It would not be long, before the gathering storm would lead Europe and most of the rest of the world to war. FDR had rightly foreseen this problem, but he only really understood it once Hitler had gotten to power. Harding had called this situation long before anyone knew or cared who Adolf Hitler was. Also Harding seemed to understand the reasons why people would turn to such extremism. This understanding seemed to escape the wit of the thirty-second President.

But in one of his many brilliantly delivered radio addresses, FDR declared that America would be neutral in the war, but that he understood all-too-well that the American people would not be neutral in their thoughts. Many Americans were horrified at what was going on in Germany, and many more rightly felt that maybe now that it had come to this, and that innocent people were directly suffering because of Hitler, that America would have to interfere.

They did not want war, and wished that leaders had followed the correct noninterventionist foreign policy advised by the Founding Fathers, as that would have prevented the war in the first place, but it was too late to go back. The concentration camps were built. Something had to be done. As it would happen, it turned out that FDR was very much the right man for that job.

In the summer of 1940, France finally succumbed to the Nazis. The Battle of Britain had begun. By November of that year, FDR broke the precedent set by George Washington, and was elected to a third term, against a fairly weak opposition, who again failed to provide a candidate who was going to seek social and economic freedom to turn the depression around.

Under the table, FDR found little ways of helping the Allies in the war. He would supply them with intelligence reports and data that aided their struggle against the Nazis. By then, a great deal of Americans knew that war was coming, they just didn't know when. FDR was warning about it from as early as 1937, again, seemingly incapable of understanding that freer trade and commerce could have prevented it. But by the time he had won his third term, everyone knew that war was just a case of when.

"December 7th, 1941. A date which will live in infamy." This was President Franklin D. Roosevelt's immortal line, summing up the horrors of the day that the Japanese bombed Pearl Harbour. His original script had the words 'world history' instead of 'infamy', but FDR's last-minute personal alterations changed it to a line that the world still remembers.

America was at war. The Second World War was now a truly global encounter.

And one of the first acts that FDR commenced as a war President was arguably his worst. He rounded up 100,000 Japanese Americans and interned them into 'camps'. Though most Japanese Americans hated the Japanese Empire (that's why they had moved to the USA, after all), this national imprisonment of citizens had never been seen before. The images of it still send a shiver up my spine. There is no real way this act made America any more safe, and even if it did, the United States was founded on a principle of liberty, even if the liberty makes things harder, or not quite as secure. This was a violation of the promise of America, plain and simple.

And it must also be said, that the Roosevelt Administration knew full-well of Hitler's 'final solution' to exterminate the Jews from as early as 1942. However, they did little save these refugees. Only once Germany had fully lost the war, did this change.

In other aspects though, FDR was truly a brilliant wartime Commander-in-Chief. Though his domestic policies reeked of the very same feeling of authoritarianism that he was trying to stifle overseas, his international diplomacy was pretty commendable overall.

For most of his time in office, FDR had been ignoring the advice of the Founding Fathers. When it came to war however, he took their heed to the fullest. This is his greatest achievement as President. He was ordered to go to war by Congress. He then told his Generals what the desired endgame result was, and allowed them to carry out the tactics that would produce this result. It was a long, hard battle, but this method of war was ultimately successful.

So while you can rightly argue that the Generals like Marshall and (especially) General Eisenhower were the real winners of the Second World War, the reason that they can claim victory, is because of the very constitutional attitude to war that FDR took.

And little wonder then, that he won his fourth Presidential election, five months after D-Day, in 1944. And even less wonder, that the American people mourned his death so deeply on April 12th, 1945, when the President succumbed to a cerebral haemorrhage.

He would leave behind him a significant new world bureaucracy. With the help of British Prime Minister Winston Churchill, FDR managed to persuade Stalin to create the United Nations. With all its successes, failures and corruptions, it would go on to be a significant player on the world stage for years to come.

THIRTY-THREE
HARRY S. TRUMAN

Took Office: April 12th 1945
Left Office: January 20th 1953
Party: Democratic
Terms: 40 & 41

THE ENTIRE NATION WAS yet again plunged into a deep mourning with the passing of President Franklin Delano Roosevelt. For many younger Americans, he was the only President they'd ever known, and more importantly, he was the reassuring voice of calm and authority during the war years. He was the symbolic head of a nation that had looked evil in face and defeated it.

By the time FDR was inaugurated for an unprecedented fourth term on January 20th 1945 (they had changed the dates of the election and inauguration during FDR's extensive time in office), it seemed to some of the more youthful in the republic, that he would be there forever.

To put it mildly, getting the top job simply following FDR's death was not the best of circumstances to take over as Commander-in-Chief. But that's the position that Harry S. Truman found himself in, (The 'S' didn't stand for anything, in case you were wondering). He had inherited the vast majority of a full term in office from his predecessor, and he had inherited a war against Japan that had not finished. And the world was eager to see what he would do with it.

POOR HARRY

In many ways, President Truman was damned regardless of what he did. Though FDR had failed to 'fix' many of the big issues of the day, his sheer length of time in office, coupled with his impressive charisma, had won him a permanent place in American hearts. Regardless of what he wanted to do, 'not being FDR' would always hang over Truman's head.

Truman was FDR's Vice President, the third man to take the position in four terms. He was only a few months into his new job when he got the call. He was asked by a staffer in the White House to come to the executive mansion quickly, but quietly.

To Truman's surprise, waiting for him was not the President, but the first lady, Eleanor Roosevelt. She looked at him with sad eyes. "Harry, the President is dead."

The Vice President was stunned. Instinctively, he asked "Is there anything we can do for you?"

"No," she said, "Is there anything we can do for you? You're the one in trouble now."

At that moment, it dawned on Truman that he was no longer the Vice President.

The surprise that Truman felt from becoming the head of the executive branch in government was nothing in comparison to the stunned reaction from the American people, and indeed the world. They held their collective breaths. What actions would this 'new man' take? Many commentators at the time did not regard the new President as a 'worldly figure.' They felt that he was just an ignoramus from the 'hick-end' of Missouri. What could he possibly do to bring America and the world back on a stable footing of peace?

It would turn out that the blunt, plain spoken President Truman was a man of confidence and decision. He had some plans up his sleeve, and was ready to use them.

GETTING ON WITH THE JOB

The new President got to work right away. He was not about to whimsically wander around the executive mansion, wondering what he should do. Before entering politics in his early fifties, Harry Truman was a businessman and farmer. In this capacity, he had risen to the dizzying heights of mediocrity. He ran (and ruined) a haberdashery business in his home state of Kansas City, and had discovered a little more success in other areas that suited him more.

In fairness, there did seem to be more than just a little common sense about President Truman. This was a man who, in the past at least, could see where he had gone wrong, and took the steps to fix it. He seemed to know where is talents resided, and would exploit them. If he discovered that he sucked at something, then he'd discard it and move on to something he was better at.

His bluntly spoken tone often upset people. In many ways, he could be a little too blunt and abrasive. But people would know exactly where he stood, and in an age of politicians clouding things over, avoiding the questions and so on, you have to admit that, even if you didn't agree with his particular brand of politics, this was an exceptionally refreshing trait.

Besides which, there's something endearing about a President who isn't afraid to swear. Some historians note with affection that President Truman was a man who would call a spade a spade. And he would sometimes call it something even worse!

And as it turned out, this blunt and plain spoken man would have to use his honesty and common sense for one of the most important decisions ever made by a President.

THE MANHATTAN PROJECT

Pretty much as soon as Truman was sworn in as President, he was told of a secret undertaking. The Manhattan Project. This project would lead President Truman to sanction one of the most significant actions in American history. Would he be the first world leader to authorise the dropping of an atomic bomb on enemy soil?

The Manhattan Project was simply the posing of that question. The nuclear technology was now up to speed. The main-stay of the war was over, but the Japanese were still fighting. There was also a great worry about the Russians. This was a perfectly valid fear. Hitler was defeated, but the communists were now using the war for imperialist aims of their own. It wouldn't be long before the Russians could place troops in northern Japan, and America's attempt to prevent the spread of an evil empire in the form of Nazi totalitarianism would quickly be replaced by a communist totalitarian empire. An empire that could create a world order just as horrific, if not more so, than the one they had fought against the fascists over.

Hitler had taken the cowards way out and committed suicide. Germany finally surrendered on May 7th, 1945. The European theatre of war was officially over. But American troops could be fighting for many years to come against the Japanese. And the spectre of an even larger communist supremacy could pose an end to freedom itself as America knew it. So what to do?

The estimates suggested that America would lose anywhere between 500,000 to a million troops just on the invasion of Japan. That's before the real fighting would even start. And, so the estimates suggested, once you had lost a few million more and won in Japan, America would be directly fighting against the Russians in an even more costly and bloody war. The rest of the world would be dragged in yet again, and World War Three would commence. And this time, the forces of freedom might well have been too depleted to fight.

President Truman analysed the costs. The huge loss of American, Japanese, Russian, and countless other nations lives in this war was absolutely too much to bare. The atomic bomb, launched on a Japanese city where the civilian population had already been told to flee, would cost significantly less lives, and might, just might, take Russia off an imperialist footing and gridlock their 'progress so far'.

The new President thought long and hard, but knew that there was only one logical choice to make. His Missouri common sense would not desert him at the time that it was most needed. With the heaviest of hearts, and with a real understanding of the ramifications, he ordered the nuclear strike on the Japanese city of Hiroshima.

Two atomic bombs were dropped. One in Hiroshima, to end the Second World War. The second in Nagasaki, to serve as a warning to the Russians, that they must end their imperialist growth. Both bombs successfully accomplished their missions.

THE NEW FOREIGN POLICY

On August 15th, 1945, Japan signed her unconditional surrender. The Second World War was over. Though it occurred very soon into his Presidency, some felt that it guaranteed Truman a second term in his own right. As we shall find out later though, Truman wouldn't have it quite so easy by the time he stood to run on his own platform.

The second atomic strike also served its purpose. The Russians did not retreat. But they no longer advanced. Holding firm, Stalin raised an iron curtain around Russia and the states that it now controlled. Places like Poland were now under the dictatorship of the proletariat. Half of Germany was under the iron curtain too. A large concrete wall was built through Berlin, separating the free west from the communist east. Those unlucky enough to be in the eastern part were controlled by communist dictatorship. This gridlock would define the world for many years to come.

The President called upon the great minds of foreign policy to devise a way of making peace with Russia, and hopefully freeing the world. He didn't need these great minds though. His big failure in this area, was to listen to most of this advice. The Founding Fathers already had all the answers he needed. We've mentioned it before in this book, and I think it comes up time and time again for good reason, but Thomas Jefferson's notion of 'peace, commerce and friendship with all nations, entangling alliances with none' was the only thing President Truman needed to instigate.

Regardless of the barriers to trade that the communists in places like Russia (and eventually China) installed, if America lowered its taxes, its import duties, reduced the size of government, started turning its debts into surpluses again and allowing the freedom of the global marketplace to do its thing, then the iron curtain would have been short lived. Alas, because President Truman understood that he wasn't an expert in this, he simply took the advice of others. It was advice from people who didn't understand the promise that noninterventionism held.

The principle idea that was created was the opposite to the anti-isolationist, noninterventionist proposal of Jefferson. Instead, these so-called 'great minds' of foreign policy devised the idea of 'communist containment'. This was an isolationist, interventionist idea.

Their basic notion that over time, the free market would prevail and that America would not need to instigate a full-on war, was correct. However, putting up barriers to trade fully with the communist nations, prolonged the time that it would take for the free market to triumph. Also, these barriers left the communist and capitalist nations on a war footing. So instead of the right approach, which would have been a free-market non-interventionist tact that would have ended the war-footing immediately, Truman was told that the only alternative to an interventionist war-approach that would have engaged another full-on war, was a third route: an interventionist, isolationist prolonged war-footing, that wouldn't turn into an outright war.

This is what he went for. This policy of containment came to be known as the Truman Doctrine. It's pretty clear that the President picked the wrong foreign policy. Suddenly America was on a permanent war-footing, by promising to support any nation that wished to fend off communist aggression. While it's commendable to promote free individuals doing this in the marketplace, getting the government involved developed the most complex system of entangled alliances the world has ever seen, with all sorts of dangerous consequences.

President Truman had to put in place the Marshall plan: he got America to give between $12-15 billion in aid to support the European nations, ravaged by war. He wanted as many 'on-side' as possible so that they wouldn't sleep-walk into Russian arms.

The pieces of the chess-board began to move. The Cold War had begun.

Not long after Truman's second election victory, China, Americas ally in the Second World War, fell to communist rule. America was becoming increasingly alarmed and paranoid about the growth of communism. When the North Korean communists invaded South Korea, the failing Truman doctrine was clear: America had to fight to repel the invasion. This battle locked into stalemate as China, with its sheer numbers, put its support behind North Korea. Then other problems occurred. North Vietnam fell to the communists too. Both sides on that war asked America for help; the communists wanted America to help them remove French imperialism from North Vietnam, and the French wanted the Americans to help them stave off the communist aggression in their Vietnamese territories. The entangling of alliances was already beginning to have what the CIA calls 'blow-back', that is to say unintended (and often disastrous) consequences. The real horrors of the Vietnam War were already being set in motion.

It can't be said enough, if President Truman had just promoted proper globalisation and limited government, none of this would have happened.

THE BUCK STOPS HERE

Truman could not help be uncomfortable with the notion that, after fighting a war that was as much to do with racism as anything else, there were still significant levels of racism at home. He passed legislation forcing the end of segregationist principles in the armed forces and in the civil service.

The economy was still in trouble though, having never recovered from the Great Depression. Truman knew, especially coming up to the 1948 election year, that he'd have to try and find a way to get America out of the economic black hole it was still in. Again, the idea that World War II got America out of the depression was always a false one.

He understood that his popularity in '48 was very low indeed. The economic hardship was beginning to overtake the euphoria of winning the war. He combated his election troubles by launching into a whistle-stop tour of the country, and giving 271 campaign speeches. Just goes to show what hard work can do. In contrast to his complacent Republican adversary Thomas Dewey (who thought that he was a shoe-in for the White House and gave only 16 speeches during the whole campaign), President Truman carried both the popular and Electoral College votes.

However, cursed with the failures of interventionism abroad, and the corruption that occurred (perhaps inevitably) in his government as the state got larger, it became very clear that there would be no third term for him.

In fairness to President Truman, his ability to make strong decisions (whether good or bad), and stick with them defined his time in office. On his desk in the oval office, he had a plaque with 'The buck stops here' inscribed. As a man who made the ultimate wartime decisions and brought about an end to the destructive conflict, he remains a figure of controversy.

Whether he was right to do what he did, and authorise the use of a nuclear weapon on a country while at war is a debate that can, will, and must continue to rage on. But one thing that must be acknowledged, is that President Truman understood very well, and fully embraced the fact, that he was the person ultimately responsible. This was not a politician who would turn-tail and run when the going got tough. He was not someone who would try and allocate blame in order to protect himself. No, he made the decisions. And he should be held accountable for the consequences. Regardless of your opinion of the man, his principles on this matter were, very, well, American.

A great deal of talk is made about the different rights and responsibilities that we have now. On the political left, they demand rights not to be offended, the right to recognise collective liability, and on the political right, they demand of the people duties to moral behaviour, and the duty to respect and comply with those in positions of authority.

But America was founded on only one fundamental right, and one fundamental duty. That's the right to do whatever the heck you please. And the duty to take full responsibility for exercising that fundamental right. In the end, it appears that President Truman fully understood how that applies to him.

While the thirty-third President was praised for ending the Second World War, one man was understood to be the real winner of that campaign – and he was not a politician. Yet. And as President Truman left office under a black cloud, General Dwight D. Eisenhower was being cheered in, on a wave of optimism.

THIRTY-FOUR
DWIGHT DAVID EISENHOWER

Took Office: January 20th 1953
Left Office: January 20th 1961
Party: Republican
Terms: 42 & 43

THE MAN THAT MANY credit as being the principle element that won the Second World War was a shoe-in for the Presidency. Unsurprisingly, both the Republicans and the Democrats courted him for their nomination, even though he had no clear interest in politics as far as anyone could see. Before he even had a chance of throwing his hat into either ring, the opinion polls were clear. There was only one man who was a guaranteed winner for the Presidency: General Dwight D. Eisenhower.

Eisenhower spent a great deal of time with both political parties. He wanted to get under the skin of their policies, and see what direction they wanted to take America. Despite having the most impressive military résumé of any other person on the planet, Eisenhower was, in many (but not all) respects, a noninterventionist.

He was more than a little uncomfortable with the constant inter-governmental engineering that President Truman was constantly instigating. Questions raced through his mind all the time. Was this really what America should be doing? Is the Truman Doctrine a really good thing? Should America 'back off' a little from this world policeman role? And shouldn't America get back to sensible economic policies at home that promote the free market and prosperity?

Though both parties weren't exactly falling over themselves to directly address these issues, Eisenhower felt that the Republicans were the ones who at the very least were leaning towards the correct answers. The General made his choice, and predictably, so did the American people. He was inaugurated on January 20th, 1953.

THE SEMI-RETIRED PRESIDENT

Like most good heads of the executive branch, Eisenhower was a reluctant President. However, he was more than a little dissatisfied with the way the Democrats handled both the Korean War and the corruption in their own house. He felt that a little more honesty, a little more transparency and maybe a little less government was needed. He was right.

So while he was reluctant to take high office, he was even more reluctant to let the country slide into what he felt was the 'wrong direction'. After his principle role in the Second World War was over, Eisenhower had spent increasingly more time back in the United States. He was unhappy with the general direction that the politicians were taking things. This was his primary motivation for standing as President.

Once he was President, there were some who teased his attitude. They said that he seemed to prefer playing golf to governing. There might be some truth to this. But if history has taught us one thing, it's that a 'semi-retired' President is usually much better than and actively interfering one.

The very first man to hold the office of President was Eisenhower's hero. He deeply respected George Washington. And just like that brilliant former General and first executive branch chief, President Eisenhower learned a great deal about the job as he went on, and became a much better President because of it. President Washington appealed to many Americans because he seemed like a non-politician. This is exactly how Eisenhower also marketed himself. However, as both these former Generals would have been able to tell you, you don't get very far in the high-ranks of the military without having more than a fair dose of political savvy. It was this savvy that would serve President Eisenhower almost as well as President Washington.

Behind the celebrity of President Eisenhower was a genuine charisma. His words were very inspirational to people, and he had that affable quality that could persuade people to get things done on his behalf. He was very much a man of great integrity and honour. The American people adored him, and it's pretty easy to see why.

The devotion to the man was quite startling. There was practically no need for there to be a big political campaign to get him into the White House – no one was ever going to beat him. But such was the enthusiasm of his fans, that a massive campaign was instigated nonetheless.

"I like Ike" posters sprung up across the United States; it was almost a social faux-pas if you had not got one. The popularity of Dwight Eisenhower transcended party-lines. It transcended most things. He was just really loved. Words can't really convey it. You just have to take one look at that big round bald head and that ear-to-ear grin and you get it.

However, many Americans weren't always totally convinced that

President Eisenhower was fully engaged with the big political issues of the day. How deep into things did he get behind the closed doors of the oval office? Was he really running things in the executive mansion, or was it his cabinet staff?

The general consensus was that President Eisenhower was essentially a man merely presiding over a cabinet. They would offer the suggestions, and he'd basically say "yes". I don't think this is fully fair. He may not have been the man pushing all the great ideas forward and he may not have been the main engine of bills and suggestions in the White House. But he was still the driver of the car, and it was still his decision on which direction to go.

Some called his time in office the 'hidden hand Presidency'. But this is really just an indulgence in erroneous conspiracy theory. The reality was that ultimately, President Eisenhower made the final decisions. It was a shame, in some ways, that he wasn't coming up with more of the proposals in the first place, but to slightly reword that famous line from President Truman, "the buck stopped here." Though his public persona might have been that he was quite aloof from policymaking, President Eisenhower called all the shots.

BIG ACCOMPLISHMENTS
Throughout history, Republican Presidents have often been voted in to bring an end to war. Despite his military background, President Eisenhower is no exception to this rule. In fact, his desire to end the Korean War was one of the main reasons for his accepting the Republican nomination.

Unsurprisingly then, one of his big achievements quite early on, was to bring about an end to the Korean War and bring the troops home. The armistice, which has stood the test of time, was a quite remarkable thing to accomplish. There was a chorus of cynics who believed that Americans would be entrenched in that war for a very long time. No level of negotiation would change that. But President Eisenhower proved them all wrong.

On a side note, one thing that maybe doesn't quite add up here, is the full nature of the armistice. Basically America agreed to not interfere with North Korea, and North Korea promised to keep to itself as well. This is the only unfortunate part of the President's plan. It imbedded an isolationism into North Korea that has lingered. And the backwards communist dictatorship of that country has lingered alongside it.

President Eisenhower was clear on one thing though: his time in office would be spent pursuing peace wherever possible. And that wouldn't just be done in treaties and the like, but in disarmament. Like President Warren G. Harding a few decades beforehand, Eisenhower instigated a massive arms reduction. He downsized the military to levels not seen for a long time. The message was clear; the Second World War, and the apparatus that went with it, were well and truly over.

In reducing the size of the military, and shrinking government down to size, President Eisenhower believed that the tax burden could be lifted too. Like Republican Presidents Harding and Coolidge before him, Eisenhower's plan produced a huge supply-side economic boom. America's classical-liberal economic boom before was called 'the roaring twenties'. The one that President Eisenhower initiated had the less sexy name of the 'post-war economic boom.' But hey, a boom is a boom, right?

However, the President didn't just want to cut spending. He felt that the reckless increases in spending over the 30s and 40s meant that investment in the basic civil infrastructure was being neglected. There were elements of this infrastructure that he thought the federal government should its increase spending in. He wanted roads. Lots of roads. And America has never been the same since.

As a military General, Eisenhower had presided over the largest military operation in history. Under his watch as President, he pushed through Congress the largest public works bill America had ever seen: The Federal Highway Act.

The entire landscape of America had, if only in a small way, changed. Suddenly there were highways, all across the country, linking the states and cities together in ways never thought possible before. The American automobile, that symbol of freedom, was being put to serious use for the first time. The internal-combustion freedom machine could now really be used to take you wherever you wanted, whenever you wanted, with as many detours as you wanted. The republic was finally a much smaller place.

Americans welcomed this change in their lives. However, a very different old spectre was a change that many resisted. Yet again, after the ugliness of slavery, the horrors of the civil war, and the hatred of segregation, America was still a country divided over the issue of racism. The divide was still predominant in between the north and the south. This stain on the American story was still ugly and predominant.

President Eisenhower almost certainly didn't want African-Americans to live in a segregated society in the south. The collectivist idea called racism was something which he didn't really understand.

And if it was something he didn't understand, it was certainly something that the Supreme Court would no longer tolerate. With their landmark ruling in 'Brown vs. The Board of Education' in 1954, they banned racial segregation in public schools. Having such public school segregation, they rightly argued, was unconstitutional.

Eisenhower was the man who appointed Chief Justice Earl Warren, who was the main driver behind the ruling. Despite this, the racially tense climate of the time made the President act in a rather shameful way. He isolated himself from the decision. Neither condemning it (and why should he, he rightly supported it), or praising it. There are some who go further and say that he actually believed that the ruling was unnecessary and a disruptive waste of the federal governments time. He believed that this sort of thing should be sorted by the states. Whether or not that's what he thought, maybe there was a valid point to be made there. Maybe it should have been sorted by the states. But because he didn't come out strongly one way or another, history has understandably treated him rather badly on this account.

While the segregation debate raged in America, Ike had his eyes on matters overseas. And this time, he ignored the noninterventionist idea of not entangling alliances. He chose to support the democratic South Vietnam over the communist North. Again, instead of just remaining impartial and freely trading with whoever in the world would agree to trade with America, President Eisenhower's decision would create a new division with the Vietnamese, and bring the United States closer to war. He supported the creation of the Bank of Vietnam (why was this job the business of an American government?) and the huge direction of federal government money in aid and support (again, what was wrong with just free trade and real wealth creation?).

TERM TWO

Overall though, President Eisenhower had shrunk the size of government (or at least, prevented it from growing quite as rapidly), had brought about peace and prosperity, and was overseeing the postwar economic boom that had come as a result of a great many of his polices. No big surprise that by a significant majority, Ike was granted a second term by the American people.

However, like so many Presidents before him, the second term would turn out to be much, much rougher for him than the first.

Part of the way through his first term, Ike had a heart attack. He was down, but far from out. He bounced back pretty well, but there was always that feeling that he wasn't quite the same. Some felt that his heart attack, combined with his fairly aloof attitude to the racial tensions in America, made him seem increasingly feeble. These feelings would fester and grow to become more pronounced in the second term.

And speaking of feelings that had been allowed the fester, the growing fear of communist Russia had expanded intensely, when the Russians finally placed a 'man made moon' (as the New York Telegram called it) into space. The rocket Sputnik had been launched. It was a success. This act was seen by many all over the globe as symbolic of communist superiority.

Many Americans, with their ham-radios and the like, often spoke of the Russian radio frequencies they could pick up over their airspace. The feeling of Russian authority looming over America was very real. What could America do to answer back? The Scientific Olympics were suddenly upon America. The space race was finally on.

Communism wasn't just spreading in space. In 1959 Fidel Castro seized Cuba. Again, if interventionist American policies hadn't turned the Cuban government into a puppet administration, maybe the emotional support for Castro's tyrannical dictatorship wouldn't have been there. But it was too late for 'if only' sentiments.

This authoritarian dictatorship took to work quickly, imprisoning Cuban political adversaries (government workers/supporters, libertarians, gays, artists, musicians, actors, priests, writers) and anyone else considered a threat to the communist totalitarian ideology. It was all taking place just ninety miles from the Florida coast. Again, Americans felt threatened. The Soviet system was getting terrifyingly close to their borders.

The kind, warm image that President Eisenhower had enjoyed (and benefited from) was suddenly something of liability. How can someone like Grandpa Ike, save us all from the communist threat? Despite his remarkably admirable sentiments against the military industrial complex towards the end of his time in office, it was pretty clear that even if he wanted it (and I doubt he did), there would be no third term for the former General. All he wanted was to leave behind a legacy of peace. But other men before him had set in place rules and global authorities that would prevent that dream from being a reality. His own interventions didn't help either.

Instead, America looked to a new man for the job. They wanted someone with youth, vigour and the ability to think in new ways, and shake up the 'old guard'.

And as it would turn out, once again they got pretty much what they wanted. Enter John Fitzgerald Kennedy.

THIRTY-FIVE
JOHN FITZGERALD KENNEDY

Took Office: January 20th 1961
Left Office: November 22nd 1963
Party: Democratic
Term: 44

THE EXCITEMENT IN THE air on January 20th, 1961 must have been electric. John F. Kennedy had become the youngest man ever to hold the office of President. At his inauguration, President Kennedy announced plainly "let the word go forth from this time and place to friend and foe alike, that the torch has been passed to a new generation of Americans."

Former President Grover Cleveland had once said that though "the people should support the government, the government should not support the people". JFK articulated the same sentiment when he said those famous inaugural words; "ask not what your country can do for you…ask what you can do for your country". It would end up being quoted for many years to come.

But the content of what President Kennedy was selling, was just mouthwash. There was a greater feeling beyond all that. A new generation of Americans were growing up, and were eager to cast aside the previous generations' hang-ups on World War Two. They wanted to live in a post-World War era. And JFK symbolised for them, the hopes that they had for their own futures.

THE CHARACTER OF A PRESIDENT

The young man from Massachusetts was fired up and ready to go. In the one thousand days or so that he was in office, he would leave a very significant mark on America and the world.

Whether he thought that an American President should act predominantly as a role model is uncertain. One thing that was certain, was that the American people loved him.

Many men of the time wanted to be just like him. He had charisma and charm by the bucket-load. Whenever things got too tense in a meeting (and with the things that occurred on his watch, tensions would arise frequently), he was always able to diffuse things with his wit and appeal.

I actually gave a good example of this in the Thomas Jefferson chapter. Once JFK had a gathering of Nobel Prize winners at a special dinner in the White House. It was an important occasion and many of the guests were tense being in the Presidents company. JFK picked up on this tension within seconds. He stood at the top of the table and declared that "I think this is the most extraordinary collection of talent and of human knowledge that has ever gathered together at the White House – with the possible exception of when Thomas Jefferson dined alone." The laughter created an effortless ease right away. The night went perfectly from then on.

He was a bright spark too. He frequently used the forces of reason to produce the results that he wanted. In fact, that's precisely how he was able to become President in the first place. A lot of the left-wing old Democratic Party elite wanted Lyndon Johnson to be their Parties nominee this time around. JFK knew that he had a great deal of popular support in America, but how could he get the Party to sign up to him?

Simple. He was certain that fighting it out with Lyndon B. Johnson in the Primaries until the bitter end, would result in him winning. But at what cost? The Party would be quite divided, and the Democrats wouldn't win against the Republicans as a result. So he used his powers of persuasion to put Johnson on his ticket as Vice President. The old-guard (begrudgingly) went on with it. And JFK became President.

Best of all, as President Kennedy saw it, he had been able to both appease and isolate the old left-wing contingency of the Party. The Vice President was a high-ranking position, but it didn't have any meaningful power at all.

That said, JFK was a highly approachable manager. Choosing not to have one of his own, he was effectively his own Chef of Staff and his door was always open. His cabinet and Congress could pop in to brainstorm and debate the big issues of the day all the time. This only added to his ability to pass legislation through that he wanted quickly, while also adding to his immense charm.

And that charm proved to be a vital weapon for fighting the Cold War. JFK, his wife Jacqueline and their three kids were like the perfect American family that you saw on TV at the time. John and Jackie Kennedy were like movie stars in their own rights. And they both had an effortless ability to light up a room with their instant congeniality.

However, JFK's charms would often lead him astray. It was only really after his death that people began to learn about his affairs and 'unwholesome' behaviour. But when he was in office, that aspect of his private life seemed to be rather outside the scope of the media. My guess is that they were all looking at him with such rose-tinted glasses that they didn't see what was right in front of their eyes. Either way, he seemed to get a free pass on his unconventional love-life.

Other aspects of his life seemed to escape the full glare of the media too. He suffered from many debilitating illnesses. You can find bits of stock footage of him occasionally having to walk around with crutches, but again, the press didn't really seem to run with it. Like FDR before him, JFK was pardoned by a traditionally unforgiving media.

And one thing's for certain: His sexual appetite and health problems definitely didn't stop him getting the job done.

GOING TO WORK
President Kennedy's brilliant mind saw with vivid clarity a truth about economics that his opponents on the left could not. In the tradition of Presidents Harding, Coolidge, and others before them, he cut taxes.

While the poor got a great deal of this cut, he cut them significantly for the rich. What happened, as he rightly predicted, was a supply-side economic boom. Sadly he didn't seem to care about the debt and deficit too much. This careless attitude has, tragically, pervaded the corridors of western powers for years.

But when he got it right, he truly got it right. Kennedy understood perfectly that if you lift some of the penalties for working, saving and investing, then everyone would be better off. It worked like a treat. Many politicians at the time, not least his political adversary and Vice President Lyndon B. Johnson, were very unhappy about this move. They didn't want plain simple economic freedom. They wanted to redistribute the wealth using government bureaucracy.

For the very left-wing members of Congress, JFK was being a thorn in their side. The fact that his policies were working, didn't seem to matter to them. For the further-left in the Democratic Party, ideology mattered much more than practicality.

However, not all of JFK's decisions were good ones. Far from it. One of his first major mistakes occurred early on. The Director for Plans at the CIA spoke often with the new President. He wanted authorisation to launch a military invasion. His secret scheme was called The Bay of Pigs. The idea was (supposedly) simple. A group of Cuban exiles would go back to their mother land and overthrow Fidel Castro's communist regime.

President Kennedy thought it over for only a brief period of time. Despite (here I go again) the warnings inherent in the recommended non-isolationist foreign policy of the Founding Fathers, the President authorised the mission. It was a total failure.

But again, President Kennedy dealt with it almost perfectly. When the truth came out about what the mission was, and how it had back-fired, the American people were not happy. However, the new President's charm worked a treat. He stood in front of the TV cameras and candidly said that "victory has a hundred fathers and defeat is an orphan". He took the entire brunt of the criticism. In a highly commendable way, he fully accepted the blame, as the Commander-in-Chief. Yet again, the buck stopped with the President.

By accepting responsibility in this way, the American people didn't just forgive him. Future Presidents take note, the opinion polls at the time were quite clear in this. By being so honest about the failure, the American people respected and trusted him more than they had ever done. His popularity soared.

And he used that popularity to embark upon a wide-range of activities. Some were good, some were bad. Some, like the Peace Corps, are still with us today. He talked often about a plan to fight poverty.

He had some very different ideas to the old-school Democrats as to how to go about ending poverty though, so his plans in that area were stifled and in some cases, completely corrupted. But there was one area of policy that he wouldn't face much significant opposition from hardly anyone in American politics at all.

CHOOSING THE MOON

The space race was well and truly on. The symbolic advances the Russians had made were worrying Americans all over. President Kennedy would start to put their minds at rest.

"We choose to go to the moon in this decade and do the other things," he said, "not because they are easy. But because they are hard." The moon was the new frontier. The only question was, could America get there before the Russians?

The very idea was monumental. The real question was how could a government bureaucracy achieve such a thing? We can only speculate, but based on his seemingly good understanding of taxes and why lowering them means more prosperity, I think that JFK understood the idea of market forces reasonably well.

The new President could see that NASA would be competing against the Russian agencies. For the first time in any meaningful way, a government bureaucracy would be subjected to the one element that was usually only reserved in the marketplace: competition. And competition breeds excellence.

The world was watching the space race eagerly. Even tiny steps of progress in one direction or another was influencing which style of governance countries preferred: Russian-style planning or American-style freedom. JFK felt therefore that it was vital for the very future of civilisation that America win the space race.

His calm, intelligence, logic and adherence to reason was beginning to serve the President well. And it would have to serve him even better with the crisis to come. JFK could clearly posture pretty well, but how could he do with a disaster scenario?

MISSILES IN CUBA

Has there ever been a more tense time for a President in history than the Cuban Missile Crisis? Maybe, but it's got to rank pretty highly up there.

The date was October 16th, 1962. President Kennedy had received a briefing from the CIA. The briefing had consisted of, amongst other things, photographs taken from America spy-planes in the air. These pictures and briefing notes showed that the Soviets were building a series of bases and installing equipment that was capable of launching short and medium-range nuclear missiles on American soil. The missiles that the Russians could launch from Cuba, could technically deliver a nuclear payload anywhere in the United States. Sweaty palms time indeed.

Just a week later, after much more intelligence-gathering, the President spoke to the nation. He was sombre. He understood the very serious ramifications of the Soviet actions. He stated that "the purpose of these bases can be none other than to provide a nuclear strike-capability against the western hemisphere." America suddenly got very nervous indeed.

We will never quite know how close America actually came to thermonuclear war against Russia. Some say that the two countries were on a knife-edge. Luckily for all of us, John F. Kennedy was the President of the United States at the time.

Unfortunately JFK didn't practise much non-interventionism during his time in office, but he was not a full-on war-monger either. He resisted the calls from the military to launch a pre-emptive strike on Cuba. This could have easily escalated the war and it wouldn't have remained 'cold' for long. Keeping the Cold War refrigerated was the main objective for President Kennedy, and he kept his head cool while all around him were burning up. He decided to settle this on the negotiating table. He managed to strike a deal with the Soviets.

It came close, but in the end, JFK managed to form a peaceful end to the crisis.

CIVIL RIGHTS AND FOREIGN POLICY

With all of these international issues abroad, you could almost forgive JFK for neglecting things at home. Almost.

While his tax cuts were improving the lot for the vast majority of Americans, there was still the difficult (and as yet unsolved) issue of civil rights for African-Americans. The base nature of the Woodrow Wilson-style segregation was still a reality for many blacks living in the south.

JFK was almost aloof to the plight of these Americans. It was only in 1963 that he personally watched some footage of the riots, demonstrations, and awful treatment of the black population in the southern states. The television reports of the violence erupting in the streets of Birmingham, Alabama were shocking to him. In Birmingham, Martin Luther King Jr was leading a protest against segregation. This right to 'peaceably assemble', as guaranteed by Thomas Jefferson in the 1st Amendment of the Constitution was being savagely violated.

The young President watched as people were being blasted with hoses, the skins peeling off their backs, while being set upon by large dogs. Not only did he feel sickened by this, but it also changed the public mood in America. Things had to change.

And unfortunately, JFK was going to spend too much time socially-engineering the world to deal with it.

Problems were arising in Vietnam. JFK became one of the principle sources of the problem. He wanted to overthrow the tyrannical communist regime in South Vietnam. He felt that to kill the snake, you only had to sever its head. On November 1st, 1963, Kennedy approved the assassination of the President of South Vietnam. From that day on, America was entrenched in a struggle in that country. Putting American troops on the ground to fight off the Northern Viet Cong suddenly seemed inevitable.

HIS LAST DAY

It was twenty days since Kennedy gave the authorisation to assassinate the South Vietnam President. It was November 21st 1963. JFK was in San Antonio, Texas, to join Vice President Johnson at the opening of a new space facility. In his usually eloquent way, he declared that America had "tossed its cap over the wall of space. And we have no choice but to follow it."

The very next day, on the 22nd, the President and the first lady went to Dallas.

A Marxist revolutionary, who had allegiances with the Soviets, who was disgusted at American capitalism, and despised both the few libertarian ideals that JFK had embodied as well as the interventionist foreign policy he was pursuing, was waiting in the book depository in downtown Dallas.

His name was Lee Harvey Oswald.

You really have to spend time in that old book depository to get a sense of the despair that it's grown to symbolise. Oswald waited for President Kennedy's motorcade to pass by the depository and he fired his rifle from the window. He hit his target. He killed the President.

The shock the nation went into is impossible to describe. The population of America effectively stalled. The outflow of grief was unlike anything many of them had experienced before. The footage of a very young boy, watching the Commander-in-Chief's funeral motorcade and somehow having the knowledge to salute the coffin as it drives past will be forever burned upon my memory.

Despite his failings in policy, President John Fitzgerald Kennedy was undoubtedly a man with a very, very good heart. And the world knew it. And so, with their feelings of him enhanced by his martyrdom, they mourned.

Finally, with the ultimate irony, left with the almost impossible task of picking up the pieces and healing the nations broken heart, was JFK's political adversary, Lyndon Baines Johnson.

THIRTY-SIX
LYNDON BAINES JOHNSON

Took Office: November 22nd 1963
Left Office: January 20th 1969
Party: Democratic
Terms: 44 & 45

HOW MANY MORE TIMES could America face the untimely passing of
their elected officials? Yet again, they found themselves with a man
at the head of the executive branch, who they didn't (directly) elect.
Lyndon Johnson was in office. And the old left of the Democratic
Party were back in power again.

Within hours of the tragedy, while the American people were
barely able to come to terms with what had happened (and a great
deal of them didn't even know about it), Johnson was being sworn in
on Air Force One. The photograph of this event occurring under such
a sombre context is one of the defining pictures taken in the twentieth century.

The real question that the American people would ask in the days and weeks after the assassination of President Kennedy, was what changes would they see in the White House? How different was LBJ going to be from JFK?

Though they saw many things very differently, President Johnson knew that anything other than the appearance of total loyalty to his predecessor would be acceptable to America. Standing before Congress, he simply referred to JFK as "the greatest leader of our time". He pledged to dedicate his Presidency to the fulfilment of Kennedy's legacy. Of course, we will never know exactly what direction the rest of the JFK Presidency would have taken. One thing is for certain, it certainly wouldn't be the direction LBJ took it.

UNDERSTANDING LBJ

Johnson was not at all happy about the way he gained high office. No doubt in private moments, he and his wife Claudia Alta (a.k.a. 'Lady Bird') were sure to speak of the 'unfortunate' nature of his ascendency. What he really wanted to do was become President outright; either after JFK failed to gain a second term in office, or after President Kennedy had successfully seen out two full terms.

President Johnson was a man of great theatre. Standing at 6' 2", the big Texan was often loud and dramatic. His personality filled any room he was in. He was desperate for power, and it's no big secret between those who knew him that he was bitterly disappointed that JFK had out-smarted and out-played him in the race for the White House. His strong competitive streak didn't die out when he finally became President. If anything, his desire for greater power and success simply grew.

LBJ didn't just want to go down in history as a remarkable politician. Why place your ambitions so low? He wanted to be recorded as the greatest politician the world had ever seen. He felt he could change society, and create a new world order. And he also believed that the world would love him for it. Evidently he had never read a history book in his life.

Unlike his predecessor, Johnson wasn't a man of great intellect. But his personal story was rather impressive. He was the very epitome of the self-made man. His family background was one of poverty. From the humblest of beginnings, he rose up the ranks of the political ladder and had finally become a formidable figure.

In an almost stereotypical Texan way, he could be very tactless, but often charming. However, these characteristics only take us to the surface of the man. Underneath was a 'school of hard knocks' kind of intelligence. You know when someone tells you that they've learnt everything they need to know from the 'University of Life'? It really normally means that they aren't that educated and are just trying to cover up. But LBJ was the real personification of the University of Life. And he had graduated with honours.

He had no significant fancy letters after his name, and as I've already mentioned, certainly didn't have the vast cool, almost objective intellect of JFK. But President Johnson had real cunning. Around the cabinet table in the West Wing of the White House, LBJ was the fox. And the rest of the cabinet were sheep.

He could be very savage. A real in-your-face kind of guy, which was pretty intimidating considering his size. And when I say 'in-your-face kind of guy', that wasn't just a figure of speech. In order to get what he wanted, he would walk right up to you, and stick his face right in your 'personal space' (as a New Yorker might call it). They called this, 'The Johnson Treatment'. Seriously, there are photos of him at cabinet meetings and all sorts where he's doing it. It's almost funny. This was a mighty contrast to the relaxed, friendly, open-door policy of JFK. President Johnson was more likely to burst open YOUR door and tell you what was what. Under LBJ's White House, the law of the jungle was at play, and you had better learn to play that game fast, or you'd be eaten. Metaphorically of course. I'm not entirely sure if he actually ate any of the cabinet. But some of JFK's appointments did have a gazelle-esque quality about them.

Like most men in power with an ego problem, LBJ was deeply insecure. His sense of self was as big as his Texas 10-gallon hat, matched only in size by his insecurity.

He had a deeply-rooted inferiority complex against the 'big-brains' that JFK had appointed as White House staff. He would push these 'ivy league' types around a lot, just to prove that he could do it. It was a flex of the muscles, a show of strength on the battlefield of politics. And really, it was quite sad.

In critiquing the personality of the thirty-sixth President, many people have gone further than I have. And with good reason. The irrational volatility of LBJ was so bizarre, so esoteric, that you may well think that the guy was nuts.

Looking at the evidence, he probably was a little nuts. And when someone believes they are 'controlling the country' while in office, their psychological state should be as stable as possible. This was not the case for LBJ. Yikes.

A NEW NEW DEAL

As well as 'The Johnson Treatment', the President would also keep his subordinates on their toes by holding meetings in unconventional places. He would call up staff to talk to him while he was in bed. He'd have meetings in the White House barber's chair, or even in the bath.

If you've seen pictures of LBJ, then I apologise for putting the following picture in your head. But he would often call members of his staff to a meeting while he was skinny dipping in the White House pool. Ugh.

And it was during one such skinny-dipping session that he called upon two of his aides to come and listen to his proposal for what he called 'the Great Society'.

America was about to be inflicted with yet another New Deal.

The nuts and bolts of the Great Society plan were pretty simple. It was a plan to setup mainly welfare programs. The government would spend a load of the American people's money, keep some of it (well okay, a lot) to pay for the administration costs and then redistribute the rest in a series of plans.

Towing the line in exchange for a series of goodies in their own districts, Congress complied with LBJ's idea. Most of the tons of new laws needed to enact the Great Society were approved. The size of government expanded, and America has never properly recovered from the mess that was created.

One of his plans was for medical care that would insure the elderly. Every American above a certain age would be eligible to join the program. This took a great deal of the medical care out of the private capitalist system and into a hybrid government/corporatist system instead. It had been moving in that direction from the early days of FDR, but as a direct result of the Great Society plans, over the years, the number of Americans who couldn't afford health insurance or weren't able to get charity or government assistance, increased. The general cost of healthcare skyrocketed as a result too. And America would go from having the best healthcare system in the world, ranked at the very top of the World Health Organisation rankings, to having one of the lowest of the western nations.

The quality of American healthcare remained the best in the world, but the cost rose to record levels, and the universality of coverage diminished too. Before the Great Society plans, Americans would pay a little bit a year to cover them for the disastrous unexpected healthcare needs that they might require. This insurance worked in the same way that home contents insurance covers you on the off-chance that your house gets burgled and someone steals the TV, or the microwave suddenly blows up or gets damaged. In those instances, the insurance pays up. Because it's unlikely that you're going to be burgled (or that you're suddenly going to have your appendix burst on Saturday afternoon), the insurance is very low and is used to pay for the unfortunate souls who get into trouble in any given year.

Now, if you wanted to just buy a new TV, you have to buy it yourself. Simple. And because there's a free market of TVs, you can go into the marketplace and get a good deal by making use of the competing businesses selling them. The same was true of healthcare. Apart from that 'disaster coverage', if you wanted say, a leg operation to fix your knee, you'd pay for it. And because of the free marketplace, you could shop around and get a good deal. Because prices were getting cheaper and cheaper all the time, more and more were finding they could afford it. And donating a little private charity for those that couldn't afford it was inexpensive too. That way, up until 1964, America had nearly universal coverage through affordability and private charity. Once President Johnson got involved, all that changed, and America suffered as a result.

From almost the start of the American republic, you can track the percentage of the population that could and couldn't get the healthcare that they needed, and the proportional costs for that service.

From the eighteenth century until 1964, the percentage covered only ever went up, and the costs only ever went down. After the initial part of LBJ's plan was instigated in 1965, the costs started to rise and the percentage of people covered went down. And the irony is, the idea that this mess occurred because America has a 'private' system was used by politicians for many decades to come. Tragically, the American people continued to listen to them.

That was just one policy of failure. Most of the rest had similar (if not quite so devastating) unintended consequences. For example, if you take just one group that was singled out for special treatment: African-Americans. Blacks in America had been treated appallingly for far too long.

But something was happening in America. Not only were attitudes to blacks changing, but African-Americans were forging out the American dream for themselves. With very little special welfare, and despite the horrors of segregation, the number of African-Americans living below the poverty line had fallen from 87% in 1940, to about 18% in 1969. Now sure, President Johnson's welfare programs to help African-Americans were instigated during his administration in the sixties. But the real money for those programs only occurred after he left office, between about 1970-1979. During this decade, poverty for African-Americans fell. It fell by a pathetic 1%, from 18% to 17%.

But, as it would turn out, policy failure at home is not what President Johnson is condemned for. Curiously, because he was seen to be 'doing something' about the problems America faced, history has remembered him quite kindly. Although I don't think he really deserves it.

The real failure that history has criticised LBJ for, is failure abroad. And that failure can be summed up in the name of one county.

VIETNAM

The war in Vietnam was something of an unfortunate inevitability by the time that President Johnson got into office. But let us be clear; it was under Johnson's Presidency that the troops were sent to fight in such huge numbers. In 1965, General Moreland told the President that he risked losing the war, unless he did something more drastic.

And drastic is what LBJ did. He mobilised the Reserves, committed more weaponry and doubled the number of troops. Within a very short space of time, the number of American soldiers fighting went from 65,000 to 125,000.

Unfortunately, LBJ was missing those vital ingredients that were needed to win the war. Firstly, there was no proper endgame strategy. Secondly, because of his sheer ego, instead of doing what FDR had rightly done so many years earlier and allowed the Generals to instigate the strategies that would satisfy the politicians' end results, he interfered. He didn't want the 'ivy league' officer-class to tell him what to do.

Despite the sheer number of troops, the war continued to look unwinnable. The President even added an extra 100,000 troops to the mix. Still no joy.

As a result, and rather unsurprisingly, the antiwar movement in America gained momentum. From outside the Oval Office of the White House, President Johnson could hear the protestors singing "Hey, hey, LBJ – how many kids did you kill today?" He was devastated.

Things were becoming strained. JFK's brother, Robert Kennedy, a man committed to some of the policies and ideas of the former President, was standing up to the bullish authority of LBJ. He wanted the removal of some of the old left wing ideas that LBJ was instigating. The Democratic Party was geared up for a pretty vicious bout of political infighting.

And even worse for President Johnson – the Viet Cong looked to be winning the war. Again, had he communicated a more divisive endgame, and allowed the Generals to do what they knew best, then maybe, just maybe, that war could have been won. But time was running out for both the US Army overseas and LBJ at home.

Under all the pressure brought about by his own making, Johnson cracked. He decided not to run for re-election. It was pretty clear that he wouldn't have been able to win anyway, if the opinion polls were any indication at the time.

Yet again, the American people wanted a change. They wanted to end the war in Vietnam. And what do they do when they want America to end a war? They vote for a Republican. The Republican they chose this time around however, wasn't exactly all that he promised he was.

THIRTY-SEVEN
RICHARD NIXON

Took Office: January 20th 1969
Left Office: August 9th 1974
Party: Republican
Terms: 46 & 47

THE GENERAL RULE OF thumb is simple: Never trust a politician. Across the board, you can usually avoid a great deal of misery if you stick to this rule. However, you can trust some even less than others.

When Americans turned to Richard Milhous Nixon for a way out of the Vietnam War, he reassured them that he had a 'secret plan' to end the conflict. So secret that he couldn't tell voters what it is? Was it because if he gave it away before instigating it, it might not work? Well that's certainly what he insinuated, but he never even really said that. Again, some politicians you can trust even less than others.

Nixon had been scheming to get into the White House his whole life. By now there had been a long tradition of Americans voting for Republicans to get them out of wars and economic disasters, and cleaning up the mess that the Democrats had left behind. When running for election against John F. Kennedy, Nixon had failed to play that card. Against someone like Kennedy, it was a hard hand to play out. Now in 1968, he finally could play the politically and fiscally intelligent card. But did he really have all of the traits required to actually instigate what he was promising and if he had, would he be using them wisely?

DEVIOUS FROM DAY ONE

The scheming for his election victory was so fiendish that you'd admire it if it were not so morally repulsive. While Nixon desperately wanted to end the Vietnam War and bring the troops home, the last thing he wanted was for the Democrats to pull a last minute 'October surprise' and bring about an end to the war.

In fairness to Nixon, on the other side, the Democrats (and LBJ included) wanted to find some way of ending the Vietnam War, even if it wasn't that satisfactory, because they were desperate to win the election too.

Both Parties were scheming, but which would win? When it comes to political manoeuvres and moral ambiguity, no one could out-do Nixon. He let on to the South Vietnamese that if they could just hang on until after the US Presidential election in 1968, then he would give them a much better support plan that would settle the war for good. They believed him, and so held on, thus prolonging the war regardless of any of the Democrats' attempts to end the war immediately.

Now both Nixon and LBJ were wrong on this. The South Vietnamese shouldn't have been made to hold on indefinitely, the steps for consolidation needed to be instigated as soon as it was viable. But similarly, the stand-down of arms shouldn't have happened straight away just to make it politically convenient for the Democrats. It needed to happen at a pace that suited both the North and South Vietnamese. Anything else would leave disastrous unintended consequences.

So before I enter into a tirade against Nixon (and believe me, I'm going there), we have to acknowledge that both sides of the political coin were being playing the same ugly game. The only difference is that Nixon knew how to fight dirtier. And that ability gave him the keys to the White House.

President Nixon, from California, was arguably one of the most experienced politicians in history. Power-crazy almost beyond the usual delirious levels of even LBJ, he was seen by many as a dangerous man.

The Founding Fathers had placed careful restrictions on the power of the executive branch of government. Many Presidents had since increased those powers, and now that a less-than decent man was in the oval office, the dire consequences of all those previous Presidential power-grabs were beginning to bare rotten fruit.

Isolated from this though, his experience in politics was truly remarkable. He had been a member of the House of Representatives, a Senator, and even Vice President under the Eisenhower administration. This gave many Americans confidence in him. That was quite understandable.

He clearly knew how to work the system to get what he wanted, so maybe he could use that influence and persuasive diplomatic talent to bring about the changes that so many Americans craved. They would end up being bitterly disappointed. He would use his talent, yes. But not for such noble aims.

POLITICS OF MISTRUST

Nixon had won many friends in Washington by the time he was President. But, some argue, he had infinitely more enemies. He kept a list of people that he felt were either against him, or didn't aid him in the way he wanted at some stage in his career. When his Vice President, Gerald Ford, heard about the so-called 'enemies list' of Nixon, he simply stated the clear truth: A man with so many enemies that he has to keep a list, has too many enemies.

Again, like President Johnson, Nixon had just another form of the same problem; an inferiority complex. What I call 'little man syndrome', pushed to the very limit.

President Nixon felt that his time in the top job should be spent punishing those who had negatively crossed his path in history. Republican, Democrat or independent, it didn't matter. In fact, most of his enemies were from his own Party; fairly noble people on the whole, who disagreed with his fairly authoritarian brand of politics. As I write that last sentence, I'm reminded of the footage I've seen of the thirty-seventh President having a meeting with one of his staff, who has just told him that some Congressmen aren't going to play ball with him on a policy. The President leans to one side in his chair, and looks at the staffer with contempt. "Well what's wrong with these clowns?" he asks. Classic Nixon.

Many historians talk of the 'demons' within Nixon. It is true that by the time he was in the White House, he brought with him a *travel case set*-full of emotional baggage. He was a very insecure man, possibly brought out by his real character of a brooding loner. His insecurity made him distrust people. Frankly, like many people with the same psychological problems of Nixon, he thought that people would behave as deviously as he would, so that made him highly secretive.

And in order to get what he wanted, instead of using the JFK-brand of open-door policies, friendly interaction and intelligent motivational persuasion, Nixon tried his own brand of the 'Johnson Treatment'. Intimidation and bullying. Do this or else. This made him loose friends and alienate people, which only exacerbated his mistrust and brooding tendencies.

And these exacerbations led to outright paranoia. If people disagreed, instead of allowing them to give him an honest assessment of their feelings, he would mistrust everything they did after that. If a political opponent happened to agree with Nixon on a certain issue (and Nixon was, it must be acknowledged, right on many issues), it didn't matter. Nixon would instantly doubt the motives of his opponent. This cynicism consumed him.

All his life, he wanted to prove himself and rise up above his middle class origins. Instead of achieving that goal by the nobility of his actions, he would always try and find a way to plot and scheme against those who might prevent his rise to 'greatness'. Some would ask, why didn't he use his great talent and intelligence, (which he possessed by the bucket load), to just be better than this adversaries? That is the ultimate question. And its answer, and the damaged psychological underpinnings of that answer, make for one of the biggest tragedies in American political history.

TRIANGULAR DISTRUST

President Nixon's constant bid for power didn't come to an end once he became the head of the executive branch of government. He always wanted the fullest authority to himself. He was not interested in 'cabinet politics'.

Like many power-hungry Presidents, he was constantly angry and frustrated at the lack of power he could take from Congress. And when it came to his cabinet, he would side-step them whenever convenient.

He circumvented both the Secretary of State and the Secretary of Defence, so that he and his National Security adviser, Henry Kissinger, could control the main aspects of foreign policy. This had never been done before, and many of the experienced people in the cabinet were quite taken aback by this.

Again, federal government was supposed to run according the Constitution. And that old document was very clear. The President took his lead from Congress. They told him the results they wanted, and he would have to follow through in the way he thought most appropriate.

But as more and more Presidents took more and more power for themselves, this line became blurred. So blurred in fact, that by the time Nixon was in power, bypassing even his cabinet was only a small step on the road to even greater power. And tragically, no one make any meaningful attempts to bat an eyelid.

Nixon was, to give him credit, a fantastic diplomat. This also reveals his great tragedy. If he used his immense skills, he could have solved so many of the world's problems. But his skills were purely used to promote his own power.

He wanted to 'run' foreign policy himself, in part, because he had a much better talent for it than most. That was true, but he also demanded have full control because he wanted the power that came with that control. The exact nature of his foreign policy strategy remains an example of one of the most unnecessarily secretive America had ever seen.

Publically, President Nixon continued to tell the people of America that he still had his 'secret plan' to end the Vietnam War. Privately, the war expanded under Nixon. He escalated the conflict by bombing Cambodia, and bringing other nations into the troubles. He also sent the Marines to invade Laos.

The problem with secrets is that they often won't stay secret for long. Especially when you have isolated and made enemies of so many people along the way. The New York Times published the details of the 'raids in Cambodia' in May, 1969.

Nixon dealt with this in his usual pathological way. Instead of rethinking the way he was doing things, he decided the best course of action was yet more paranoia.

He was furious at how the information had gotten out. Despite the dubious (to put it mildly) Constitutional legitimacy of his actions, the President ordered wiretaps on many government officials. Some elected, some not. He also allowed the bugging of phones and homes of journalists and the like.

He was determined to get to the source of the leak, even if that meant stepping outside of the law. He didn't seem to understand that the President was not above the law. The Founding Fathers had created a system whereby the President was highly accountable for his actions, and a that violation in such a way would result in a much-deserved impeachment.

While the war against the Viet Cong had intensified under Nixon, he also had a plan to end it. The plan was radical, and if not done for such power-hungry motives, might well have worked. As we have already mentioned, the Presidents big talent was politics. He knew how to 'grease the wheels' so to speak. He wanted to use his diplomacy skills to bring the interested parties of the conflict together and bring about a peaceful solution. Unfortunately, he couldn't help wanting to turn it into a power-struggle.

The system that President Nixon and Henry Kissinger came up with, was referred to as 'triangular diplomacy'. The idea was to disengage from Vietnam, while getting China and Russia to play-off against each other. Again, instead of using his diplomacy to engage and build friendships with these nations and end the war, Nixon insisted on entangling alliances and turning it into a complex game.

History had already shown the President what a mistake this is, and how it always turns out. However, the Nixon didn't care. It was all about power for him.

Nixon was right that a peaceful settlement in Vietnam in which both North and South Vietnam would coexist, could be achieved by the United States having a good relationship with China. This is where Nixon headed.

He forged a diplomatic relationship with the communist government in China. It seemed to work. He brokered an agreement in 1973. This lead to the official ceasefire in Vietnam.

America was relieved to hear the President state on national television that "we today, have concluded an agreement to end the war, and bring peace with honour in Vietnam". This should have been his great moment, and the Commander-in-Chief would have secured a favourable place in history as a result. This was certainly the reason for the landslide re-election victory for his second term. However, Nixon's power-play wasn't quite done yet.

He continued his triangular diplomacy and exerted leverage over Russia. He forged more close ties with the Soviet regime too as a result. So far so good. He's ticked the boxes of peace and friendship with these two nations. All that was needed was to allow individual Americans and businesses to begin less restricted commerce and he would have been one of the great American heroes. But Nixon used this power-play to his own personal advantage. He began posturing against the Russians and Chinese. He made them play against each other. He started to entangle his newly-formed alliances.

And as things abroad started to sound a little shaky to some, his trouble at home would bring about his downfall.

WATERGATE

The Watergate scandal was heating up during the end of President Nixon's first term. It wasn't long before this would blow up into something quite shocking.

The President had continued to wiretap the phones and homes of reporters, some of whom were, ironically, investigating his less-than legitimate surveillance methods. The government had also infiltrated a number of American groups.

The student movement, the Black Panthers, and lots of other political groups were being permeated by Nixon's administration. They were all beginning to realise it. Something was about to give.

Nixon did what he could to prevent being sent down for the crimes of intrusion that he instigated. He couldn't hold out much longer. The calls to impeach him were growing. The Constitution was quite clear, if the President was found out to be engaged in criminal activity, then he had to be impeached.

"People have got to know, whether or not their President is a crook", he once famously said on national television, with a biting and bitter fury. "Well I'm not a crook. I've earned everything I've got."

In July 1974, after fourteen months of Congressional hearings on the Watergate tapes, the house judiciary committee passed an article of impeachment, which charged Nixon with obstruction of justice. In honesty, whether he really knew what had happened at the Watergate hotel remains cloudy. But he certainly did get in the way of allowing the investigation to follow through unhindered. The impeachment call was sound.

But before the House of Representatives could vote to impeach, (and it looked like they would), Nixon announced he was standing down. He resigned on August 9th, declaring that he could not continue to do the job if people felt that he was an obstruction to the truth. As he said himself; "There could be no white-wash, at the White House."

Angry at both his enemies (and certainly by now, in fairness, at himself), Nixon was walked to Marine One, the Presidential helicopter on the White House lawn by Vice President Ford. He got into the helicopter, and was waved off.

Ford them walked back into the White House, and took the oath of office. In a manner that must have bewildered him, he suddenly found himself to be the thirty-eighth President of the United States.

THIRTY-EIGHT
GERALD FORD

Took Office: August 9th 1974
Left Office: January 20th 1977
Party: Republican
Term: 47

HE COULDN'T HELP LOOKING like a bunny in the headlights when he stood in front of the television cameras for the first time. And you could see the incomprehension on his face when he walked away from President Nixon's helicopter, and headed across the White House lawn, back into the executive mansion. "Okay, what happens now?" he must have been thinking.

In the same way that Harry S. Truman was stunned at suddenly finding himself as the Commander-in-Chief after the unexpected death of FDR, Gerald Ford was frankly bewildered at the way that he elevated to the top job. Despite the bizarre nature of the proceedings, as soon as he was inaugurated, just minutes after Nixon had flown away, President Ford, with all the composure he could muster, impressively spoke the words that the nation needed to hear. "My fellow Americans, our long national nightmare is over."

And with that, the United States of America had its thirty-eighth President. The man from Michigan who would do all he could to turn the nation's attention away from the disaster of Nixon. The question was, would it be enough?

CLEANING THE DECKS

The oval office had been a place of secrets. Indeed, the White House itself had fallen into chaos in the last few weeks of Nixon's Presidency.

It would be Gerald Ford's job to change all this. As a personality, he certainly had the ability, if anyone possessed such a thing.

There were a great many issues of the day to deal with. The most prominent was the criminal indictment of President Nixon. Just because the power-hungry thirty-seventh President was no longer in the top job, that didn't mean that he was let off the hook. The law was the law, and no one should have been above it. The big question everyone wanted to ask President Ford, was would Nixon be brought to justice for what he had done?

On top of the demand for Nixon's indictment, people were becoming increasingly disillusioned with the powers that be in Washington. The Nixon farce had highlighted for them what was wrong with American politics in general. They felt like they weren't being listened to. The people in government were just there to cling onto power. Standards of living were increasing and there was more social mobility, sure. But people were rightly beginning to understand that most of this progress was occurring despite the political class, not because of it.

America was founded on the principles of people being the architects of their own destiny. It would take until Ronald Regan stood for high office until they could finally get someone back in the White House who was more 'on-message' with the Founding Fathers.

President Ford also had other issues to deal with. Congress felt that the powers that belonged to them had been taken away under a progressive series of power-hungry Presidents. They wanted to be the ones swinging the big sticks again. And of course, the spectre of an impending problem in Vietnam was still hanging over the whole political scene.

The character and temperament of the new President was completely different to that of the scheming Nixon. It was just what America needed. Maybe here could be a man who would change things for the better. America, while disillusioned with politics in general, held a slight candle of hope in the window of Ford's oval office.

President Ford was a consensus builder. He had worked to bridge many gaps between the Republicans and Democrats during President Johnson's time in office. He had no way near the same political skill as his predecessor, but was an honest and straightforward kind of guy. This way, he could bring people together and make the necessary compromises to get to a result that most people could be reasonably happy with.

This cordial quality had won him a lot of support and showed that putting him on the Vice Presidential ticket was certainly a smart and calculating move by Nixon. Now the admirable character that Ford had would need to show the world that he could restore normalcy, (as President Harding would have so reassuringly called it), to the White House.

FRUSTRATED PRESIDENCY

Unlike President Kennedy's tax breaks in the early sixties, Ford decided to aid the economic slump that LBJ's policies had ignited by issuing tax credits. This was a mistake, which would be repeated by President George W. Bush in the early Presidency of the 21st century. However, instead of people engaging with the merits of Ford's policies (some good, some bad), and the laws passed by Congress at the time (mostly bad), the country wanted to talk about just one thing. Watergate.

Unfortunately, try as he might, President Ford's ability to move the country on from the black stain of the Nixon scandal just proved impossible.

Whenever he was having a press conference, regardless of what the conference was about, he found time and time again the controversies of Nixon's indictment took up half of his time. Something had to be done.

The American people (and certainly the press) knew full-well that President Ford would be the man who got to decide Nixon's fate. He and he alone had the ability to give him a Presidential pardon. I can't say I've ever liked the idea of the Presidential pardon myself. It seems to undermine the core underpinning and principles that the American republic was founded on.

President Ford could have leant in the same direction. He could have said that he disagreed with the principle of the pardon, and so would not exercise it. He could have therefore placed the ball firmly in the court of Congress. That way, he could carry on governing and would have minimised the amount of Watergate-questions he was constantly bombarded with.

Instead, he took each question as it came. He constantly rose to the bait, and reminded everyone all the time that he would be the man who made the final decision regarding Nixon. This mistake caused the majority of his Presidency to be overshadowed by the misdeeds of the previous occupant.

Enough was enough. He had to weigh up the options. By failing to remove the Presidential pardon from the table, Ford sealed his own doom. And he knew it. He felt that he had two options. Either wait for the indictment to surface, allow President Nixon to be convicted and have the saga continue to overshadow the proper business of government, or he could put an end to all of this by announcing that he would pardon Nixon. Either way, Ford must have known, he would almost certainly not have a chance in the next Presidential election.

For the sake of making the rest of his short time in office count, Ford gave a full Presidential pardon to Richard Nixon. Many in the nation felt disgusted. President Ford would have no shot of a term in his own right.

People felt that President Ford had not been in the White House for long enough. He had not built up enough legitimacy in his own right to make that kind of decision. That's why officially renouncing the possibility of a pardon from the start would have been the wisest move. But by the time he made the decision, it was almost too late fix things.

And, along with the continuing troubles of inflation, an increasingly bigger, more controlling state, and other domestic difficulties that America faced, there was a significant foreign problem on the horizon.

SHAMEFUL VIETNAM ENDING

On the other side of the world, the tensions being built between North and South Vietnam were ready to burst. President Nixon decided not to allow commerce and freedom to ignite in both nations, which would have brought voluntary cooperation to the table. Instead, he had simply set groups of people up against each other. The peace would not last; it was built on a house of cards.

North Vietnam broke the peace accord and launched a large-scale offensive into South Vietnam. The atrocities they committed are too numerous to mention here. Suffice to say that the attacks were brutal and sickening. Nixon had, understandably, promised the South Vietnamese that America would intervene if the North tried to take over the South again by force. President Ford therefore, had to act.

The President pleaded with Congress for military and economic aid to stop the South of being dominated. He felt that maybe, just maybe, stopping this offensive and then instigating a more honest noninterventionist foreign policy in the region could solve the problems in Vietnam for good. He was right.

Congress however, were not going to play ball. They were fed up with the mess of Vietnam. Instead of allowing the steps President Ford requested – steps that could have ended the conflict and brought about a lasting peace – Congress decided to betray the South Vietnamese. Many years of suffering, reunification camps and horror awaited thousands of innocent Vietnamese citizens as a result of this decision by the legislative branch.

In the years to come, the noninterventionist policy that Ford wanted to apply (long term) would be implemented, and America would trade with Vietnam again. The world would see the lowering of communist oppression in the region and things would get better. But in the late 70s, that all seemed like a long way off.

It does have to be quickly mentioned of course, that a lot of this is President Nixon's fault. I know, why not blame Nixon – he's the 'bad guy' so it's fun! Nixon's agreement that the South Vietnamese would be protected if the North broke the peace accord, was made in secret. Congress didn't even know about it. The Viet Cong from the North knew that Congress in America didn't know about it. They also knew that they wouldn't have the guts to support it. That is why they decided to attack the South: They knew they could get away with it. It was as simple and as tragic as that.

On April 19th, 1975, Saigon fell to the communist North. People in South Vietnam who believed in freedom, who had supported the CIA and had believed that America would use force to protect the humanitarian liberty that they had fought for, were utterly betrayed.

The image of one of the last helicopters leaving the US Embassy in Saigon, with people climbing over the walls to get to America and freedom, became one of the all-time defining images of American military failure. It should never be forgotten.

President Ford did all that he could to prevent that outcome. But, clouded under the scandal of Watergate and the unpopular pardon he gave Nixon, combined with the desire from most of the American people and Congress to leave Vietnam regardless of the immediate ramifications and the refusal of aid from the legislative branch, left him with little ability to do anything else.

The election of 1976, two hundred years after the forming of the republic, would not be one that would see President Ford back in the White House. Instead, the American people were sold on the idea of a character who was outside of the political elite in Washington.

The electorate was keen for change, even if they weren't quite able to quantify what that change would mean. The Democrats, who were seen as a shoe-in due after the ugly nature of Nixon's brand of Republicanism, had an answer to the 'change' question that the American people were asking.

Voters were down-trodden by federal politics. The actions of the people in power there no longer filled them with confidence. They wanted optimism. They wanted someone who could portray honesty, simplicity, and virtuous morals. They wanted mouth-wash. They wanted a one-term governor from Georgia. They wanted a homely peanut farmer. They wanted Jimmy Carter.

THIRTY-NINE
JIMMY CARTER

Took Office: January 20th 1977
Left Office: January 20th 1981
Party: Democrat
Term: 48

THE MOST EXCITING ASPECT of Jimmy Carter's bid for office, was that he came from almost nowhere. In a typical 'American Dream' style, Carter was a virtual unknown, who the Democrats felt would be able to win them back the White House. Because he was a Washington 'outsider', and even though people felt that his policies were vague and 'gee-wizz' in nature, he captured the immediate desire of America to clean its political decks.

In many ways, his Presidential bid was rather like that of George W. Bush a few decades later. Carter had a life-altering religious experience as an adult. He profited from the immense backing that the evangelical movement gave him. He promised a series of things, and delivered something quite different. There was no real campaigning for any significant increase in government, but that's exactly what they got. Carter promised a more humble foreign policy, but expanded America's role in the world greatly, and entangled intergovernmental associations more than anyone could have guessed.

The idea of a Republican that was even tenuously linked in some ways to Richard Nixon was not going to fly. While many people voted on strict Party lines, I don't think it's unfair to say that almost any one of the Democrats running in the Presidential primaries would have gone on to win the majority of the Electoral College votes.

But due to the 'outsider' image that Carter brilliantly spun, he won the Democratic nomination. As a result, he was all but guaranteed to be the next head of the executive branch.

CARTER'S CHARACTER

Jimmy Carter had spent most of his life in Georgia. He ran a peanut farm. One of his big iconic campaign images was a caricature of himself as a human/peanut hybrid. It had both the dark peanut shell and the big Jimmy Carter teeth. It must have given children in the late 1970s nightmares of the very worst kind.

As he ran for President, he promised to never tell a lie. That's probably the first lie he told on the campaign trail. Other lies, including the idea that America under him would become "a strong nation, like a strong person, [which] can afford to be gentle, firm, thoughtful and restrained", would soon follow.

However, generic platitudes and friendly-sounding gestures were just what America needed. The economy was tanking. Though it was obvious, from an intelligent economic standpoint, that America's troubles would not be fixed if Carter's ideas were implemented, the optimism he espoused did put some people into the right frame of mind. It would be four years later before they could elect someone who would let them practice what they were feeling though.

His small-town boy image worked. He appealed to a certain desire for getting back to the simpler things in life. You can almost hear his supporters today, saying "if only everyone was like Jim, then maybe the world would be a better place". Was this a naïve and inaccurate view of the world? Sure, but it was how people were feeling at the time. He managed to tap into their hope, and capitalised on it perfectly.

He knew that image was important, and the visuals could help him spin things his way. Oddly enough, a great deal of the spin he instigated during his Presidency still resonates with people today, which you can detect when historians give their sycophantic, dewy-eyed recollections of the thirty-ninth President.

His ability to paint a picture that people liked got him inaugurated on January 20th, 1977. He certainly wasn't going to give up this image-manipulation any time soon. He started from day one.

After taking the oath of office, he refused the Presidential limo to the executive mansion. It had all been planned beforehand of course, but he was able to make it look spontaneous, friendly and informal. President Carter walked the entire inaugural parade route from the Capitol building to the White House – just like Thomas Jefferson had done way back in 1801. The crowd loved him for it. The move worked like a charm.

Other visual cues of spin included the way he used his family. The rather cynical image of the President's 'nuclear family' was used to its fullest for the first time with President Carter. His children were always part of the scene and even his beer-swilling brother Billy became a somewhat two-dimensional character. In fact while some describe President Carter's political spinning as 'mouthwash', his brother capitalised on the idea in a much better way, by producing and selling his own label of beer: *Billy Beer*, to be precise.

President Carter was not as soft-headed as his image might have indicated. He was a graduate of the US Naval Academy and served in the Nuclear Submarine programme. How many other Presidents can claim to be nuclear engineers?

Unfortunately his desire for 'marketing' and surface-based politics, made him a very interfering President. He micro-managed every aspect of the job, instead of simply getting the best people to perform in an optimal fashion.

Raised as a Southern Baptist, he was a deeply religious man. The Secret Service code-name for Carter was 'Deacon' as a result. But even his religious conviction was used to political advantage. He was able to win-over the religious Democrats in the South and this almost certainly helped get him the nomination.

TRYING TO CONTROL THINGS

Despite the almost laid-back attitude to things that Carter seemingly demonstrated while running for the Presidency, once he had obtained the job of his dreams, it turned out that he had quite different ideals.

He wanted to control the way that things were run. He wanted to alter the way that societies could be ordered. Despite his election promise of a "thoughtful, restrained" foreign policy, he felt that in many policy areas, he could somehow socially-engineer the world. Like all men who think that things would be better if only they were in control, he ended up feeling very dismayed by the unintended (and frequently disastrous) consequences of his actions.

The President felt that he could make things better by getting the markets to decide less things and getting government to reallocate more things. He thought that if he just took more (and more) money from those who were producing the wealth, and redistributed it to more of those who weren't, then maybe the whole nation would somehow be able to improve its lot.

It didn't. As a result of the tax increases and forced income redistribution that Carter commenced, the economy just got worse and worse.

The social and economic difficulties that America was facing in the 70s because of the financial instigation of President Johnson's Great Society policies, finally exploded under Carter's watch, when combined with his own big-government policies. The thirty-ninth President's straw broke the camel's back. And the camel had been overloaded because of the thirty-sixth President.

The failure of President Carter's idea of control was highlighted by Ronald Reagan, who, when running against the President from Georgia in 1980, summed up the Carter Administrations political philosophy and why it was failing in a typical, elegant-yet-simple Reagan-style: "If it moves, tax it. If it keeps moving, tax it some more. And when it stops moving, subsidise it."

When Carter didn't get what he wanted, he threw his toys out of the pram. There were games that the political class in Washington played. In order to get things done, you often had to play those games too. Refusing and demanding that Congress should 'obey' you because you're the President was, frankly silly. Not to mention rather unconstitutional.

The President can and does inspire and motivate Congress. But that's not due to any technical authority. Carter seemed frustrated that he couldn't 'run' both Houses of the legislative branch. His job title wasn't enough. If he had a good idea (that happened every now and then), he needed to provoke Congress and awaken them to the good that would come out of that idea. He couldn't just sit there and grumble because people didn't agree with him, which is unfortunately what President Carter did all too often.

ACHIEVEMENTS AND FAILURES

This growing increase of governmental control over various industries was beginning to turn ugly. Which industry would cause a serious problem first? It turned out, that the energy production sector would be the first to lash out. Suddenly, everyone was talking about oil.

The summer of 1979 provided images that summed up the Carter years. Pictures of cars, circling block after block, waiting in endless lines, desperately trying to acquire gasoline. The gas shortage was a monumental mess. The President seemed impotent to do anything about it.

The increased taxation of the wealth creators was causing them to spend less money investing in their businesses and less in the economy in general. Of course it was – how could they invest more and keep the economy going if more of their money was taken away from them by the government?

But things weren't all bad for President Carter. Okay, they were mostly bad, but the 1978 Camp David Accords were something monumental. It has to be understood, that President Carter was, on the whole, failing in his domestic agenda and his naïve attitude to controlling the world was making him seem weak. The Soviets were having a field day under Carter. They saw that the President was a weaker man than most, and that they would (and did) run rings around him.

But in between these monumental failures, history has recorded some significant achievements. Carter's time in office did, it must be acknowledged, bring about the liberalisation of certain governmental policies. In a number of respects, the President was actually against the statist position that a lot of his fellow Democrats held dear. This laid the foundations to give certain areas of the economy breathing space, so they could get back on their feet again.

As I said, the Camp David Accords in 1978 have to rank pretty highly in achievements too. Finally peace was successfully brokered between the Egyptians and the Israelis. It took thirteen days. But President Carter finally managed to get the leaders of both countries to agree on a framework of peace. This was without doubt, a truly remarkable accomplishment from a peanut farmer from Georgia.

He wanted to achieve a great deal more peace-brokerage in the Middle East. However, most of this would fail. Again, how many times does it need to be said; non-interventionism works. Entangling alliances doesn't. If America stood back and concentrated on expanding its freedom at home, the beacon of liberty always aids the expulsion of tyranny abroad. And it does so in a way that doesn't give America the blow-back of negative (and sometimes violent or evil) unintended consequences. Like so many before or since, President Carter just didn't get it.

But America as a country was beginning to get it. In fact, they were finally beginning to understand that government couldn't solve the nation's problems. At last, they were beginning to see that the government was the primary cause of the nation's problems.

And Jimmy Carter's time in office was almost certainly going to end as a result of this newly-found clarity from the American people. But before his time in office was up, he had one last significant issue to face. Would this end in success or failure?

IRANIAN CRISIS

The news came as a shock. The Carter policy of 'controlling' the world was beginning to have significant levels of blow-back. In October 1979, Islamic militants stormed the American embassy in Iran. As well as killing some, they took 52 Americans as hostages.

America fell into a deep shock. They saw American diplomats, just regular people like them, being paraded around in front of the cameras while blindfolded. The level of this humiliation was unlike anything that America had ever witnessed before. And America was finally in a constant televisual-news age. There was no getting away from the footage on TV.

President Carter refused to engage in military response. He wanted to go down the slower path of diplomacy. This made even more Americans than before believe that he was too weak to be President. Maybe you think that Carter was taking a noninterventionist approach? Not at all. His interventionism had caused this mess. A noninterventionist would have not got America into that trouble in the first place. But as soon as the situation had occurred, they would have attacked militarily, (after trying any immediate peaceful solution, making it clear to Iran that the next step would be an aggressive one). This would have resolved the situation quickly, and probably before any fighting needed to take place.

Carter instead thought that he could negotiate despite not compromising on his interference in the Middle East. This was a pipedream. And not only did it bring him no respect at home, but the Iranians felt it was laughable too.

The President's image was further weakened by the failed military rescue attempt in 1980. He couldn't make it work on the negotiating table, and he couldn't make it work militarily either. Coincidentally, the 1980 Presidential election took place on the one-year anniversary of the hostages being taken in Iran. Carter wasn't going to win the election anyway, but that didn't do him any favours.

Upon the inauguration of the fortieth President, Jimmy Carter was informed, just minutes after he was no longer Commander-in-Chief, that the Iranians had let the hostages go and that they were safely on their way home. The Iranian authorities had no respect for Carter, but feared that his successor would be infinitely more strong-willed at getting the hostages back. So before the new President

could even take steps to combat the situation, it was already resolved.

Perhaps the Iranians understood what the American people
knew. That the era of governmental expansion over so many decades
had weakened both the liberties and success of America, and increased the oppression and tyranny abroad. It was time for someone
who could bring about the ideals of the Founding Fathers once more,
and end the nuclear gridlock between the free and dictatorial super-
powers.

By an overwhelming landslide, the American people elected a
former b-movie actor and hack radio announcer from California to be
their next President: Ronald Reagan.

FORTY
RONALD REAGAN

Took Office: January 20th 1981
Left Office: January 20th 1989
Party: Republican
Terms: 49 & 50

GOVERNMENT WAS NOT THE solution to our problems. Government was the problem. The American people were, it seemed, finally beginning to understand that again. Many scoffed at Ronald Reagan, the Illinois-born hack radio announcer from General Electric, turned B-movie actor, turned Californian Governor. His bid for President was, by the left-wing elite in the media, considered a relatively silly move. They considered him an imbecile. He would end up proving them all wrong.

Once he had won the Presidency with an overwhelming landslide majority, his critics turned their teasing to something more urgent. They worried that he was an ignorant cowboy, who didn't understand the complexity of Soviet geopolitics. They argued that his description of the Soviet Union as an 'evil empire' was dangerous talk. But Ronnie knew better. He could see that not only would the communist system inevitably collapse, but that confident defiance in the face of their 'sad old relic' of a political system would expedite the empire's final destination on the "ash heap of history" as he so wonderfully put it.

And they warned that his idea that government shouldn't be used to redistribute the wealth was a dangerous idea too. They questioned his supply-side economic ideal, Reaganomics they called it. They said that if the rich paid a lower percentage of their income in tax, then they would pay much less and the poor would suffer. They warned that the rich would get richer, and the poor would get poorer. But they didn't seem to understand the beautiful simplicity of classical-liberal economics that Reagan did. They couldn't get it around their heads quite how right about the economy he really was.

The world watched his remarkable inauguration speech, and wondered. This 'increase in freedom and prosperity at home, while ending tyranny abroad' that he was promising – could he really deliver? They were going to find out that the answer was, in so many ways, an overwhelming yes.

MR. NICE-GUY

There was probably no man liked, even loved, quite so much as President Reagan in Washington. Like so many great men, he didn't have a large number of close friends, but virtually no one who really knew him could bring themselves to dislike him. It wasn't just the American people who took him so closely to their hearts. The political class in D.C. did too. And he didn't just soundly beat Jimmy Carter. He swept his way into office. He beat President Carter in 44 of the 50 states.

During the election campaign, Reagan spoke simple, elegant and (usually) articulate truth. He understood America's role as a bright beacon of liberty and hope in the world. He understood that the freer America was on its domestic issues, then the freer other nations would become too. They would seek to replicate the prosperity and free-will that America would demonstrate as a shining example.

Reagan was the oldest man ever to be elected to the office of President. And to this day, those who served with him still can't quite comprehend how he was able to break the 'rules' of campaigning and win over so many American hearts. His Democratic adversaries would always try and exploit his age, but it never worked. Maybe it was the friendliness and humility that he had that just allowed him to brush that sort of thing off. When re-running for President in the mid-80s, he said during a televised debate that he personally promised to not make age an issue. Not once, he promised, would he exploit his "opponents youth and lack of experience".

When he was dealing with the difficult economic problems he had been left with, he would often (rightly) explain how the Democrats in Congress and in the White House had created a serious mess through inflation, regulation, bureaucracy, wealth-stifling and social-engineering. When a member of the White House press corps asked him if he was to blame at all for any of this, he simply said "Yes. Because for many years, I was a Democrat."

This light-hearted approach and constant joke-making won many people over. And the footage that Americans were constantly exposed to, seemed to endear them to him even more. This wasn't just a stunt for the cameras. He was genuinely a really decent, upbeat and optimistic character. They saw him enjoying a Mexican lunch with his Vice President (and political adversary) George Bush, they laughed at him feeding the White House squirrels, and at lowering tensions between rival nations with friendly affection and endearments.

John Hinckley, a loner obsessed with the actor Jodie Foster and her character in the remarkable Martin Scorsese movie Taxi Driver, tried to assassinate the President. But even this couldn't dampen Reagan's ability to see humour. His calm reassured the nation when he jokingly said "when I saw all those doctors around me, I said 'I hope they're all Republicans'!"

He was the life and soul of any party, and would brighten up any room he was in. There was a certain magnetic charm, people were genuinely drawn to him. And there was more to it than just the fact he was a funny guy, who enjoyed politically incorrect jokes. They could see something important, something real, behind that winning smile and twinkle in the eye.

And his abilities as a performer were second to none. A striking example of this can be seen in that footage of him addressing a packed Congress, during a State of the Union address, where he wanted to explain how overly bureaucratic the systems of Washington had become. He brought with him the documentation from one bill. A few thousand pages. He slammed it on the desk next to his podium platform, grabbing his hand, pretending that it hurt slightly from the sheer weight of the thing. The members of Congress all laughed. He made his point very well. And making his point, was something that he was awfully good at.

He gave his cabinet secretaries a lot of freedom. But, despite the slander from his opponents to the contrary, he was very much the one making decisions. Many complained that he fell asleep during cabinet meetings. This was nonsense of course, and he could have come out and angrily attacked his critics. But instead, he allowed humour to again paint over the ugliness of the remarks.

His first White House Chief of Staff, James A. Baker, has a doodling that Ronald Reagan gave him on day after attending a meeting. At the bottom of his doodles, the President wrote: "Dear Jim, see, I don't fall asleep in ALL the cabinet meetings! Sometimes I do this – trying to get to sleep."

THE GREAT COMMUNICATOR

Very few people in the theatre of politics anywhere in the world have ever been as good as communication as Reagan. Beyond his impressive oratory skills, the language he used also conveyed the right things at the right time.

Some mocked this idea. They thought he was a bumbling puppet, who was being fed his lines like any hack actor. But in the years to come, we would be able to see that in fact most of the really significant stuff he actually wrote himself.

There's too many examples, but here's one that I've copied verbatim (complete with his shorthand and all), from a little speech he wrote himself called simply "America's Strength." Reagan writes: "Our system freed the individual genius of man. Released him to fly as high & as far as his own talent & energy would take him. We allocate resources not by govt. decision but by the mil's. of decisions customers make when they go into the mkt. place to buy. If something seems too high-priced we buy something else. Thus resources are steered toward those things the people want most at the price they are willing to pay. It may not be a perfect system but it's better than any other that's ever been tried."

It's worth reading that passage out loud. The simplicity, truth and brilliance of it defy anything a series of spin doctors could construct. And he was knocking out stuff like this all the time.

He didn't possess the so-called 'common touch'. This is a trite political devise. He was so effortlessly in touch with the common ideals, that he didn't need something so hackneyed. He would spend a great amount of time in the oval office, (always in a suit and tie – he felt that room deserved that respect), endlessly writing personal letters to pen-pals and acquaintances he had met from around the country over the years. He never once thought that such a task was beneath him now that he was the President. If anything, such decent standards were now more important to him than ever before. There was something decidedly Jeffersonian about this. I'm reminded of the third President, and the fact that (as I've often said in this book) it was often Thomas Jefferson who would be the one to answer the door to people who called in at the White House, the President never once thinking that he was too important to ignore such common courtesies to the people he was serving.

Some today consider Reagan a military hawk, but that was far from the case. He desperately wanted to see an end to the Cold War. He knew the war would end of its own accord. But hastening its demise was necessary to speed up the rate at which the oppressed people in the Soviet Satellite-States and indeed Russia herself could claw their way out of poverty and oppression. "A nuclear war", he once said, "cannot be won and must never be fought".

His nickname, The Great Communicator, was defined perfectly on the day that he addressed the nation following the Challenger disaster. The space shuttle had exploded during takeoff, thousands of feet above the earth. The American people were hit with a real shock at the fragility of human life in its attempt to conquer space. President Reagan understood it too. And he bonded so closely with the nation when he described how "We will never forget them, nor the last time we saw them, this morning, as they prepared for their journey and waved goodbye. And slipped the surly bonds of earth, to touch the face of god."

EXPANDING FREEDOM AT HOME
At the time of his election, there were those who felt that the Reaganomic plan of lowering taxes would destroy the government

revenues. And for the most part, they still believe it did. However, the data from the time tells us the real truth.

President Reagan implemented a system developed by Art Laffer. Laffer was the creator of the so-called Laffer Curve. This graph demonstrated the realities of dynamic scoring. Basically, this obvious and intelligent system explains that if government taxes on something like income, are say, at 0%, then the government wouldn't get any revenue. But dynamic scoring and the Laffer Curve show us that also, if government taxes income at 100%, then they also won't receive any income. Incredibly, even today, some try and suggest that this wouldn't be the case. But think about it, why would you bother working to earn money, if the government was going to take all of it in taxes? You wouldn't. And before you get to 100% taxation, there is a huge period (usually anything after 30% at the most) where government revenues will go down due to increased taxation.

That was the basic philosophy of Reaganomics. And it was spot on. He believed that if he lowered the taxes on those who earned lots of money, then they would declare more of their income rather than funnel it elsewhere, and they would actually work more because they got to keep more of their own money, and these two things would actually increase government revenues. Even today, people say that this was not correct, and point out the fact that government debt increased during Reagan's time in office.

However, the facts show us something different. The amount of revenue generated by Americans declaring income at the top rate (in the 70% range in Carter's America) found that now the top rate was a mere 28%. Unsurprisingly, they declared an incredibly huge amount of extra income as a result. And the money that the government received from that 70% tax rate, (somewhere in the two hundred million dollar range), skyrocketed to nearly a billion dollars when that same money was taxed at 28%. As a result, the rich actually ended up really paying their fair share. Government revenues increased dramatically.

Yes, it's true that the national debt grew, but that was because President Reagan was massively funding the military to win the Cold War and prevent it from becoming a 'hot' war. And considering that he succeeded and finally freed the world from the constant tyranny of nuclear annihilation, it was arguably a pretty good price to pay. Both of Reagan's successors would benefit from Reaganomics, by keeping taxes fairly low (certainly not increasing them back to the Carter-era), and not expanding government too much. As a result, by the end of the 90s, the books on American government were balanced again. Really remarkable, and tragically Reagan never receives credit for it.

Others argue that Reagan's economic freedom was a negative thing because the rich got richer and the poor got poorer. This is often said with an unchecked bluntness. However, just like the fallacies against the supply-side Laffer Curve and dynamic scoring, this rich/poor disparity is also a total falsehood.

Did the rich get richer and the poor get poorer? No. They both got richer. And the poor got richer at a much faster rate. I'm serious – the facts are pretty clear. According to the data from the Urban Institute, the bottom quintile of earners saw their incomes rise by 28% during this time in real terms, compared with a rise of 11% for the top quarter of American earners. The facts are staggering.

It's funny now to hear people talk about how ignorant President Reagan was about such complex sciences like economics. But it was clear that he understood it with much more clarity than his opponents ever did. And just 30 minutes listening to his radio addresses (all of which that he wrote himself) shows you just how in tune he was with the 'Austrian' school of economic thought. His familiarity with the work of the likes of F.A. Hayek and Ludwig von Mises shows you just how engaged he really was. And the evidence, (rather than the distorted versions of history that have been passed around), show you just how right he was as well.

EXPULSION OF TYRANNY ABROAD

The incredible overall success of Reagan's domestic agenda didn't quench his appetite for success abroad. He understood that things needed to change overseas. He would grow to mature his opinions of foreign policy. By the end of his time as President, Reagan finally started to realise that it was unhealthy for America to interfere with the "irrationality" (to use his own word) of Middle East politics.

But in other aspects, he was all-too aware that he had inherited a mess that had never been solved. The Soviet empire had caused America to entangle too many alliances with nations, and with his decentralised approach to the cabinet politics, one of these unethical deals would hit him head-on.

It appeared that some in his administration had engaged in what became known as the Iran Contra-Affair. This would be the darkest moment in Reagan's Presidency. The President didn't know any-thing about the illegal scheme that was instigated to fund anti-communist rebels in Nicaragua with proceeds from covert arms sales to Iran. But someone in his staff must have, and it did stain his time in office.

It would appear that some in the National Security Council didn't really buy into the whole noninterventionist thing. They kept Reagan out of the loop (thus breaking all sorts of rules) and instigated the awful deal. However, despite it not really being his fault at all, the President accepted full responsibility. Despite being the Great Com-municator, it would be his most bumbling speech ever, where he said that "a few months ago, I told the American people that I did not trade arms for hostages. My heart, and my best intentions still tell me that's true. But the facts and the evidence tell me it is not."

But his main goal was for the expulsion of tyranny abroad. A second term would be needed to fully instigate this plan. With the economy in incredible health, he was re-elected, and was brought back into office even more impressively than in his first term, winning 49 of the 50 states. And if he had been so cheeky as to ask for a recount, he probably would have gotten a total clean-sweep. He asked Americans bluntly if they felt they were better off. They thought about it, realised that they were, and voted him back into office in record numbers.

Now he could end the Cold War. Not that many people thought it would be that simple. But old Ronnie had a strategy that would finish it for good. It was simple and brilliant.

The general idea was that he would confidently talk down communism, boost America's prosperity, and use taxes to increase military spending to such obscene levels that the Soviets would not be able to compete. Reagan, and almost Reagan alone, felt that this three-pronged attack would accelerate the downfall of a system that was destined to collapse anyway. Turns out, he was dead right.

With the American economy in a giant boom, the first part of his plan was working brilliantly. The Soviets could see with envious eyes how capitalism and freedom was increasing the prosperity for all Americans, while their people had to wait in line for bread that wasn't even there.

He would constantly describe the antiquated and backward nature of the socialist system that Russia had built. He would often use a confident humour to explain it. The careful, weak-willed peace accords that lesser American Presidents, fearful of the 'great' Soviet empire had put in place were things to be joked about by Reagan. "Détente," he once asked, "isn't that what a farmer has with a turkey until Thanksgiving?"

His confidence in America continued to weaken the Russian confidence in their system. But humour against them only went so far. It was when he was at his most serious and biting at their way of life, that the real political damage was done. Reagan's messages of the Soviets collapsing under themselves, inspired the people of places like Poland, who finally thought that maybe they had a real shot at gaining liberty.

Think how inspiring it must have been for people living in the satellite states of the Soviet dictatorship, hearing on pirate radio signals an American President with the courage to say that "communism is another sad, bizarre chapter in human history whose last pages even now are being written." He was the man who finally penned it as the 'evil empire' and, with the world hooked on George Lucas' Star Wars saga at the time, really understood the differences between the free rebellion fighting for a republic, over the dictatorial empire. Interestingly enough, supposedly a deleted scene from the first Star Wars movie contained a line about how the empire would start nationalising private farm ownership. I wonder if Lucas made a conscious decision to develop such a clear analogy?

And another type of fictional Star Wars, of course, proved decisive in the victory over the Soviets. With America's prosperity on the rise, and communism in the dumps, the President only had one final thing to do to secure victory before the decade was over. He had to increase military spending.

He was doing this fairly well, and the Soviets had taken notice. By the time he spoke of the Star Wars system, that would defend America totally even if the Soviets tried to launch a nuclear attack, the powers in Moscow realised that there was no way they could keep up. Peace and a stand-down of arms was inevitable. Of course, the Americans had no way of developing the Star Wars programme. It was a work of fiction, dreamed up by President Reagan. But it worked – the Russian leaders felt that tangible American military strength was already too high for them to combat. Star Wars was a defensive military programme-straw that broke the communist camel's back, if you excuse the bizarre use of that metaphor.

Standing in front of the Berlin Wall, the President called for the Soviets to "tear down this wall." At the time that he said it, people thought he was totally unrealistic. They all felt that Reagan's plan would not work, and that the Soviet Empire was going to last for a good few more decades at least. They said that the Berlin Wall would last much longer than old-man Ronnie would. However, his demand came true. And once the Soviet empire collapsed in 1989, he was invited over to wield one of the sledgehammers onto the Berlin Wall himself. It was a truly joyous moment, and on a personal note, one of the greatest events in my lifetime.

There are still those today that fail to understand how President Reagan's plan worked. They just think he's like the 100th customer in a shopping mall, who got lucky by being at the right place at the right time. That notion is nothing but nonsense. The plan Reagan initiated, could have been started under any of the previous Presidents before him, and it would have ended the Cold War much sooner. If he had not taken the Soviets on in the way that he did, then I'm sure that the 'evil empire', and all the misery with it, would have continued into the early part of the 21st century.

But one man, Ronald Reagan, demanded an end to this suffering of humanity as soon as possible. He put his talent, courage and brilliance into the struggle and won. He changed the course of American politics, and the politics of the world. He ignited an economic success that, bumps in the road aside, remained for decades. The world was profoundly better after his two successful terms. Hardly surprising then, that, because they couldn't vote for him a third time (the Constitution now forbid it), they turned to his Vice President, despite the fact that he didn't really share a lot of Reagan's values and politics deep down.

When President Reagan finally died in June of 2004, after a long spell of Alzheimer's disease robbing his ability to recall his past achievements, the entire nation went into a period of deep mourning. Though in his last years he would not have been able to recall his vast accomplishments, a great many Americans do. It's important that no one allows that light of historic truth to be extinguished.

It's worth wrapping this discovery into Ronald Reagan's Presidency with this little moment that yet again sums up the character of the man and why America loved him and his charming self-deprecation. When he was asked how he will spend his time after he leaves the White House, considering all the incredible things he had achieved, he simply said "I'm looking forward to going home at last, putting my feet up and taking a good nap." Then, after a beat, with a twinkle in his eye: "I guess it won't be that much different after all."

FORTY-ONE
GEORGE HERBERT WALKER BUSH

Took Office: January 20th 1989
Left Office: January 20th 1993
Party: Republican
Term: 51

THE FUNDAMENTAL DIFFERENCE BETWEEN Reagan and Bush, was that Reagan understood the people should be and were better than the government at solving the problems of the day. Reagan's opponent for the Republican Presidential nomination of 1980, George Herbert Walker Bush, believed deep down that government could fix most things. However, like most politicians who believed this, Bush didn't know how to spell it out properly. In order to keep the Republican base happy, Reagan had Bush as his running mate (but gave him very little to do in terms of real importance once in office).

When, two terms later, Bush ran for the Presidency, he had to retract from his previous rhetoric. The American people loved Reagan, and the success of his economic strategy was very clear. Bush had to conveniently forget that he called the supply-side economic system "voodoo economics". He had to promise that he wouldn't return to his old beliefs. On the campaign trail, he said time and time again "Read my lips. No more new taxes".

Though his heart still wasn't into Reaganomics, and though many of the American people suspected this was the case, he was seen has slightly more 'Reagan' than his Democratic challenger, so the American people chose "better the devil you know, than the devil you don't". On January 20th, 1989, George H. W. Bush was sworn in on the steps of the Capitol Building as the 41st President of the United States.

ASSESSING THE MAN

George Bush became the first sitting Vice-President to an election since the mutton-chopped Martin Van Buren back in 1836. But his résumé was long and distinguished. He had been a Texan member of the House of Representatives for two terms, a UN Ambassador, and was even at one point the head of the CIA – the first President to have previously had that role.

He was born in the state of New England, and had made his fortune as a successful oil man in Texas. Somehow he was able to juggle his busy and thriving work life with looking after the six children he and his wife Barbara had. Graduating from Yale, he had a competitive streak that really came out from his love of sports. Right into his old age, he would end up skydiving and all sorts.

He was loyal and fairly smart. But one of his most significant traits was his patience. He would happily wait for the pieces of the diplomatic puzzle to form before he would move on to advance his own agenda. He was a man quite comfortable with waiting for the right time to strike.

Some of his critics had a hard time attacking him. While many of the Reagan-Republicans disagreed with many aspects of President Bush's political philosophy, some of the left fundamentally shared his belief that the supply-side system was "voodoo economics". This put the left in a tough position. If he believed in bigger government in many areas, how could they come at him? Bizarrely, they took his Yale-graduate image and portrayed him as a bit of a wimp. Now I might not be the world's biggest fan of President Bush (certainly when compared to Reagan), but to call him a wimp is quite a stretch.

After all, George H. W. Bush was a World War Two hero. Period. He flew airplanes and was blown out of one of them when fighting the Axis powers. I mean seriously, he should have died, but managed to just about get out in time and onto an American naval vessel. You can (and I will) criticise President Bush for a lot of things. But you have to live on another planet to call him a wimp.

REAGAN-LITE
President Bush wanted to show the world that he was basically the continuity candidate from Reagan, at least to get elected. However, he was concerned that some of the criticisms of his predecessor would stick to him as well. As we've covered better than you'll find almost anywhere else, Reagan was far from an aloof President. He was thoroughly engaged with the big issues of the day. In fact, he was often the driver of the main issues.

But the media had portrayed Reagan (inaccurately) as an impassive President. Many, despite the clear evidence to the contrary, still do today. President Bush didn't want this to happen to him. He wanted to be seen as fully engaged with everything important.

He would run around all day long, getting photo-ops and would have to be at the head of every major discussion. I have to be fair here. President Bush was a fairly smart guy, and he had lots of really important stuff to contribute, but a lot of his engagement was just empty posturing.

He cared deeply about public opinion. Reagan did too, but Reagan only cared in so much as he wanted to change opinions, and shape the direction of the country towards a more freedom-focused agenda. President Bush on the other hand wanted to know what the public was thinking so that he could get into the centre of that opinion and claim to represent it. The difference between Reagan and Bush are the differences between a President who has conviction and a President who wanted to please the centre-ground.

So did President Bush violate the direction that Reagan had moved the country? Only in marginal ways of little significance. And, like all politicians who incorrectly thought that there was no truth in supply-side economics, he ended up, in many little ways, being a victim of its rules.

A good short example of that: he wanted to make it seem like he was clamping down on 'outrageously rich' people, (by the way, who cares if they're 'outrageously rich'? As long as the poor are getting richer at the same time and even at a faster proportional rate, who cares? But that's what happens when you pander to the centre). So what would be a symbolic way of showing that you're going to take these 'super-rich' folk down a peg or two? He created an additional tax on the purchase of yachts in America. You might think that made sense: Rich people buy yachts right?

Again, if he understood supply-side economics, he would have realised the foolishness of this action. The followers of Reaganomics predicted exactly what would happen as a result. They were spot on. Basically, rich potential yacht-buyers, in order to avoid paying his yacht-tax, bought their boats outside of the United States, where they paid no tax to the American government. The yacht industry in the US suffered as a result, meaning many poorer/working class people employed by yacht companies lost their jobs, (going on welfare as a result), and as well as having to spend more on unemployment bene-fit, the government made less money in revenue than it would have if it had just done nothing. There are many examples of this incom-petence throughout American politics. Such a shame that it didn't fully die out once Reagan had so brilliantly made the case against it.

THE TWO BIG WARS

President Bush and his executive branch legacy are defined however, not by the retractions of Reagan economic policy, or even the slight expansion and control of government in the domestic arena, (though this expansion is what brought about his downfall in the end). Bush is remembered for two things: the end of the Cold War, and the commencement of the Gulf War against Saddam Hussein.

Following on from the passionate call to arms that Reagan had instigated, Bush was lucky enough to be President when the Berlin Wall finally came down. However, he played it very smartly. He knew that there could be a lasting peace if he exercised his calm and decent patience and didn't use this as an opportunity to ruffle the egotistical feathers of the Russians.

A politician in Washington at the time made the remark "if it was me [in the White House] right now, I'd be dancing on top of the Ber-lin Wall." But Bush knew he had to be smarter than that. Coming across as smug about it all and bruising the Soviet ego would not help finally dismantle the empire, and may prolong the agony. This carefully intelligent and humble policy allowed the Cold War to end with a whimper and not with a bang. And for that, we all should be thankful.

In the August of 1990, President Bush finally had his most diffi-cult foreign policy task. The dictator of Iraq, Saddam Hussein, a man whom the Americans had effectively installed previously, (yet again, violating the Jefferson policy of non-interventionism), invaded neighbouring Kuwait. With a solemn tone in his voice (or as solemn as he could try to be), the President pointed out that Iraq had "thus far, turned a deaf ear to the voices of peace and reason." Maybe if America had not installed Saddam Hussein in the first place, this wouldn't have been happening.

Publicly on TV, President Bush was strongly condemning the actions of the Iraqi leader. Behind closed doors however, he was pulling every diplomatic string that he could. While he was (rightly) emphasising the humanitarian nature of a military venture to defend Kuwait, there was also another issue at stake for the President: protecting the energy reserves of the Persian Gulf. America needed that oil. Too many rules against domestic drilling existed, so the Gulf oil supplies were needed and significant alternative renewable energy resources were a long way off.

The President worked hard and successfully built a coalition within the United Nations to tackle Saddam. He was fairly honest, and made the case for protecting the oil reserves, which seemed to serve the interest of most of the political leaders in the West. He successfully built an international coalition of 34 countries to remove Saddam Hussein from Kuwait. He very much cared about what the other nations thought, and was especially keen to keep many of the Arab nations on his side too. He would let them see what he was doing and for what purpose. He also persuaded them that supporting the Gulf War was in their interest too. Whether or not you can agree with it, his ability to achieve this coalition was really quite a remarkable feat.

Once the war had begun, and an endgame was set, President Bush set the agenda out clearly. When visiting the troops, he said "we are not here on some exercise, this is a real-world situation. And we're not walking away until our mission is done; until the invader is out of Kuwait." The 'endgame' strategy was not to undo the

American interventionist mistake of the past and destroy Saddam Hussein's regime. That policy, with all its negative results, would have to wait until one of President Bush's sons took power years later.

There was less than six weeks of aerial bombardment from the American forces. Then the ground assault against Saddam Hussein's Republican Guard began. Within hours, the Iraqi Army was in full retreat from Kuwait. Saddam's soldiers were surrendering on-mass.

Bush was quite happy for Saddam Hussein to be targeted and killed during the war against the Iraqi Army, as he was the leader of that Army and therefore was a perfectly valid war aim. But to go after him afterwards was not on the agenda for President Bush. For the time being, the Iraqi dictator would remain in power. Opening free-markets up with Iraq immediately after the war might have seen Saddam toppled by his own people, or at the very least, there would have been a policy shift in Iraq towards more freedom. However, unfortunately, that didn't seem to be on President Bush's agenda either.

After the success of the war, and with Kuwait free, Bush's approval ratings soared to 84%. The odds of him being re-elected in 1992 seemed likely. But the slight switch to less free-market policies, and an incapability to shrink the size of government down as Reagan had intended after the Cold War, was causing a significant debt that the American people were rightly getting anxious about.

FINAL FAILURE
Unable to make the case for a more limited government, and because he couldn't really understand the supply-side system, President Bush had to do the only thing that was left. Raise taxes. Suddenly the argument "read my lips, no more new taxes" sounded silly when he was introducing large tax increases and government intervention in

the markets in so many ways.

Unsurprisingly, this caused the President to be unseated after just four years by a very charismatic man from Arkansas who openly promised the left that he would increase certain areas of the government and nudge up taxes, and quietly suggested to the right that he'd return to Reaganomic normalcy by keeping the taxes low overall and allow the budget to balance. In the end, he would turn out to sit firmly in the centre. And America seemed just fine with that.

FORTY-TWO
BILL CLINTON

Took Office: January 20th 1993
Left Office: January 20th 2001
Party: Democratic
Terms: 52 & 53

AFTER TWELVE YEARS OUT of the executive mansion, the Democrats were finally back. William Clinton, from Arkansas, understood that the American people loved the era of freedom and prosperity under Ronald Reagan. He knew that in order to both win over those people and his base on the left, he would have to lead from a position of moderation and the centre.

And it worked. Those on the left who were fed up with the Republicans and those who were missing the era of Reagan both saw a little bit of what they wanted from Clinton. By leading from the centre ground, he would end up pleasing and annoying both groups.

Clinton was a real personality. However, it seemed a bit like he didn't have much substance behind his personable approach. Sadly, rather like George W. H. Bush, he was someone who would pander to opinion. Whereas Reagan wanted to know what public opinion was so that he could shape it, Clinton wanted to know what public opinion was so that he could tell people that he represented that opinion.

THE ROCK 'N ROLL PREZ

President Clinton was the first man in the executive mansion who appeared to want to be a real celebrity. He played the saxophone and if he couldn't be a rock star, seemed like he would settle for being the President instead.

His campaign for office was youthful and, despite the lack of real substance, was energetic and full of passion. The Clinton political campaign was a bit like a vague student rally: "What do we want?" "Erm, something good," "When do we want it?" "Now!"

And who cares about policy? This was a man who revealed on MTV what type of underwear he preferred (I didn't look it up, sorry – couldn't bring myself to do it). Also other areas of intrigue were beginning to emerge. Clinton was spending quite a chunk of time during the campaign trail, having to play down the allegations of extra marital affairs.

Like a number of Presidents before him, Bill Clinton came from a working class background, and had used his significant IQ to better his situation. He was literally another success story from the application of the American Dream. And in Washington, there were few people quite so adept at the game of politics. He was a real natural.

He had an incredible ability to inspire, even if the real messages he was given were rather vague and 'gee-wizz' in nature. If he was at a fundraiser for example, when he got up to the podium and spoke, he'd be able to make it feel like he was personally communicating with every individual in the room. People would walk out at the end of the speech thinking "Wow, Bill was really speaking to me back there".

And of course, we have to talk about the infamous Bill Clinton handshake. It's a political technique that many in business try to replicate, and very few can do it quite so well as President Bill. He would start by grabbing your hand, then his other hand would move in (two hands, very sincere you see), and then the other hand would go up your arm and before you know it, he's got you in an all-embracing bear hug.

Following on from this 'phony empathy' hugging gesture, it's unsurprising that President Clinton was the author of the rather vacuous phrase "I feel your pain". It's a faux-sincere verbal posture. He could therefore play the heartfelt card, without having to actually be heartfelt in any meaningful way. Clinton's form of empathy was like eating junk food. It would fill you up, but probably had no significant good nutritional value. Incidentally, Clinton really *LOVED* junk food, which might explain why he put on so much weight after leaving the oval office.

President Clinton was a Yale graduate and Rhodes scholar. His management style was rather chaotic – people would turn up to meetings in jeans, everyone would be late (especially Clinton himself) and productivity would often suffer as a result. But in government, having an executive branch that was slowing itself down is probably a good thing, don't you think? If they're able to get a few less laws passed and so on, then all for the better.

CENTRE GROUND

Just think for a moment of Clinton, spending time in the White House bumbling through with all-night policy talks, massive personnel meetings, and formal discussions in casual dress. Sounds noble, and in many respects a lot of it was. But on the whole, President

Clinton was just constantly trying to gauge opinion more than anything else.

He would bring together a lot of people from all different sides of a debate, and figure out which perspective was the most popular to the American people. Whichever one he decided to throw his weight behind, was usually done out of a sense of increasing his popularity rather than a personal 'right or wrong' morality.

But while he was weighing up the value of everyone's opinions to a degree of equality, the one person who had the most influence over his policy directions was his wife, Hillary.

When he was running for the office of President in the first place, it was always made clear that it was going to be a "buy one get two" deal for the American people. Bill Clinton would be the President, but Hillary would have a great degree of authority.

Hillary was the first Presidential spouse to have an office actually in the West Wing. This almost caused unconstitutional scenarios where there were virtually two Presidents. A member of the cabinet or Congress could take an issue to Bill and be turned down, but if you could get Hillary on-side, there was a chance that she'd be able to change his mind. Old news footage from the 90s of Hillary Clinton talking from the Presidential podium, with her husband, (the actual President, remember), down and to her side, are still very odd to look at indeed.

Clinton had made some progress. He had successfully signed the North American Trade Agreement, or NAFTA, that allowed much more free trade between Canada, Mexico and the United States. Some rightly wondered, why get government involved in a scheme like that at all? Why not just let the free market operate with less oversight and control?

He had areas of total failure though. For example, his healthcare reform bill was rejected by Congress. They rightly saw that government intervention in the healthcare system had caused many problems for decades. Yet more intervention wasn't going to fix anything, it was just going to make things worse.

In foreign policy, Clinton's actions also had mixed results. He pushed (and managed to get) a NATO-based strike on Kosovo to halt a genocide, and he was unsuccessful at galvanising the failing peace process between Israel and Palestine. Generally he was an interventionist, and the policies of interventionism that he both inherited and continued would grow to have horrifying unintended consequences after he left office.

EXECUTIVE VS. LEGISLATURE

Congress were often launching investigations into various scandals from the executive branch. Travelgate, White water, and many other concerns surrounding Clinton were being raised. One of the most notable scandals had to be the filing of a sexual harassment charge and lawsuit against the President from Paula Jones.

And their power continued to get more pronounced. In the 1994 mid-term elections, the continued desire by the American people to see a return to Reagan-style government saw the Republican Party regain both the House of Representatives and the Senate for the first time in forty years. The fight between the executive and legislative branches of government started to seriously begin again.

In a great many respects, ironically, this is what made Clinton's time in office fairly successful. Because Democrat Clinton himself didn't want to raise taxes that much, the Republican Congress fought to keep the rises to a minimum. And whenever he wanted to expand government, the Congress fought most of his significant measures. So you had a stalemate of government, which the American people greatly benefitted from.

By limiting the speed of which government expanded, and by

keeping taxes reasonably low to promote the increase in economic prosperity, there came an inevitable point when the governments' books finally balanced.

Ironically President Clinton, the man who had fought for this not to happen (by constantly pushing for new government spending all the time), was given a lot of the credit. Credit he gratefully accepted.

As a result, President Clinton secured a very decent second term against Dan Quayle, George H. W. Bush's Vice President. Quayle was a man who, during the campaign trail, accidently revealed that he couldn't spell the word 'potato'. So on second thoughts maybe the victory for Clinton wasn't quite as impressive as some think.

So the on-going fight between the legislative branch (Congress) and the executive branch (Presidency) caused a bit of a 'stall' in the federal government. This stall meant that government interfered a lot less than it otherwise would have done into the everyday lives of the American people.

Unsurprisingly, this stall allowed the Americans to work, save, invest and generally improve their lives without the government breathing down their neck and standing on their shoes. Prosperity and social mobility improved as a result.

All this made President Clinton even more of a political centrist, keen to capitalise on the goodwill that the people had. The reason for the goodwill was of course, slightly misguided. Because Clinton was doing less than he otherwise would have wanted, America prospered. But a great deal of the American people saw the President as the cause of this improvement.

I know it sounds crazy when you spell it out like this, but people just don't really think this logically in their everyday lives. They just think "well, I'm doing better now than I was four years ago. And for the last four year that Bill Clinton guy was the President, so I guess another four more years of him will be a good thing because he must be in some way responsible."

And while on the most part, the economic and social prosperity for most Americans persisted during Clinton's second term, the scandals involving his love life were growing. And they would end up dominating a significant chunk of time in office.

SCANDAL

The President had been fighting for some time with Congress over the federal budget. It was simply a difference of political point of view. By and large, the Republicans were in the right – expanding the government budget would undermine the good economic progress of America and could bankrupt the government at a time when the books were actually looking pretty good for the first time in an age.

The refusal to compromise in 1995 led to a government shutdown. A great many Washington staffers had to go home because they would not get paid. Just think of it – people not working or able to things done in Washington; no wonder the progress of the American people was so astronomical at the time!

Clinton eventually won a lot of the battles that were going on during this shut down. He was able to use all of his charisma, political cunning and ability to spin to blame the shut down on the 'heartless, uncompromising' Republicans. In the end, the Republicans had no choice but to make the compromises Clinton was accusing them of not wanting to do.

So while battling Congress, and while painting the Republicans as being the cause of the government shut down, the White House found itself with very few members of working White House staff. In order to maintain the basic infrastructure, Clinton hired interns. One of these unpaid interns, by the name of Monica Lewinski, was able to get unusually close to the President.

Just into President Clinton's second term in office, when finally the federal budget balanced for the first time since Andrew Jackson's Presidency, everything went wrong.

In August 1998, President Clinton's oval office affair with Monica Lewinski became public when Lewinski was called to testify in the Paula Jones case. Now we don't know how many of the women that claimed Clinton slept with him actually did, but if you ever get a chance to see photos of them, have you ever noticed how they all look rather similar? The big hair, overdone make up and 'glam' image? Just worth mentioning...

Any way, it was pretty clear that Lewinski and the President had been getting up to some naughty shenanigans in the oval office. However, Clinton decided to lie about it. "I did not have sexual relations with that woman," he said. He should have taken a leaf out of Grover Cleveland's book: when there's a scandal, just confess, say you're sorry, and move on. The American people praise your honesty and it's all done with. But Clinton chose to drag it out, with awful consequences that his last years in office were sucked into. The sympathy that came out for his wife however, was pretty strong. She would go on to dominate the political scene for many years to come.

By lying about the affair, on December 19th, 1998, he was impeached. He was the second President in history to be so. Just like with Andrew Johnson back in the mid-late 1800s, when the impeachment decision had reached its conclusion, the actual process of removing him from office stalled. And in fairness, with regards to Clinton, who wants to remove a President for something so pathetic?

And what was really pathetic, was while America was worrying about sex in the oval office at home while feeling indifferent about the continued foreign interventionism abroad, a twisted and bitter man called Osama Bin Laden was in the mountains of Afghanistan planning an attack on American soil of such horror and devastation, that it would define the next Presidency.

But who would be the next President? As it would turn out, the American people would bizarrely not get to know the answer to that question over a month after the day of the election.

FORTY-THREE
GEORGE WALKER BUSH

Took Office: January 20th 2001
Left Office: January 20th 2009
Party: Republican
Terms: 54 & 55

THE CRUCIAL CHOICE IN the 2000 Presidential election was basically a choice between either beige or grey. Al Gore, President Clinton's Vice President, ran under the angle that he was the continuity candidate. But he lacked real personality. He had a strong left-wing instinct, but seemed like he was going to keep that under wraps to appease the American people. He tried in vain to tell Americans that he was his "own man", but many just didn't buy it.

And the Republicans made an interesting choice. Deciding to sideline the maverick (and slightly too interventionist) John McCain, they instead picked George W. Bush – son of the forty-first President. He shared some of his fathers' looks, and some of his fathers' policies. Some were wary that, like his dad, he didn't really understand supply-side economics and the benefits of decentralised government. But he was certainly saying the right things, even if they were platitudes. He promised a real return to non-interventionism. He said that America needed to return to a "humble foreign policy". That sat well with a number of the Reagan Republicans, who were still feeling sidelined from the process since Ronnie left the White House.

As it turned out, he would u-turn practically all of these principles. But before we even get to that, we need to explain how a Presidential election between two of the dullest candidates seen in a generation turned into one of the most hotly contested legal fights in American political history.

ELECTORAL FARCE

Days and weeks after the Presidential election, it seemed like the winner would never be found. The race was simply too close to call. There are some that say that Al Gore won the popular vote (that's still the official line from when they stopped counting) and that George W. Bush won the Electoral College votes (again, that was the final official verdict).

People on both sides, who were fairly indifferent before, suddenly were galvanised into pushing for 'their man'. But who really should have won? It's still a question that invokes grand debate. But it really shouldn't, once you look at the figures properly.

Basically the number of votes cast were very close. That's it. We'll never quite know who really won the popular vote because even if the main contentious state (Florida) went to Al Gore instead of George W. Bush, then Bush's people would have demanded a recount on some of the other contentious states that went for Gore. If they had done that, a number of those states would have almost certainly swung back to Bush, meaning that either way Bush would have won.

Al Gore, to his credit, seemed to understand that. So despite the Supreme Court finally handing the election to George W. Bush on what appeared to be purely partisan (5-4) lines, Al Gore decided not to take it any further. In fact, letting the unjustified resentment that some of his supporters had continue to boil ("we were robbed!") meant that he was able to capitalise on this and go on to make a successful career as a highly partisan 'environmental' campaigner, producing, amongst other things, the alarmist anthropogenic global warming polemic *An Inconvenient Truth*. This won the Academy Award for best documentary.

So Al Gore recognised that it was incredibly close, and didn't quite go his way. He moved on. Maybe everyone else should have done that too.

9/11

When elected, George W. Bush, a Yale graduate, joined John Quincy Adams as the only Presidential son to win the White House. He was the only President ever elected with an MBA – he was actually smarter than his often bumbling inarticulate speech suggested.

He would go on to run a pretty tight ship too. In contrast to the Clinton White House, with all its chaos and over-relaxed meeting style, President Bush did things very differently. Everyone had to be very punctual, or they would miss their meeting with the Commander-in-Chief. If you were late, it was considered rude and unacceptable. Everyone would be in their suits – no 'jeans and t-shirt meetings' here. The meetings were prompt, brief and formal.

Many believed that based on the incredibly close election he had won, that he would run on a fairly centrist line. A great number in the media predicted, (even hoped) for a small, fairly indifferent Presidency. However, this would not happen for two reasons. The first, his own personal instincts for a bigger government and increasingly centralised control in the hands of the executive, which despite playing these beliefs down during the election, became very evident very quickly. And secondly, the horrific and evil events of September 11th, 2001.

I happened to be just down the road from President Bush on September 11th 2001. He was up at a school in Florida to talk about education. He had created a new layer of federal bureaucracy in the education system called 'no child left behind' which, like so many of these things, ended up as yet another overall federal government failure. While he was sitting in a classroom, listening to the children recite from a book, he was informed of the news. A plane had been hijacked by terrorists and had crashed into one of the twin towers of the World Trade Centre in New York. America was under attack.

After taking a minute to take the information in, and in order not to panic the children in the class, as well as the nation at large, I think that President Bush acted appropriately. And the teacher who was in the classroom at the time agreed. She later said when interview that "I did not vote for him during the election, but [based on the way he acted] on that day I would have voted for him."

He composed himself, stood up, and told the class and the public that something had just occurred that required his urgent attention. Even at that moment, the real horror of what was happening had not quite fully manifested itself.

Two planes had hit the twin towers of the World Trade Centre, causing both towers to collapse. Another plane had been forcibly crashed into the Pentagon. A forth, United 93, had deliberately crash-landed into a field, seemingly by the brave passengers who knew what was going to happen and did what they could to stop it. Their actions, it has been suggested, prevented the White House or some other important symbol of America from being destroyed.

Almost every one of us in the United States at that time was hit with contradictory senses of fear, brotherhood, and defiance. America was shaken, but stood united and bold. Standing on the ruins of the twin towers, President Bush told the people of New York "I hear you, America hears you, and the people who knocked these buildings down will hear all of us soon."

Despite his usual lack of articulation, the President hit the rhetoric on the head. The Americans wanted to hear defiant words in support of freedom and the American tradition of liberty at such horrific times. Though highly scripted, the way President Bush handed his key speeches in the days after 9/11 were spot on. In the very evening following those awful events, he described perfectly to the American people how the countries way of life, its very freedom came under attack in a series of attacks. But he rightly reminded them that "these acts shatter steel. But they cannot shatter the steel of American resolve. No one will keep that light from shining."

DISASTER SOCIALISM

With the overwhelming support from the American people, and with military support of many other nations, (particularly Great Britain – America's strongest ally – who suffered a great number of citizen losses in the 9/11 attacks too), President Bush commenced a military strike on Afghanistan.

And from then, things went wrong. Instead of pounding the mountain-ranges between the borders of Afghanistan and Pakistan, knocking Al Qaeda (the terrorist network led by Osama Bin Laden who had caused 9/11) into the Stone Age, a difference approach was taken.

The strikes were more careful, and were designed not just to retaliate and make the prospect of attacking America too horrifying to any other would-be terrorist group, America tried to carefully target the Taliban, the backwards draconian dictatorial government who ran Afghanistan. This brought about the prospect of nation-building and increasing foreign interventionism all over again. America's one-month strike would turn into years of difficult, potentially unwinnable struggling, infrastructure-building, and guerrilla warfare.

This laid the foundation for a neoconservative agenda. Some rightly call this philosophy 'disaster socialism'. It's the creation of big government interventionist policies based on the idea that catastrophe and "another 9/11" were just around the corner unless America gave the federal executive branch more power and authority. Again, it would seem, the dwindling Reagan Republicans and more libertarian-minded politicians were going to be isolated from the political scene once more.

And while we're talking about libertarians, of course, those good ol' boys the Founding Fathers already had the perfect solution to defeat Islamofascist terrorism. Noninterventionist foreign policy and free trade. Had America just poured hell-fire on Al Qaeda, then proceeded to drop all the trade barriers with Afghanistan and the rest of the Middle East, then it really would have been "mission accomplished", as President Bush wrongly called it so early into the campaign. The horrific governments in states that were harbouring terrorists would have fallen as their people craved more and more trade with free nations like America. Then the world truly would have been safer. This would have been the full success of a non-isolationist/non-interventionist foreign policy.

However, by declaring nation-building as part of the American project in Afghanistan, President Bush allowed many of the fascist Middle East dictatorships to posture against the United States, and the grievances (mostly imagined) against America were allowed to fester. As a result, Al Qaeda and other such terrorist networks found that it was easier to recruit weak-minded people into sacrificing themselves for 'the cause'.

Bush's isolationist/interventionist policies came to a head with Iraq. Saddam Hussein had a series of WMDs (Weapons of Mass Destruction) left over from the previous Gulf War. Had he destroyed them? Or more likely, was he keeping them for another attack some day? The President was given evidence from the CIA, MI5 and secret service agencies all around the world, which suggested Saddam still had his weapons. As part of his 'War on Terror', Bush targeted Iraq next. Along with North Korea and Iran, he declared that Iraq was part of the 'Axis of Evil'.

Many say that the war in Iraq was about oil. Actually, not going to war with Iraq was really where the unethical oil money went. The UN was a big joke to Saddam Hussein. By effectively paying off France, Russia and China (three of the five permanent members of the Security Council), with cheap oil, he had 'bought the jury' and it meant that the UN wouldn't ever allow Britain and America to commence a military strike against Iraq, regardless of the evidence. So George Bush, like his father, had to string together another so-called 'collation of the willing' to fight if need be. Unlike the forty-first President though, Bush Jr. had to put his collation together outside of the UN.

After the UN weapons inspectors continued to be messed around by Saddam (was he stalling them long enough to destroy and/or sell off his WMDs perhaps?), America and the rest of the collation finally struck.

Once more, instead of targeting the weapon-stocks and opening the barriers to free trade, (and accelerating the demise of Saddam's government), the President attempted to nation-build again. This dragged Britain, America and other nations into a long and bloody war that lasted years instead of weeks.

Despite mainstream belief, there actually <u>were</u> WMDs in Iraq. The republican guard fired some of the rockets that are internationally recognised as WMDs on American troops. What wasn't found though, were the chemical and biological weapons, and the significant building-blocks of a nuclear arsenal. However, the evidence that was discovered suggested that these had either been dismantled or removed in the run-up to war. Seemed like Saddam had taken Bush's military threat to heart. The UN dithering had allowed him to brush away a great deal of the evidence. The mainstream media seemed to disregard this interesting fact as news though.

REPUBLICAN SOCIALISM

Bush solidly won a second term against Democratic challenger John Kerry. Kerry had flip-flopped on the war in Iraq and when asked what he would have done differently, instead of making the case for noninterventionist policies, would simply say that unlike Bush, "I would get the job done right". To this day, I don't think anyone, even John Kerry, knew exactly what that meant.

While the failure of interventionism and disaster socialism was becoming more apparent abroad, President Bush was also pushing through oodles of legislation that I call 'Republican socialism'. He created massive new authoritarian federal bureaucracy called the 'Department of Homeland Security'. He increased the size and the budgets of many of the federal departments, sometimes at eight or more times the rate of inflation.

He centralised government in a way never thought possible. And, it must be said, in a way that would have horrified the Founding Fathers. Government didn't just get a little bigger under Bush, it got obscenely massive.

According to the Competitive Enterprise Institute, in 2007 alone fifty agencies brought 3,595 new rules into play. Of these new rules, 45% came from just five agencies; Commerce, Agriculture, Homeland Security, Environmental Protection and the Treasury.

And the rules and regulations on banking were easily the worst. American banking policy had changed a great deal since its free-market origins in the late 1700s. Some of the draconian regulations from the early part of the 20th Century had been removed by Congress bit by bit over the decades. But they hadn't just been removed; for every piece of backwards-regulation struck from the books, there were fifty pieces of woolly, light-touch, bureaucratic, loophole-inducing regulation added that caused all sorts of perversions of the market. They caused all sorts of unintended consequences that the free market would not have done.

These pieces of regulation, measuring in their thousands, had over the years combined with thousands more from the IMF and World Bank, as well as more from the rest of the nations of the world, to turn the free-market banking system (that never had any serious recessions) into the most regulated industry the world had ever known. This new disaster-prone recession-crazed boom-and-bust economy was something Americans and citizens of the world had become used to. They couldn't even imagine going back to a time before the Federal Reserve, Bank of England, etc. when the free market used to prevent such things. However, as we've seen from the Great Depression and so on, whenever there's a crash in the market due to the regulation, governments usually step in, blame the free market and 'greedy' people, and regulate some more, leaving disastrous results for the future. The same was true towards the end of President Bush's time in office.

THE CREDIT CRUNCH

Every politician loves it if they can say that standards of living have improved on their watch. They can take the credit, and either win re-election, or go down in history favourably. That is why, over the years, governments had regulated how banks gave out mortgages to homeowners.

Instead of allowing the free market to do its thing, they intervene. In the free market system, the bank would assess whether or not it was economically viable to give a certain person (or persons) a mortgage. If they were unlikely to pay it back, then it probably wasn't worth the risk. When the overall economy is good, they can take more risks, and also more people are better off and can afford a mortgage. When the economy is in bad shape, they give out fewer loans, because less people can pay them back and the money supply is limited. Over time, in a free market, the economy would be better and more stable, and more people would be able to afford a home loan. Simple.

But then politicians get involved. They wanted more people being able to afford homes all the time, so they can say that tangible living standards have improved on their watch. So most Presidents in the twentieth century set up policies and rules in the banking industry that forced banks to give out mortgages that weren't as economically viable. Mortgages that were literally 'sub prime'. They forced the banks to loan more with 'easy money' policies, with the unwritten guarantee that the big banks that play ball were 'too big to fail' (i.e. the big corporatist special interests were going to be bailed out if need be, so long as they play along).

Eventually, towards the end of President Bush's second term in office, the economic crash that most libertarian 'Austrian-school' economists had predicted finally occurred. Powered on by large government controlled/run financial institutions like Fanny Mae and Freddy Mac, a credit crisis hit America.

Bush decided to cope with this by launching a multi-billion dollar Keynesian stimulus package. Like all other packages of its kind in history, this was destined to failure. The only major question that the libertarian economists wanted to know was, how long would it take for the free market to overtake the bumbling incompetent regulation and restore normality to the markets?

As a result of this market crash, and most of his foreign and domestic policies, George W. Bush left office under a cloud with very low approval ratings.

His successor promised to do things differently. He described his vision in generalised terms – he talked about how America was a country founded on hope, and despite setting up basic straw-man arguments, used his incredible oratory skills to galvanise America to his side. Some rightly suspected that despite the rhetoric for 'change', he might be 'George W. Bush on steroids', and expand the federal government even more.

But these were all questions to be answered in time. What was most interesting for some in 2008 was that America voted for their first black President. But there was something even more incredible than that: in less than two full terms after the attack on 9/11 by Islamofascist fundamentalists, to their infinite credit the American people voted, (mostly on the basis that they hoped he had the right policies), for a man with the name Barack Hussein Obama.

2923635R00187

Printed in Great Britain
by Amazon.co.uk, Ltd.,
Marston Gate.